THE Jews

Their Religious Beliefs and Practices

ALAN UNTERMAN

sussex
ACADEMIC
PRESS

BRIGHTON • *PORTLAND*

4 6 8 10 9 7 5 3

First published 1996, reprinted 1999, in Great Britain by
SUSSEX ACADEMIC PRESS
Box 2950
Brighton BN2 5SP

and in the United States of America by
SUSSEX ACADEMIC PRESS
5804 N.E. Hassalo St.
Portland, Oregon 97213–3644

British Library Cataloguing in Publication Data

A CIP catalogue record for this book is available from the British Library.

ISBN 1–898723–41 9 (paperback)

Front cover picture: a scribe carrying a new *Torah* scroll into the synagogue. Back
cover picture: a Kabbalistic plaque showing the tetragrammaton surrounded
by angelic names, placed in front of the cantor's desk so he can focus on the
deity while leading prayers.

Printed by Biddles Ltd, Guildford and King's Lynn
This book is printed on acid-free paper

The Jews

The Sussex Library of Religious Beliefs and Practices

This series is intended for students of religion, social sciences and history, and for the interested layperson. It is concerned with the beliefs and practices of religions in their social, cultural and historical setting. These books will be of particular interest to Religious Studies teachers and students at universities, colleges, and high schools. Inspection copies available upon request.

<u>Published</u>

The Ancient Egyptians   Rosalie David

Buddhism   Merv Fowler

Gnosticism   John Glyndwr Harris

Hinduism   Jeaneane Fowler

Humanism   Jeaneane Fowler

Islam   David Norcliffe

The Jews   Alan Unterman

Sikhism   W. Owen Cole and Piara Singh Sambhi

Zoroastrianism   Peter Clark

<u>In preparation</u>
The Diversity of Christianity Today   Diane Watkins
The Doctrine of the Trinity: God in Three Persons   Martin Downes
Death and Afterlife: An Introduction to Christian Eschatology
Tony Gray
You Reap What You Sow: Causality in the Religions of the World
Jeaneane Fowler
Christian Theology: The Spiritual Tradition   John Glyndwr Harris
Jainism   Lynn Foulson

<u>Forthcoming</u>   *Bhagavad Gita (a student commentary)*
Confucianism   The Protestant Tradition   Taoism   Zen

Contents

Preface

Preface to the First Edition

This book is about the religion, ritual and attitudes of the Jews. It concentrates on those areas of Jewish life which uniquely identify the Jew, and therefore there is little in it about the ethical norms which are common to all members of modern Western society. It is indeed true that there is a difference of nuance between the approach of the Jew to such things as hospitality, charity, good neighbourliness, honesty and responsibility for one's fellow man, and the approach of the non-Jew. For the traditional Jew ethical norms are part of religious ritual and determined as much by the Bible and later Jewish literature as by the heart. Nevertheless there is a sufficient similarity of attitudes on these issues amongst those cultures which base themselves on biblical values, not to require a discussion of Jewish ethics within the space available.

I should like to thank Dr Paul Gardner, and the executive of the Hillel Foundation of Victoria, for their encouragement whilst the work was in progress, and Mrs Margaret Kilpatrick of Monash University for typing most of the first draft of the book. To Nechama, Yael, Yossi and Avi many thanks for their patient forbearance.

Preface to the Second Edition

In the last fifteen years the world has changed dramatically. The Soviet Union has collapsed, a Middle East peace process is underway, and most of the surviving perpetrators and victims of the Holocaust are now well into old age. I have made some reference to the short-term effects of those developments in this second edition. Since, however, beliefs and practices change very slowly the substance of the book, apart from small additions and revisions, has not changed.

Transliteration and Abbreviations

Transliteration

The transliteration of Hebrew, Aramaic and Yiddish words generally follows modern Israeli usage according to the simplified system of the *Encyclopaedia Judaica*, except that I have occasionally opted for some greater simplification to aid the reader. Thus, for instance diacritical marks have been replaced with ordinary letters. Some terms which have a widespread use have been transliterated to approximate their usual spelling, so the English reader should have no difficulty in recognizing them.

Abbreviations

Abbreviations have been kept to a minimum in the text and notes. The only ones with which the reader may not be familiar are: BCE = before common (or Christian) era; CE = common (or Christian) era; M = *Mishnah*; R = Rabbi; TB = *Babylonian Talmud*; TJ = *Jerusalem Talmud*. Biblical books follow the accepted spelling and have not been italicized. All other books in the text or notes have been italicized. Translations from the Hebrew or Aramaic are the author's.

For
Mori Chami Hagaon R. Alter Halevi zal

"Some trust in chariots, and some in horse, but we will invoke the name of the Lord our God." (Psalms 20:8)

Introduction

Knowledge and Acquaintance

The Jewish religion may be defined as that complex of beliefs, attitudes, legends, laws, rituals and institutions predicated on the religion of the Bible but specifically associated with the Jewish people after the destruction of the Second Temple in 70 CE. It is a religion which is reflected in, and lays claim to, a vast literary heritage most of which can be unambiguously identified as Jewish religious literature. The main components of that heritage are the Hebrew Bible; the rabbinic corpus of the *Mishnah*, the *Jerusalem* and *Babylonian Talmuds*, and midrashic collections; biblical commentaries; legal responsa and codes; mystical texts; works of ethical (*musar*) instruction; theological and philosophical writings; and numerous other works of a heterogeneous nature. Jewish teaching as expressed in this literature is commonly referred to as *Torah*, a term which is also used in a narrower sense to mean the Pentateuch.

None of the above literary products has a purely historical interest for Judaism; they are all living texts possessing different degrees of sanctity. They are used for reference, as proof texts, as guides to ritual and moral behaviour, or in the formulation of belief. The texts do not always agree among themselves and thus a mere working knowledge of Jewish literature may not, on its own, guarantee more than a passing acquaintance with Jewish religion. Some works are much more important than others, some are referred to only occasionally and others continuously, some are interpreted literally and others homiletically.

To understand the religion in its contemporary setting we must be sensitive to the way in which the past lives on in the minds and activities of modern practitioners. Literary evidence is, anyway, only a partial reflection of Jewish religion and an attempt to understand Judaism must take the actual behaviour, thought patterns and attitudes of committed Jews as its point of departure. We shall try to blend together textual and contextual elements of Judaism to provide both knowledge about, and an acquaintance with, the living faith and its manifestations.

Judaism is the religion of a particular ethnic community and in order to understand the former we must know something about the latter. A certain amount of material of a historical or sociological nature about Jews is thus a pre-requisite for the study of their religion. Indeed certain Jewish attitudes can only be fully understood if we take into account the experience of the Jewish people living in exile, subject to persecution and expulsion as an insecure minority often living among a hostile host majority.

It is often not practical to bring in all the refinements and qualifications that one would want to make in describing a Jewish belief or practice, if only because there are many different Jewish sub-groups with their own customs and lifestyles. The generalizations in this work should be sufficiently well-grounded, however, to serve as guidelines to the reader through a complex, and often disputed terrain. The notes and bibliography enable the serious student to gain a more detailed overview.

Translation and Interpretation

All religions suffer distortion when discussed in a language not their own. Judaism is no exception and is heir to a history of both wilful, and unintended, misdescription generated by the particular theological bias of European languages. English, for example, necessarily assimilates Jewish thought-forms to the Christian assumptions implicit in the English cultural milieu. In this respect Judaism has suffered more than Islam, and considerably more than Hinduism and Buddhism, because Christianity shares some of its basic texts. It thus seems obvious that there are ready-made translations for many Jewish concepts, whereas some of these translations are in fact terms already heavily laden with Christian values.

In order to avoid reinforcing this process of conceptual baptism many Jewish concepts have been transliterated in this book, and their meaning explained both directly and contextually. A glossary is also provided so that the reader can refer to it for clarification. This has the advantage of allowing the central concepts of Judaism to speak for themselves, unencumbered by those prior assumptions which might distort their meaning.

It is a common mistake among Christian students of Judaism to see the religion of the Hebrew Bible (the Christian 'Old Testament') as 'Ancient Judaism' and the religion of the Jews in Palestine at the time of Jesus as 'Modern Judaism'. This, of course, ignores the last two thousand years of religious development, and expresses the Christian bias that somehow Judaism came to a stop, was frozen in time, when Christianity began. Part of the purpose of this book is to show that this is completely false.

1

Some Basic Categories and Complexities

In What Sense is Judaism a Religion?

Whether or not we wish to characterize Judaism as a *religion* will depend on our approach to that somewhat over-used term. Such a characterization is useful as long as we bear in mind the peculiar features, to be discussed in the course of this book, which separate Judaism from what we may commonly accept as the defining paradigm of religion.

Traditionally Judaism did not conceive of itself as a religion, it saw itself as the teachings and commandments consequential to the covenanted relationship between God and Israel. The idolatrous worship and behaviour of other peoples were not seen as religions to be contrasted with the Jewish religion, but were alien ways which represented a threat to the maintenance of the Covenant. As in other ancient texts there is no concept of religion as such in the Bible.

In a modern context there is considerable resistance among traditional Jews to the characterization of Judaism as a religion, for this seems to them to imply a belittling of its status. They do not consider Judaism of a class with Christianity, Islam, or Buddhism, it is unique and in a category of its own as recording the divinely revealed teaching mediated through God's Covenant with Israel.

While these attitudes may serve as useful reminders that we must not impose procrustean religious categories on a religious tradition, there is no denial of the particularity and uniqueness of a religious tradition in classifying it within the wider context of the study of religions. The leading figures of medieval Jewish theology did just that when discussing the beliefs of Christianity and Islam in comparison to those of Judaism – though their purpose was admittedly polemical.

One additional feature needs to be borne in mind when talking of Jewish religion. Until comparatively recent times there was no dichotomy between the religious and secular aspects of Jewish culture and civilization. Jewish cultural self-awareness, Jewish historical consciousness, Jewish identity and Jewish existence in its totality were united within an essentially religious framework. It was perhaps this feature which contributed as much as anything else to the lack of a fully-fledged concept of religion within Judaism.

Judaism and the Jewish People

The *Torah*, and its associated life-style and thought patterns, is inextricably bound up with the experience of the Jewish people and their notions of self-identity. This bond creates an ambivalence in Jewish theological reflection on the nature of the Jewish teaching. On the one hand the *Torah* would seem to contain a message from God to man, a message admittedly mediated through Jewish prophets but of universal validity. On the other hand the *Torah* is part, indeed the central part, of the particularistic covenant between the God of Israel and his specially appointed people the Jews.

Both these universalistic and particularistic elements co-exist side by side within Judaism, and are perhaps not always perceived from within as separate, and in some ways conflicting perspectives.

Accompanying the universalistic element is a positive attitude towards proselytization and active missionary effort. The Judaism of the Roman Empire, before the rise of Christian hegemony, saw itself as a religion with a message to the gentile world. Conversions to Judaism were common, although it is not clear to what extent the rabbinic leaders were themselves active in this area, nor whether they approved of all aspects of the enterprise. The words of the New Testament,

> Woe unto you Scribes and Pharisees, hypocrites, for you encompass sea and land to make one proselyte, and when he is made you make him twice more the child of hell than yourselves[1]

though undoubtedly reflecting anti-Pharisaic bias, do point to a situation of active proselytization. We also know from Josephus that converts to Judaism were found in both Greek and Barbarian cities[2] and even among the wives of the anti-Jewish activists in Damascus.[3]

This universalistic perspective finds its most distinctive religious expression within Judaism in the following teaching of the third-century rabbi Eleazar ben Pedat:

> The Holy One, blessed be He, exiled Israel among the nations only in order that they should add proselytes to their number.[4]

It was the particularistic perspective, however, which dominated the religious outlook of the Middle Ages and which has largely persisted among traditional Jews into modern times. The external background to this particularism was the experience of a militant Christianity, and later on an equally militant Islam. Conversion from Christianity or from Islam to Judaism meant the risk of serious penalty for the convert, and for those Jews who had converted him. It need not be assumed that the emergence of these particularistic attitudes were merely the result of external pressure against Jewish proselytizing activity, for there was an internal theological rationale to abandoning Jewish missionary work among gentiles.

Christianity and Islam were clearly daughter religions of Judaism, which had taken over many of the basic ideas and practices of the mother religion. The missionary work of the former could therefore be seen as a direct continuation of the Jewish task of being 'a light to the gentiles'. Christianity and Islam were bringing Jewish religion to the gentiles, and Judaism saw itself as relieved of the burden of active proselytization and free to concentrate on refining its own religious self-development.

The above attitude is implicit in the remarks of the greatest of classical Jewish theologians, Moses Maimonides, writing towards the end of the twelfth century CE, in a passage deleted by the Christian censor from most printed editions of his *Mishneh Torah*:

> And all of these matters concerning Jesus the Nazarene and the Ishmaelite who arose after him were only to lay out a path for the Messiah, and to rectify the whole world to serve God together. How so? The whole world is now filled with the idea of the Messiah, of *Torah*, and of the commandments.[5]

Here we see Maimonides preserving a qualified universalism in a situation which was turning Judaism towards a thoroughgoing particularism. Not all Jewish thinkers were willing even to go as far as Maimonides' qualified universalism. Their attitude was based on more particularistic tendencies, already found in rabbinic literature, that *Torah* was not meant for gentiles who were merely bound to keep the Seven Noachide Laws: (1) to set up courts of law, (2) to prohibit blasphemy, (3) not to worship idols, (4) not to indulge in sexual immorality, (5) not to commit murder, (6) not to rob; and (7) not to eat a limb torn from a living animal.[6] Thus a gentile should neither study the *Torah*[7] nor keep the Sabbath,[8] but if he genuinely desires to take upon himself 'the yoke of the Kingdom of Heaven and of the commandments', he would be accepted for conversion. He need not convert, however, since if he keeps the Seven Noachide Laws he is considered a righteous gentile who has a portion in the World to Come.[9] Although the more particularistic attitude predominated in the Middle Ages, views to the contrary were still expressed by individual rabbis. Thus R. Moses of Coucy, a leading French rabbi of the thirteenth century, warns Jews to mend their ways, so that gentiles will not be put off by their bad example since the making of converts is the purpose of Israel's exile.[10]

In more modern times together with a renewed emphasis on the universalistic aspects of Judaism among Progressive Jews, there has been an accompanying relaxation of rules for proselytization. The majority of traditionalists remain opposed to an easier conversion procedure and to the ideology behind it. Jewish particularism is, in some ways, a more acceptable attitude for the contemporary Jew since he is not thereby automatically committed to deny other religious traditions. It fits more easily into an environment of religious pluralism and tolerance. A thoroughgoing universalism carries with it the implication that the only path to God leads through Judaism, whereas particularism may allow for different paths to God. On such a view Judaism is simply the path which has been divinely ordained for Jews to follow.

The classical formulation of a Jewish pluralistic particularism is found in a letter of Moses Mendelssohn, written in 1769 to a Christian acquaintance, J. C. Lavater:

> According to the principles of my religion I am not permitted to try to convert anyone not born into the tradition of Israel. This missionary spirit, which some people so desire to ascribe to Judaism and to find its origin there, is completely alien to it. All the rabbis unanimously agree that the written and oral laws that are basic to our revealed religion are only binding on those of our faith.

All other nations, we believe, were commanded by God to maintain natural law and the religion of the Patriarchs. People who live according to the religion of nature and of reason are called the pious of the gentiles and have a portion in the World to Come. . . . Were we to find among our contemporaries a Confucius or a Solon I would, according to the principles of my religion, love and respect such a great man without considering the ridiculous idea of converting Confucius or Solon.

Halakhah, Culture and Belief

The Jewish tradition not only teaches certain fundamental ideas about God, revelation, and man, it also expresses these beliefs through ceremonies, rituals and behaviour-guiding laws which in turn give rise to religious institutions, and distinctive styles of Jewish life and culture. Being Jewish is therefore not necessarily synonymous with being a believing Jew, nor does the religious Jew identify himself primarily with doctrinal formulae. For some Jews their Judaism is more the participation in the life of a given ethnic community than any rigid adherence to rituals or beliefs. For others the primary dimension of Judaism is the set of halakhic proscriptions and prescriptions which determine normative behaviour, with theological issues relegated to a shadowy existence on the sidelines.

A modern exponent of this last view, Professor Yehoshua Leibowitz, claims that the religion of Israel, embodied in *Torah* and *mitzvot*, was the only thing which gave continuity to Judaism and preserved its identity. All the other features of Jewish existence, such as the philosophies, the ethics, the literature, the poetry, the folklore, the politics and the social organisation were not specifically Jewish, but were of a general human character. 'All the different, changing ideas and opinions in Judaism were only supra-structures erected upon the *Halakhah*.'[11]

This approach, which gives primacy to the *halakhah*, the 'path' or legal side of Judaism which deals specifically with the *mitzvot*, or 'commandments', is found among a small but influential group of Orthodox thinkers. It has provided fertile ground within Judaism for the development of an inward-looking scholasticism which does not try to connect Jewish religion with issues of a general religious nature. This has enabled those who subscribe to it to overcome the problems besetting the Jewish thinker in the modern world by divorcing their intellectual activities from wider theological issues.

There is a secular parallel to this attitude which separates the milieu of normative action from theological investigation. The secularized version sees all the religious components of Judaism, including the halakhic dimension, as merely outgrowths of Jewish ethnic culture, primary to which are a shared sense of common history, a series of Jewish life-styles, the use of Judaic languages, community habits, folk-ways and ethical values. Whereas secularists naturally gravitate towards this cultural or ethnic Judaism, it is often the ultra-Orthodox who advocate its more extreme halakhic form.

The vast majority of Jews, be they Orthodox, Conservative or Reform, accept a wider perspective on Jewish religion and Jewish life. Although different emphasis is put by different groups on the various components, Orthodoxy stressing the halakhic dimension more than Reform, they are all caught up in the interplay between practice and belief in Judaism, and the tensions set up between Judaism and the modern world. The free and open contact between Jews and gentiles in the Western world has sharpened the Jew's awareness of his own doctrinal position and its problematic status, as well as generating a crisis in Jewish identity because of assimilation and inter-marriage. The emergence of a Jewish state in the historic Holy Land has made Jewish nationalism an integral feature of contemporary Jewish consciousness which needs to be reconciled with the emancipated Diaspora Jew's more localized nationalism. The major social and moral issues of our times have revived Jewish interest in the attitudes of the traditional *halakhah* to normative behaviour, and its ability to cope with the permissive society.

The most sensitive area of these tensions is that of education, where Jewish children are fully exposed to the ideas, attitudes, and values of the general community. One solution which is adopted by a significant minority of Jewish parents is to send their children to Jewish schools. This is meant to cushion the effect of the gentile environment, enhance social contact with fellow Jews, limit the prospect of inter-marriage, and provide a modicum of Jewish education. Jewish schools, however, generate their own problems since they increase the sense of alienation felt by the Jewish child, his awareness of the invisible walls of the cultural ghetto which divide him from the gentile world. Another solution, admittedly adopted by only a small proportion of Western Jews, but contemplated by a much larger number, is emigration to Israel. This removes the severe strain imposed by an emotional identification with the State of Israel on the sense of citizenship of the Jew, and on his loyalty to his host country.

The Dimensions of Jewish Identity

An analysis of the various elements constituting Jewishness, in its broadest sense, is important for understanding both the Jewish and the gentile perception of Jewish identity. Briefly we can isolate four categories which go to make up Jewishness: (1) biological origin, (2) religious affiliation, (3) membership of community/culture group, (4) ethnic or national belonging and language use.

Each category is independent of the others, and thus it is possible for someone to belong to only one category, e.g. to be biologically Jewish without religious, community, or national affiliation. Most Jews would be Jewish according to the majority of these categories, and unequal weight is given by different Jewish groups to the different categories, some being considered sufficient criteria of Jewish identity and others not. Let us examine these four categories in greater detail.

BIOLOGICAL ORIGIN

According to the *halakhah* it is sufficient for someone to have been born of a Jewish mother for them to be considered a Jew. Historically this has meant that the children of Jewish women who were raped by non-Jews, a not infrequent occurrence in pre-modern Europe, were accepted by the Jewish community as full Jews. The same rule is not applied by the traditional *halakhah* to children born of a Jewish father and a gentile mother. They are considered gentiles, although some elements within Reform Judaism accept them as Jewish.

The biological category is further complicated by the fact that gentiles do not usually recognize this internal Jewish classification, and may well think of someone as Jewish if either of their parents were Jews. This has certainly been true of anti-Semitic attitudes to Jewishness, and is exemplified in the Citizen Laws of the Nazi Reich which defined someone as Jewish if they were of Jewish blood with one Jewish grandparent. This meant that some of the people persecuted by the Hitler regime as Jews would not have been recognized as such even by radical Reform Judaism, and indeed did not identify with anything Jewish.

An atheist, anti-religious, Jew who was born of a Jewish mother would still be considered halakhically Jewish, and therefore accepted as such by his fellow Jews. The only real identity problem arises for the Jew, born of a Jewish mother, who converts to another religion. Here we face a clash of categories, i.e. biological origin versus religious affiliation, and the traditional Jewish attitude is that such a person is to be considered a Jew in some respects but not in others.

A case of this nature came before the Israeli Supreme Court in 1962 when a Carmelite monk, Brother Daniel, tried to register as an Israeli citizen under the Law of Return, which gives immediate citizenship to Jews settling in Israel. Brother Daniel, originally Oswald Rufeisen, was born in 1922 into a Polish Jewish family. He converted to Christianity in 1942 while hiding in a Catholic convent from Nazi persecution. The court, in a majority ruling, turned down Rufeisen's application though not specifically on halakhic grounds. It held that applying the term 'Jew' to someone who was a practising member of another faith would contradict Jewish national consciousness and common usage.

RELIGIOUS AFFILIATION

In the formal halakhic sense a gentile can become a Jew by undergoing the process of conversion (*giyyur*). There has been considerable dispute between Orthodox, Conservative, and Reform Judaism as to just what should constitute this process. The traditional halakhic conversion, as a purely ritual procedure, involves the acceptance by the convert of all of the commandments incumbent on a Jew, followed by immersion in a *mikveh* – a specially designed pool which is an extension to a storage pool of 'living water', e.g. rain water. For the male convert (*ger*) it also involves ritual circumcision prior to immersion.

A period of study precedes conversion when the convert must not only assimilate what is entailed by becoming Jewish, but can also rethink whether or not they genuinely wish to take the step. This period of study and reflection prior to conversion is longest among Orthodox Jews and may be prolonged to as much as four or five years. The conversion has to take place in the presence of three rabbis who constitute a *bet din*, or court of law. If no *bet din* is present then there is some disagreement among the classical rabbinic authorities about the validity of the conversion.

Orthodox Judaism still follows this traditional procedure for conversion. Any changes which may have been introduced are purely cosmetic. For instance the female convert (*giyoret*) today may well wear a loosely fitting smock during immersion. This satisfies the requirement that the water of the *mikveh* should be in contact with all parts of the body, while avoiding embarrassment to the convert or the three rabbis who must witness the act.

Conservative practice closely approximates the traditional procedure in this as in many other rituals, but may not always follow the details of the ritual to the letter. Orthodox rabbis do not, in general, recognize Conservative conversions either as a matter of policy or because they doubt the validity of both the ritual itself and the rabbis who have supervised it. Reform Jewish conversion differs in the degree it emulates traditional practice in different countries. Since, however, Reform rabbis are not acceptable as religious authorities either to the Orthodox or Conservatives, the Reform ritual is not regarded as valid by them, even when circumcision and immersion are used. The present situation is, therefore, a very fluid one with different criteria of conversion being applied and accepted by different groups.

This, of course, leads to identity problems of enormous dimensions since Orthodox Jews will not marry Conservative converts, and neither Orthodox or Conservative Jews will marry Reform converts, although the converts may think of themselves as fully Jewish. So far the three trends within modern Judaism [12] have not really begun to tackle this issue which may in the long run divide Jewry into three endogamous groups.

In the modern State of Israel, where problems surrounding conversion lead to political crises from time to time among the members of the religious/secular coalition government, Orthodox practice generally prevails. Yet the secular law of Israel will accept anyone who has undergone conversion of whatever type in the Diaspora as a Jewish citizen under the Law of Return. Since much of the support for Israel and Zionism comes from Conservative and Reform circles in North America there is a growing agitation for Israeli recognition of converts to Judaism from these groups for purposes of marriage, divorce and personal status which are currently controlled by the Orthodox rabbinate in Israel. While it is true that the Israeli rabbinate is usually more flexible on the subject of conversion than Diaspora Orthodoxy, and runs special training schemes for would-be converts as well as shortening the waiting period before conversion, it will not accept non-Orthodox conversions under any circumstances.

MEMBERSHIP OF COMMUNITY CULTURE GROUP

Central to Jewish life is the idea of the Jewish community, either in the sense of the macro-community of all Jews, known as *Kelal Yisrael*, or the micro-community of a given body of Jews in a specific location. In ancient times the Jewish community was not made up exclusively of Jews. A gentile living in the Land of Israel who agreed to abide by the Seven Noachide Laws was known as a *ger toshav*, or resident alien, and was given limited rights and responsibilities within the community. A modified form of this practice was still widespread among Jewish communities of the pre-Christian Roman Empire, when many Greek-speaking gentiles attached themselves to Diaspora synagogues without actually undergoing conversion.

The status of the *ger toshav* no longer exists today and, in theory at least, all those intimately associated with a given Jewish community would either be Jews or would think of themselves as such. In practice, however, since the life of the Jewish community includes social and cultural elements, as well as religion, there will be individual community members who are not born of a Jewish mother or converts to Judaism. It sometimes happens, for instance, that a male member of the Jewish community marries a gentile and brings up his children within the community. Problems inevitably arise when these children grow up and seek to participate in the religious life of the community or to marry a Jewish spouse in a synagogue ceremony.

ETHNIC/NATIONAL BELONGING AND LANGUAGE USE

With the emergence of the modern State of Israel a new dimension has been added to Jewish identity. Jews from all over the world have made *aliyah* (i.e. 'gone up, ascension') to Israel some with their gentile spouses. There are young Israelis, born in Israel, who speak Hebrew, serve in the Israeli army, and identify as Israeli Jews rather than Israeli Christians or Moslems. Yet they are not halakhically Jewish.

They are invariably the children of mixed marriages in which the mother is a gentile.

Since the traditional *halakhah* affecting personal status is operative in Israel these non-Jewish Jews represent a specific problem area in the life of the Jewish state. The Orthodox establishment has often been able to overcome the problems involved by converting those who are willing to undergo conversion. There are some, however, who claim Jewish national status but refuse conversion.

In 1968 an officer in the Israeli navy, Benjamin Shalit, requested that the Israeli-born children of his gentile wife be registered by the Ministry of the Interior as of Jewish nationality. The Israel Supreme Court, to whom Shalit had turned, acceded to his request though it pointed out that as far as religious laws governing personal status in Israel were concerned the Shalit children would be considered gentiles. After considerable protest from religious parties the Israeli government eventually altered the law of registration of citizens so that only those born of a Jewish mother or converted to Judaism could be registered as Jews.

The situation as it now stands leaves other young Israelis, who are in a similar position to the Shalit children, in an identity limbo. The problems surrounding Jewish identity arise because Israel is a Jewish state which has a population including not only a large number of gentiles, but also a sizeable proportion of secular Jews. The Israeli legislation itself is mixed, with some areas covered by religious law and others by secular law. Each Israeli citizen has to carry an identity card on which his or her *leom*, i.e. ethnic grouping, is recorded. This card is issued by the Ministry of the Interior, which is not officially bound by halakhic considerations in deciding on someone's *leom*, though in practice the ministry has been dominated by the religious parties. The *leom* of the majority of Israel's citizens is recorded as 'Jewish', which, religious Jews argue, must be determined not by civil servants but by halakhic categories.

The importance of which criteria are used to determine Jewish *leom* is brought out by the fact that Israeli laws of marriage and divorce for all Jews are controlled by Orthodox rabbis, with parallel control for Moslems or Christians by their religious authorities. A national or ethnic 'Jew' who does not qualify as such according to the *halakhah*, and cannot be classified as a Moslem or Christian, has no way of marrying in the State of Israel. If he or she marries in a civil ceremony abroad then the marriage is recognized by the

Israeli secular legal system under international agreement. Identity problems for such ethnic 'Jews' living in Israel can be of a severe nature, and though as yet they affect a small proportion of the population they are a potential flash-point for secular-religious power struggles.

With the influx of immigrants to Israel after the demise of the Soviet Union these problems have become more marked since many, some estimates say 30 per cent, of the Russian *olim* ('immigrants') are not halakhically Jewish They are the spouses of Jews, children or grandchildren of a gentile mother and a Jewish father, or simply Russian gentiles who acquired Jewish identity papers by bribery in order to leave the poverty of Russia for a new life in the West.

2

Main Religious Doctrines

The Nature of the God of Judaism

Monotheism is usually understood as the belief in one God, but behind this overtly simple definition lies a host of complexities. In the course of its long history Judaism has always felt itself committed to belief in one deity, but the meaning of this belief and the theology which surrounded it has differed markedly from period to period. In any given age varying concepts of God have coexisted with each other, and shaded into one another. In what follows we shall indicate the main components which go to make up the complex picture of Jewish belief.

Jewish Belief

1 ANTHROPOMORPHISM

People use language drawn from the relationship of human beings to each other and to the world to apply to God. This is characteristic of Jewish God-language from earliest times to the present day. It is central to Jewish theology though it is extremely problematic, and caused the medieval Jewish philosophers to expend considerable intellectual energy trying to neutralize its stranglehold on men's minds. To talk of God as a Father or a King, as angry or happy, as creating a world and being disappointed with His creation, etc., brings home the message of man's relationship to God in the most vivid terms available to man. It also encourages the formation of a picture-image of God incompatible with other Jewish teachings about His nature. The talmudic rabbis would often preface their more extreme anthropomorphisms with the phrase 'as if it were possible' (i.e. to talk about God in these terms).

Anthropomorphic language does affect the kind of monotheism which is couched in its terms. It emphasizes the continuity of God's being with man's being, projecting God as a more powerful, more moral, manlike entity. God emerges as personal, caring about man and needing to be placated by him. Apart from the Bible and talmudic literature, the main repository of anthropomorphic thought is the traditional Jewish prayer book.

2 TRANSCENDENTALISM

There is also an emphasis on the otherness of God and his essential difference from the created world. This transcendentalist factor in Jewish thought is the main contrast to the anthropomorphic perspective. It views all human language about God as merely man's attempt to grasp the incomprehensible. At its extreme it separates God from the world by positing an abyss between the two. His 'thoughts', are not our thoughts and His 'ways' are not our ways. Philosophically minded Jewish theology has invariably opted for a transcendentalist position, though it is not confined to the Jewish philosophers – the Bible veers between outright anthropo-morphism and counterbalancing statements of a transcendentalist nature, while early forms of Jewish mysticism contained in the *Merkabah* tradition are imbued with a strong transcendentalism. Idol worship, which is anathema to Jewish monotheism, is seen as a direct challenge to transcendentalism and the unity of God. God cannot be identified with any aspect of his creation.

3 PAN-EN-THEISM

We also find a belief that God is in everything though He is not to be identified with the totality of the created world and certainly not with any part of it. This conception of God is a relatively late development and popular among Jewish mystics from the medieval period on. While anthropomorphism is a very problematic way of thinking about God, reducing him to the dimensions of man's experience, transcendentalism too often divorces God from reli-gious experience and produces a form of deism. Pan-en-theism tries to resolve the dialectical tension within Jewish theology between the God of the philosophers and the God of the Patriarchs by positing a God who is the reality behind all appearances. He is thus different from, but intimately related to, the created world. Such a conception was opposed by non-mystics, either because it was mistakenly understood to be identical with pantheism ('the totality of what exists is God'), or because it seemed to have anti-nomian consequences. If everything is a manifestation of God, as in pan-en-theism, then the distinctions between holy and profane, and between good and evil, can become blurred.

4　PARTICULARISM

It is often stated in the Bible that God is the God of Israel, who has entered into a special covenantal relationship with the People of Israel. God is active as a Redeemer in Israel's history, and Israel owes allegiance to Him alone. Together with this particularistic picture goes an assumption about the Jewish people and its special status and destiny. Particularism is characteristic of each era in Jewish history but it does not necessarily predominate in them all. It is in tension with more universalistic tendencies.

5　UNIVERSALISM

It is equally often stated that God is the creator of heaven and earth, the God of human history, who cares and is active in the affairs of mankind in general. Although there is no necessary relationship between universalism and transcendentalism, in contrast to particularism and anthropomorphism, there is an intellectual connection. If God is totally other, different from any aspects of his creation, He may easily be viewed as relating to the whole of His handiwork. Anthropomorphic images, implying an immanence or at least a personified relationship, are more easily assimilated to a particularistic tendency when God is Israel's 'Father', or 'King'. These five components are all present in the Jew's conception of God, although different rituals may involve only one particular perspective on God and the theologian, mystic and simple pious Jew may operate with divergent central images. With the emergence of modern Judaism and its bifurcation into traditional and progressive streams, a more self-conscious assessment of the Jewish conception of God began. The process has reached the point where none of the traditional images may seem quite adequate to the modern Jew, particularly in the post-Auschwitz era. Nevertheless, the basic commitment to monotheism remains, the oneness and unity of God are still the central pivot of most Jewish thought about God in the twentieth century. The interpretation of the meaning of Jewish monotheism, however, is an issue of dispute among different contemporary schools of thought.

Immanence, Transcendence and Idolatry

Although we have pointed out five main components within Jewish belief about God, there is one polarity of concepts which is of prime importance for an understanding of Jewish theology, and that is the difference between divine immanence and divine transcendence. In Judaism there is a dialectical tension between the immanence, and closeness of God, and His absolute transcendence. Maimonides (twelfth century) writing in the spirit of medieval philosophy states categorically that to believe in the corporeality of God is to treat God in a heretical manner.[1] Elsewhere, Maimonides tries to solve the problem of religious language, particularly of anthropomorphisms, by explaining that we cannot ascribe any positive attributes to God, we can only know Him negatively. 'He is not' rather than 'He is'. Thus anthropomorphic language is seen by Maimonides as a shorthand way of denying limitations and imperfections when talking about God.[2] The God of the philosophers which emerges seems to leave no room for the 'Eternal Thou', the personal God whom the Jew meets in prayer and on every page of the Bible. The anti-Maimonidean reaction rejected the transcendent impersonal deity, which his theology had forged, and re-affirmed the immanentist God preserved in the vivid language of anthropomorphism. As such, this left all the problems which Maimonides found associated with anthropomorphism unsolved. The Jewish mystics who were among the foremost critics of Maimonides tried to preserve anthropomorphic immanence by giving it a mystical significance. Human categories could be applied to God not because God was man-like but because, in some Platonic sense, man was God-like. Each aspect of human experience was a reflection, albeit a pale reflection, of the divine structure, the deeper meaning of which being given to mystic contemplation.

In the modern era, with its rejection both of naive anthropomorphism and of Jewish mysticism, there has been a re-thinking of the immanence/transcendence dichotomy. Immanentist theology has turned to the human personality and psyche as the matrix for an understanding of God's relationship to man, while transcendentalist thought specifically associated with the Reconstructionist movement in the United States,[3] has developed an impersonal God image identified as the projection of the ideals and values of Jewish civilization. Perhaps the best known immanentist theologian is Martin Buber, whose writings on the nature of the I–Thou relationship in which God, the Eternal Thou, is revealed, have been influential outside the boundaries of Jewish thought, especially among Christian thinkers.

Man and God

The biblical account of the Creation in Genesis Chapters 1 and 2 is understood by Judaism to teach the central importance of man among all created beings. Such key ideas as men being created in God's image (1:26, 27), the command to man to fill the earth, subdue it, and have dominion over all earthly creatures (1:28), and the idea that man is separated from other creatures and can find no companionship among them (2:20) are developed in Jewish thought into a highly anthropocentric structure.

Man is so highly regarded in Jewish thought that there are a number of passages in talmudic literature which imply that man, and more especially the Jew, is superior to the angels. Thus, for example, Adam, the human prototype, is of greater intelligence than the angels, as is evident from the following midrashic description of a conversation between the angels and God:

> The ministering angels said to the Holy One, blessed be He: Master of the Universe, what is man that you should know him? A man is like a vain thing, and he cannot even rule over his physical nature. He replied to them: Just as you praise me in the upper worlds, so he unifies me in the lower worlds, and what is more can you give names to all creatures? They tried, but were unable. Adam tried and gave names to all creatures. (Genesis 2:20)[4]

Though there are also contrasting opinions expressed about man's status *vis-à-vis* the angels, both in talmudic literature and among medieval Jewish thinkers (e.g. Abraham Ibn Ezra (1089–1164) and Maimonides), this strong anthropocentric view indicates the value placed on man in Jewish religion. Man is free to act as he wills, he bears responsibility for his acts, and he is the recipient of the divine teaching through revelation.

Saadiah Gaon, the tenth-century scholar and philosopher, sums up this trend of thought in Judaism as follows:

> Although we see that there are many creatures, nevertheless we need not be confused as to which of them is superior, and when we investigate through natural reflection we will find that man is the superior being.

[Then follows a series of arguments from reason and scripture to prove man is the goal of creation]

> Should anyone think that these superior qualities are given to something other than man, then let him show us these qualities, or even part of them in some other creature. Such a thing will not be found. It is fitting, therefore, that man should be subjected to commandments and prohibitions, reward and punishment, for he is the axis of the universe and the goal of creation. The reason why the wise God has made man with these superior qualities, is so that man may be the recipient of His commands and prohibitions.[5]

The idea of man's superior status as the axis of the universe is thus bound up with man's responsibilities and duties towards God and the created world. The wicked man is thought of by the rabbis in the *Talmud* as living a dead life, his potential as man, the goal of creation, remains unfulfilled.[6] The *Zohar*, the most important Jewish mystical text, puts the idea in a more picturesque form when it asserts that man's control over the animal kingdom, and the subservience of lesser creatures to him, is dependent on man manifesting his superior spiritual qualities. When the animals cannot perceive man's higher form, his soul, because he is not living a life of righteousness, then they lose their awe of him.[7]

Ideas on the Soul

Though biblical theology is somewhat reticent on the topic of man's nature and spiritual destiny, rabbinic Judaism in talmudic and medieval times is concerned to spell out these issues at great length. No single talmudic, philosophic or mystical doctrine of man won universal approval in traditional Judaism, but all of

the major views had their supporters. Since there were no direct
practical consequences associated with theological speculation, a
very loose and ambiguous doctrinal framework was all that was
deemed necessary for dogmatic purposes. Generally speaking, the
idea that there will be a Resurrection of the Dead in the messianic
era is expressed as normative doctrine in the *Mishnah*, but the implications of this doctrine are left vague.[8] This is because the notion of
bodily resurrection implies a view of the soul as not having a fully
independent existence distinct from the living, embodied person.
Otherwise the judgment taking place at the Resurrection could
just as well be passed on the disembodied soul. The Rabbis, who
increasingly tended towards the idea of separately existing souls,
explained the need for the resurrection by means of a parable:

> A king had a beautiful orchard in which were fine ripe figs. He
> placed two guards there, one lame and one blind. The lame guard
> said to the blind one, 'I see fine ripe figs in the orchard. Come, carry
> me and we will gather them to eat.' The lame guard rode on the back
> of the blind one, and they gathered them and ate them. Eventually
> the owner of the orchard came and asked them where the fine ripe
> figs were. The lame guard answered, 'Have I legs on which I could
> walk?', and the blind one said, 'Do I have eyes to see with?', What
> did the owner do? He placed the lame guard on the shoulders of
> the blind one and passed judgment on them as one unit. In a similar
> manner the Holy One, Blessed be He, brings the soul, throws it into
> the body, and judges them as one unit.[9]

This explanatory parable is ascribed to R. Judah the Prince (second
to third century CE) and represents a reply to the question of
whether the soul or the body is responsible for man's actions
on earth. It seems to be an aggadic attempt to deal with the
problems arising from asymmetrical conceptions of the nature of
the soul. Is the soul the real man, the active responsible component
of personality, and the body merely a vehicle? Or is the soul not a
personality structure at all, but a spiritual life-giving element? The
parable seems to imply the second alternative, but expresses it in
terms of responsibility rather than ability. The responsible human
personality is only found in the conjunction of soul and body.

On the one hand we find a conception of the soul which after
death is devoid of personalizing individuation, and rests in heaven
awaiting the Resurrection either in the 'store of souls', or under the
throne of glory.[10] On the other hand we see the emergence of a
somewhat different conception. The Talmud [11] discusses whether or

not the dead are aware of what is happening on earth. According to R. Chiyya (third to fourth century CE) the dead are unaware of what is happening on earth, and in support of this view Ecclesiastes 9:5 is quoted 'But the dead do not know anything.' The other view, that of R. Chiyya's contemporary R. Yonatan, is that the dead are indeed aware of what is going on, and any scriptural evidence to the contrary needs to be interpreted in a non-literal manner.

This idea has its origins in the Bible where the souls of the dead live on in *She'ol* after death, but preserve an awareness of what is happening on earth.[12] In the post-talmudic period concern for the spiritual life of the soul after death predominated over the conception of souls awaiting renewal at the Resurrection. The latter, however, was doctrinally supported, and this caused some serious theological problems. Maimonides, though he enumerates the belief in the Resurrection as one of his doctrinal principles, does so briefly and ambiguously. In his more philosophical works he deals only with the eternity and nature of the disembodied soul. His less philosophically minded colleagues accused him of negating or undermining the doctrine of the Resurrection, and he was eventually led to write an essay on the topic of the Resurrection to explain his position. Popular Jewish piety, which accepts both the doctrine of the Resurrection and the belief in the life of the soul after death has continued to find Maimonides' viewpoint enigmatic.

The situation grew more complicated in the Middle Ages with the rise of Jewish mystical speculation. In the kabbalistic teachings the soul has an inner structure, and is made up out of separate elements. At death these elements break up and reform in combination with other elements to be reincarnated in a new body, i.e. transmigrated. This doctrine of transmigration of souls, or soul components, had been rejected by previous Jewish religious authorities, such as Saadiah Gaon in his *Book of Beliefs and Opinions* (ninth to tenth century) who considered it alien to Judaism. Since transmigration may be viewed as an extension of the idea of resurrection, a doctrine of multiple resurrections in fact, the implications for the conception of the soul are not as such new. Side by side with this conception, however, the Kabbalah also held a strong underlying belief in disembodied souls having their own conscious existence, which was also a central belief of exoteric Judaism from at least the third century.

It will be seen from the foregoing that a series of different, and somewhat incompatible, views of the soul exist side by side in

Judaism without too much attempt at resolving the innate conceptual tensions. In modern times all of the traditional strands have
been held in one form or another. Reform Judaism has generally
dropped the belief in the Resurrection in favour of the eternity of
the soul after death. Orthodox thinkers have tried to find a means of
conceptually uniting the various notions, although transmigration
has never received the same of kind of support as the other ideas,
outside of the narrow circle of mystics and mystically influenced
Jewish folklore.

Torah

In its narrow sense the *Torah* merely signifies the Pentateuch, but
it also has a range and depth of meaning for Judaism which
extends far beyond the narrow reference. Indeed it is one of the
central concepts of Judaism, operating on the levels of religious
law, theology and mysticism, at the same time. The *Talmud* sees the
Jewish sage as a living embodiment of *Torah*, so that after studying
and immersing himself in it, every thought and action of his is
an expression of *Torah*. It is in the light of this that we have to
understand a series of stories in the *Talmud* of how pupils followed
their masters even into the toilet to learn from their example, and
how one student hid himself beneath his master's bed to find out
how he and his wife made love. To objections at this unseemly
behaviour they replied: 'This is *Torah* and I need to learn.'[13]

The talmudic concept of *Torah* is further brought out in the
teachings that the *Torah* pre-existed the creation of the world[14] and
that it is indeed the craftsman's blueprint underlying the whole of
nature.[15] This idea may be seen as a direct descendant of certain
notions in biblical Wisdom literature. There Wisdom is elevated to
a pre-existent feature of the creation:

> God founded the world through Wisdom, and through understand-
> ing He established the heavens.[16]

and even seen as a co-worker in the process of creation:

> And I [i.e. Wisdom] was with Him as a craftsman.[17]

Though Judaism, unlike Christianity, never took up or developed
the doctrine of the *logos*, the *Torah* itself may be seen as a *logos*

equivalent within Jewish theology. Ben Sira (second century BCE) would seem to have been the first to formally identify biblical Wisdom with *Torah*, but this became a standard practice in talmudic times.

The more rationalist Jewish philosophers of the Middle Ages played down the pre-existence doctrine, but for the kabbalistic mystics, who taught an emanationist theory of creation it was apparent that the pre-existent *Torah* was actually to be identified with a stage of divine emanation. The *Torah* thus became simply the clothed form of an aspect of the Godhead. By studying *Torah* and living a life in accordance with its teachings one was thereby in direct contact with the divine sub-structure of reality.[18] R. Chaim of Volozhin (eighteenth to nineteenth century) develops this idea of the mystical identity of the *Torah* and God at great length in his work *Nefesh Ha-Chaim*,[19] an identity already found in a number of medieval mystical texts.

In terms of general Jewish religious consciousness, and particularly among those influenced by mystical ideas in popular dress, this meant that the highest ideal of Judaism was a life of *Torah*. Parents would be willing to undergo privation to enable their sons to study *Torah* without hindrance, indeed to support them as full-time students after they had married. The typical greeting to a parent of a new-born child is 'that you may be worthy to bring him up to *Torah*, to marriage, and to deeds of loving kindness'. The man of *Torah*[20] in a community was a figure of authority and commanded respect whether or not he was an ordained rabbi, or held rabbinical office.

Torah, for the traditional Jew, may be compared to a combination of the harmonious pulse of all creation and all social action and at the same time a system of religious law, ethics and ritual, functioning independently of religious experience with its own notions and authority. Even God studies the *Torah*[21] and He is pictured as a teacher instructing the Jewish people. The morning liturgy contains a number of benedictions which must be recited by the devout Jew in thanks for the gift of *Torah*, one of which ends with the words 'Blessed are you, O God, who teaches *Torah* to His people Israel'.

Mitzvah

The concept of *Torah* in Judaism goes hand in hand with the equally fundamental idea of *mitzvah*, the action-guiding commandment of

God extending into all areas of human behaviour. Thus a *mitzvah* is not only a prescription derived through scriptural exegesis, it is used far more extensively to apply to good deeds in general and to Jewish customs and rituals sanctioned by tradition. In studying the *Torah* the Jew sees himself as in contact with the will and mind of God, and such study is thus one of the highest religious activities. In carrying out *mitzvah* (including the commandment of *Torah* study) the Jew is obeying that divine will, and through ritualized action he orientates himself towards God. The *mitzvot* are both the discipline of obedience, and the contact point between man and God. In rabbinic Judaism the *mitzvot* proper are preceded by a benediction: 'who has made us holy through His *mitzvot* and commanded us to . . .' The mystics, particularly the Chasidic mystics of the nineteenth century, introduced a short prayer of meditation which was recited prior to each *mitzvah* benediction. These meditations sought to bring out the mystical meaning of the *mitzvah* about to be performed, the angels or divine names specific to it, and its consequences for higher levels of reality. A typical Chasidic meditation would run:

> For the sake of the unification of the Holy One, blessed be He [the divine masculine principle] and His *Shekhinah* [the divine feminine principle], in awe and devotion I am prepared and ready to perform *mitzvah* X or Y to fulfill the command of my Creator.

While the kabbalists developed the mystical interpretation of the role of the *mitzvot* within the religious life of the Jews, as acts of cosmic significance whose effectiveness reaches far beyond the world of man into the sphere of the divine, other groups within Judaism had their own interpretations. The moralists saw each *mitzvah* as incorporating a particular teaching of *musar* or ethics, the theologians saw them as the path of discipline leading man away from this-worldliness towards spiritual perfection. Performing *mitzvot* was *imitatio dei*,[22] it was the distinctive task of the Jew marking him off from the gentile, it sanctified him as a member of 'a kingdom of priests and a holy nation'. Ideas about the place of ritual in Judaism have changed in the modern period, and whereas some *mitzvot* have been selectively retained by Progressive Judaism[23] as having symbolic, social or even therapeutic value, others have been rejected as archaic. The traditionalist, however, still sees the *mitzvah* as the most direct, if not the sole, valid response of the Jew to God. Conscious tampering with the *mitzvot*, and their evaluation in terms of usefulness or ethical probity, seems to the traditionalist to be a form of blasphemy in which man makes himself judge over the decree of the Creator.

Sin and Repentance

According to the rabbinic view man has within him two inclinations, a good inclination (*yetzer tov*) and an inclination to evil (*yetzer ha-ra*). The former inclines man to follow the demands of the *mitzvot* and maintain the covenant with God, while the latter may lead man 'after his heart and after his eyes' into sin. The kabbalists saw the *mitzvot* as expressions of the deeper nature of the soul, the performance of which was not simply obedience to an externally imposed rule but the self-expression of the divine element within man. The *yetzer tov* is therefore closer to the real motivation of man which may become obstructed by his misuse of the *yetzer ha-ra*. This view would not seem too distant from that expressed in the *Talmud* that 'no man sins unless a spirit of foolishness enters him.'[24]

The transgressor has always the possibility of repentance, of *teshuvah* ('returning'), which brings him back into a right relationship with God. True repentance, involving *teshuvah* from love, rather than from fear of punishment, can have the consequence of transmuting past sins into deeds of righteousness.[25] Even *teshuvah* undertaken from less exalted motives can wipe out past transgressions, though it cannot transmute them. The gates of *teshuvah* are always open, and honest self-scrutiny is encouraged in the pietistic literature so that the Jew should reflect on how far his performance falls short of the divine command. This aspect of *teshuvah*, which is reiterated throughout Jewish literature, has the consequence of allowing the Jew both to begin again when he has strayed far from the path, being then classified as a *baal teshuvah*, and simply to rectify the occasional lapse which might prey heavily on his conscience.

Reward and Punishment

Built into the notion of *mitzvah* is the idea of reward and punishment either in this life, after death, or in the great judgment to come following the Resurrection. It is only while in bodily form that man can perform *mitzvot* and repent of past transgressions.[26] There is therefore a sense of urgency in many of the pietistic works reminding man that there can be no question of procrastination in matters affecting his status for all eternity. These ideas are summed up in two teachings from the mishnaic tractate *Avot*, which deals with matters of an ethico-theological nature:

> R. Jacob (second century CE) says: 'This world is like an entrance hall before the World to Come. Prepare yourself in the entrance hall so that you may enter the (royal) chamber.'[27]

And in a more urgent tone:

> R. Tarfon (first to second centuries CE) says: The day is short, and there is much work, and the labourers are lazy, and the reward is great, and the employer is insistent.[28]

The actual nature of any future reward or punishment is usually cloaked in the hyperbole of aggadic description. In general the righteous receive their reward in the Garden of Eden, and the wicked their punishment in *Gehinnom*. *Gehinnom* is both hell and purgatory, and even the righteous have to spend some time in *Gehinnom* after death so that they may be cleansed of their sins. This is the rationale behind the recital of the *Kaddish* prayer by a mourner for eleven months after the death of his parents. To recite the prayer for a full twelve months would imply that the deceased was wicked, needing the full period in purgatory. Indeed the very wicked remain in *Gehinnom* even after their period of cleansing is at an end, whereas the only moderately wicked leave after a temporary stay, though what their fate is thereafter is unclear.[29]

The vivid descriptions of the sufferings undergone in the fires of *Gehinnom*, as well as those of the delights of the Garden of Eden, were variously interpreted by Jewish thinkers. Philosophers emphasized the spiritual meaning of the symbolic descriptions – man becomes at death what his own self-discipline or desires have made of him. The mystics did not try to explain away the doctrine in symbolic terms, although for them every idea was meaningful on a number of different levels at the same time. Popular Jewish consciousness, and Jewish folklore, have elaborated on the whole topic and have accepted the various aggadic motifs as a literal description of the fate of the soul.

The relationship between the fate of the soul after death and the Resurrection is given no totally coherent expression, many of the passages possessing an ambiguity of reference. A talmudic passage on the condition of the righteous in the World to Come, taken to refer albeit ambiguously to post-Resurrection existence, has it that:

> The World to Come is not like this world. The World to Come does not have in it eating or drinking or procreation or business dealings or jealousy or hate or competitiveness. Only the righteous sitting with their crowns on their heads enjoying the radiance of the *Shekhinah*.[30]

While traditional Jews today are content to work within this doctrinal framework, even if they feel free to reinterpret some aspects, Progressive Jews have shelved large parts of what they take to be religiously opaque images and medieval assumptions.

Although underlying the conception of *mitzvah*, with its notions of reward and punishment, is a doctrine of salvation by works rather than faith, this does not necessarily imply a mechanistic view of salvation. The words of Micah 'and what does the Lord require of you, but to act justly and love mercy, and to walk humbly with your God' (6:8) and those of Habakkuk 'The righteous man shall live by his faith' (2:4) are quoted approvingly by the *Talmud* as representing the essential core of Judaism.[31]

The tension between the value of quantitative *mitzvah* performance, and that of the qualitative inner dimension, of how a *mitzvah* was to be performed, with what motivation and intention, affects Judaism from its earliest period. It is this tension which at different times led to revivalist movements within Judaism of a mystical or *musar* (ethical) nature. These movements wanted to reassert the place of faith, of morality, and of man's inner condition, against overly mechanistic tendencies which seemed to have grown out of the Jewish ritual base and dominated the life and consciousness of the Jews.

Redemption

Besides the monotheistic belief, the assumptions about the special covenantal relation between God and the Jewish people, and the expression of this covenant in *Torah* and *mitzvah*, there is one other fundamental structure of Jewish religion. This is the belief in historic redemption, the messianic era brought about by a messianic figure or figures. Associated with messianic redemption is the ingathering of the exiled Jews to the land of Israel, the rebuilding of the Temple, the resurrection of the dead, and the judgment of mankind. The exact order of these events, and their nature, was differently interpreted by different schools of thought. Their significance, however, is common to all trends within Judaism until the modern period when Jewish modernists subjected them to a reassessment along with other traditional doctrines and practices.

During the long 'night of exile' in the centuries following the destruction of the second Temple, when the Jew became painfully aware of the contradiction between his ideal status as chosen by, and beloved of, God and his real situation as spurned and often persecuted by man, the idea of messianic redemption was singularly important. Although suffering the Jew lived with the hope and vision of a golden age to come. He could look forward to a time when the true nature of Israel would be revealed to the world, and when the nations would come to bow down in the House of God in Jerusalem. These two ideas, that of the unrecognized exalted status of the Jewish people and that of the redemption, are expressed forcefully in the *Aleinu* prayer which is recited at the conclusion of every liturgy. The original form of this prayer was composed by a talmudic sage for use on the New Year festival, but was adapted by the liturgy to be said thrice daily, presumably because it captured a thought which needed constant reiteration in the face of despair and recalcitrant circumstances.

We should praise the Lord of all things, ascribe greatness to the Creator, who has not made us like the nations of the lands, nor placed us like the families of the earth. For He has not apportioned our lot as theirs, and our destiny as that of all their masses. For they bow down to vanity and emptiness, and pray to a god who does not save. While we bend the knee and bow down, and give thanks before the King, King of Kings, the Holy One, Blessed be He . . . He, and no other, is our God. Our King is true, others beside Him are naught . . . Therefore we direct hope to you, O Lord our God, to see the glory of Your power quickly; to take away idols from the world, and to surely cut down [false] gods; to rectify the world under the Kingdom of the Almighty, and all sons of flesh shall call on Your name; to turn all the wicked of the earth to You. Let all the dwellers on earth recognize and know that to You all knees should bend . . . Let all of them accept the yoke of Your kingship, and You shall quickly rule over them for ever.

Doctrinal Principles

Although we have set out some of the main parameters of Jewish belief, there is no general agreement within Judaism on the content of a doctrinal platform necessary for traditional orthodoxy. Until the period of the medieval theologians there were no attempts at constructing such a platform and the whole question of doctrine was in a state of considerable fluidity. The *Mishnah*[32] enumerates those categories of Jews who forfeit their portion in the World to Come: those who deny that the resurrection of the dead is taught by the *Torah*,[33] those who deny that the *Torah* is from heaven, and the Epicurean. Other sages add to this list also those who read the external books (containing heretical ideas), those who whisper an incantation over a wound, and those who pronounce the divine name as it is written. Clearly, however, the *Mishnah* is not setting out the conditions for doctrinal orthodoxy, but limiting itself to a specific area. For all the fluidity of rabbinic discussion there were any number of commonly shared doctrinal assumptions the denial of which would place someone in the position of a heretic or sectarian. It is the meaning of these assumptions, and their detailed character, which is the subject of debate and differences of opinion in talmudic literature.

The attempt to formulate a doctrinal platform really begins in the twelfth century with Maimonides' commentary to the above *Mishnah*, where he sets out thirteen principles of belief. Seven of these principles concern the belief in God: His existence, unity, incorporeality, eternity, that He is the sole object of worship, knows men's thoughts and deeds, and rewards and punishes. Four principles deal with revelation: the belief in prophecy, that Moses is highest in rank of all the prophets, that the *Torah* was given by God to Moses, and that the *Torah* is unchangeable. Finally two principles concern the coming of the Messiah and the Resurrection.

In the post-Maimonidean period there was considerable discussion of whether these principles were all necessary or sufficient to determine normative Jewish belief. Criticism of Maimonides ranged from those who detected an arbitrary selection process in the choice of principles, since clearly they are not all of equal importance, to those who castigated Maimonides for having limited the list to thirteen. In the course of time, despite the caveats, the thirteen principles became the unofficial creed of many sections of Judaism and found their way in different forms into the standard prayer book, to be recited at the beginning or end of the morning liturgy. Jewish pietists, however, remained wary of using them since they seemed to reflect an atmosphere of medieval philosophy which was rejected as an alien import into Judaism and anathema to the more mystically minded.

The possession of a doctrinal platform helped Jews sort out their differences with Christianity and Islam, and more particularly with Jewish sectarian movements, and thus the need for a formal creed represents a certain phase within the Jewish history of ideas. The issues which beset the modern Jew are of a different nature and turn on questions of meaning, of the extent to which a doctrine is wholly or partially to be understood literally or re-interpreted in modern categories. The mode of formulation of Maimonides or other medieval theologians is only partially intelligible to the modernist, and the central concerns of the latter differ markedly from those of the former. The hyperbolic manner of expression of the talmudic sages on matters of doctrines, for all the bewildering complexity of the differences between one sage and another, seem to wear better over time. Rabbinic *aggadah* by its very nature calls out for exegesis, and thus allows the modernist to find a relevant meaning-dimension for problems associated with God, revelation or man. The lines drawn by the medieval thinkers, by contrast, were much finer and, as attempts to make final statements about doctrine, too bound-up with the medieval philosophical coinage.

Outside of Orthodoxy a much more free-ranging examination of Jewish doctrine has taken place within Judaism in the nineteenth and twentieth centuries. The modern Reconstructionist movement, founded in North America in the 1920s, for example, has replaced Maimonides' thirteen principles in its prayer book by thirteen criteria of Jewish loyalty. The argument is that loyalty can no longer be a credal matter, but the experience of life enriched through the Jewish heritage. The Reconstructionist criteria are generalized, moral principles for reflection and the guidance of action, representing what the Reconstructionist Jew seeks from Judaism.[34]

3

The Bible and Revelation

History and Tradition

Although theological interpretation of historical events is characteristic of major sections of the Hebrew Bible neither biblical religion
nor rabbinic Judaism was interested in history as it is understood
in the modern world. In line with biblical paradigms Judaism was
not interested in purveying objective historical data. The value of
history was its religious and ethical content, and little attempt was
made to distinguish fact and interpretation.

The past was continually being re-interpreted by Jewish theologians to throw light on the religious ideas of the present, and
rabbinic exegesis saw the heroes of biblical religion as paragons
of rabbinic religious piety. This somewhat playful approach to the
past, as exemplified by the midrashic interpretation of the Bible,
characterized Jewish thought up to the modern era. Individual Jewish thinkers may, on occasion, have tried to unravel the essentially
homiletical structure of the *aggadah* to reveal its factual basis, but
they were the exception rather than the rule.

Just as the first-century Jewish historian Josephus, like many of his
gentile contemporaries, thought nothing of putting long speeches
into the mouths of historical characters he was writing about, so
the talmudic sages allowed their current debates about religious
ideas to be read back into the past. Since the *Talmud* exerted
considerable authority on medieval Judaism, attaining the status of
a semi-canonical text, it was considered impious to dismiss rabbinic
historiography as heuristic anachronism. Those Jewish thinkers who
maintained an independent stance in such matters came in for
severe criticism, and were accused of heresy, by conservatives for
whom every word of the *Talmud* was sacred lore.

The aftermath of the medieval controversies has spilled over into the modern period, and the fact that Judaism was more interested in the working of Providence in human history than in the sometimes less convenient details of that history, has created problems for contemporary Jewish theology. A number of Orthodox intellectuals feel committed, by the authority of the past and particularly the talmudic past, to a view of the history of the cosmos, of the human race, and of the Jewish people and Jewish religion, which is at variance with modern ideas on these subjects.

The recently deceased leader of the New York based Lubavitch Chasidic group, R. Menachem Schneerson (1902–94), who incidentally received university training in engineering science, revived the nineteenth-century viewpoint that the world was created complete with the fossilized remains of prehistoric animals and with various geological strata. Since, according to Jewish reckoning, the world is only a little over 5,700 years old, any scientific findings which seem to negate this figure are based on a false premise – namely that the fossils or geo-physical data represent real temporal development.

It is this area of the literal acceptance of traditional Jewish conceptions about the past which is one of the dividing lines between Orthodoxy on the one hand, and Conservative and Reform Judaism on the other. The latter two groups have been willing, in different degrees, to see the rabbinic and medieval viewpoints as not religiously binding on the modern Jew, though containing important insights for him. The former group, by the very nature of its belief in the authority of the *Talmud* and post-talmudic literature, is less open to such flexibility. Whereas some Orthodox thinkers have been willing to give the Genesis account of creation a non-literal interpretation, and even to accept a modified version of the theory of Evolution as not contrary to Jewish teaching, few have been able to reconcile modern views on biblical literature or Jewish history with traditional teachings.

In the early 1960s British Jewry was rocked by a controversy over the published views of a member of the rabbinical establishment, Rabbi Dr Louis Jacobs, which were sympathetic to a critico-historical view of the Bible. The Orthodox rabbinical hierarchy in London vetoed Jacobs' appointment as head of Jews' College, an institution for the training of Orthodox rabbis, on the grounds of the incompatibility of his views with traditional Jewish belief.

In 1964 a similar situation developed in Israel when the historian Cecil Roth, a Jew of Modern Orthodox persuasion, was appointed to Bar Ilan University. Roth, in one of his works on Jewish history, had presented both traditional and critico-historical views without claiming he supported the latter. Nevertheless there was a protest against his appointment from some leading Israeli rabbis and Bar Ilan University, which is an Orthodox institution, was under considerable pressure to withdraw its offer of a professorship. Eventually Roth resigned and left Israel to take up an appointment in the USA.

One of the hurdles which Orthodoxy still faces is the clarification of its position on the whole issue of modern biblical scholarship. Two directions seem open, either the development of some kind of synthesis between traditional and modern views, or a defence of the traditional position using generally accepted historical and scientific criteria. So far Orthodoxy has elected to maintain a low profile and only a handful of Orthodox scholars have sought to argue for the traditional position in this way, and even then using an oblique approach. This has to be contrasted with attempts at synthesis between theories of the age of the world or the evolution of life and Jewish belief, which have been forthcoming from more modernist Orthodox intellectuals. The whole subject of biblical criticism is a very sensitive one, and whatever the private views of individual rabbis there is a general feeling that the Orthodox position on revelation and the authority of Scripture and tradition would be undermined by the acceptance of critico-historical assumptions. An Orthodox rabbi advocating such an acceptance would be viewed by his colleagues as declaring himself outside the sphere of Orthodoxy.

Even the mere entertainment of the ideas of modern biblical scholarship, particularly those denying Mosaic authorship of the Pentateuch, is anathema to most Orthodox thinkers. The possibility of studying such ideas and defending the traditional view of the dating and authorship of the Bible is therefore closed to them. We find a leading Orthodox rabbi of the last generation complaining about the lack of response to challenges of critical scholarship on the part of his Orthodox colleagues:

> The spade of criticism has been lifted up by modern scholars particularly against the book of books, the perfect *Torah* of God, in order to dig with it under the received tradition and to undermine its foundations. The works of Welhausen and Kittel are translated into Hebrew, and to our grief and distress these words of poison and destruction find willing ears also among many of our own, traditionally-educated, young people. But to our grief not one of

the great sages of Israel has gone out to fight a holy war against
those who wish to uproot everything.[1]

By contrast Progressive Jewish theologians, who have accepted
the critico-historical picture of the Bible as a collection of traditions
edited over a long period of time and reflecting a variety of different
religious standpoints, are faced by the problem of building a new
framework for the idea of revelation. Once the classical Jewish
model of God literally revealing the Bible to Moses and the prophets,
word for word, is rejected questions of the authority of Scripture
and the relevance of the biblical commandments for modern man
become paramount. These questions are still being grappled with
by thinkers within both Conservative and Reform Judaism, and no
ideological solutions have as yet won general acceptance in either
case.

For Orthodox Judaism the problem is made more complex, and
at the same time more amenable of solution, by the very fluidity
of doctrinal statements. Thus while the *Talmud* makes any number
of statements about prophecy and revelation, and even lists which
biblical books or parts of books were written by which prophets, it
pictures Moses as not being able to understand the Judaism of the
second century.

> When Moses ascended on high he found the Holy One, blessed be
> He, sitting and binding crowns on the letters. He said to Him: Master
> of the universe who necessitates this from You? He replied: There is
> someone who will appear at the end of a number of generations,
> and Akiva ben Joseph is his name, who will exegetically derive
> mountains upon mountains of laws from each and every stroke.
> He said to Him: Master of the universe show him to me. He replied:
> Turn backwards. He [Moses] went and sat at the end of the eighth
> row and he did not know what they were saying. He felt weak.
> When a particular point was reached the pupils said to him [i.e.
> R. Akiva]: Rabbi, from where do you know this? He said to them:
> It is a law of Moses from Sinai. His [i.e. Moses'] mind was put at
> rest.[2]

It is certainly possible to interpret this story as saying that
Judaism undergoes religious development and that the talmudic
rabbis recognized that it had grown and changed by the mishnaic
period into a form incomprehensible to its biblical progenitors. This
story has to be set side by side with other teachings on the nature
of the religion revealed to Moses which claim that not only did

Moses receive the Pentateuch from God, but that he also received the *Mishnah*, the talmudic discussions, the *aggadah*, and even what a mature student will expound before his teacher in future times, at Sinai.[3]

The Bible as Jewish Scripture

The Hebrew Scriptures are more or less identical with the Old Testament of the Christian canon. Some Christian denominations include works which are not part of the Jewish canon, e.g. *Esdras, Maccabees, Tobit, Judith,* etc. These works are known as the Apocrypha and their inclusion is due to the fact that they are found in the Septuagint, the early Greek translation of the Bible, which influenced Christian discussions of canonicity. The term 'Old Testament' is a specifically Christian one since it contrasts the Hebrew Bible with the New Testament of Christianity. The implications of the use of these two terms are that the Covenant between God and the old Israel (Judaism) contained in the Old Testament has been superseded by the Covenant with the new Israel (Christianity) contained in the New Testament. The term is thus rarely used by Jews who prefer more neutral descriptions such as the Hebrew Bible or the *Tanakh*. This last term is made up of the initial letters of the tripartite division of Jewish Scripture: *Torah* (the Pentateuch), *Neviim* (Prophets), and *Ketuvim* (Hagiographa). Other common terms for Scripture among Jews are the Holy Writings, or simply *Torah* used in its wider sense to refer to the whole collection of scriptural books.

The concept of a canon of Scripture is not found as such in classical Judaism. In mishnaic times, i.e. to the end of the second century CE, there seem to have been various kinds of distinctions at work with regard to the biblical corpus. A group of writings, known as the Holy Writings, were recognized as inspired to different degrees and to which other writings, known as Extraneous Books, were contrasted. The latter, possessing merely secular status, contained works of purely human wisdom. The rabbis spoke out against some of them to prevent confusion between them and sacred writ,[4] and especially against those which were heretical works purporting to be inspired.[5]

Whereas some of these works of human wisdom, e.g. *The Wisdom of Ben Sira* or *Ecclesiasticus*, were often used and quoted by the sages despite misgivings that they might be accepted as divinely inspired, the heretical works were rejected outright. Among these are presumably to be counted some of the early Christian proto-gospels. The distinction between 'Holy' and 'Extraneous' texts was still a matter of controversy in mishnaic times, as was the issue of whether all of the Holy Writings should be allowed to circulate freely or some be withdrawn from circulation. The first controversy is reflected in a discussion in the *Mishnah* about the ritual impurity of the hands from contact with works of Scripture:

> All of the Holy Writings make the hands ritually unclean. The Song of Songs and Ecclesiastes defile the hands. R. Judah says: the Song of Songs defiles the hands, but there is a dispute about Ecclesiastes. R. Jose says: Ecclesiastes does not defile the hands, but there is a dispute about the Song of Songs . . . R. Simeon ben Azzai said: I have a tradition . . . that the Song of Songs and Ecclesiastes both defile the hands. R. Akiva said: Heaven forbid. No man of Israel has ever disputed about the Song of Songs, claiming that it did not defile the hands. For the whole world is not worthy of the day that the Song of Songs was given to Israel. For all the scriptures are holy, but the Song of Songs is the holy of holies. If there was a dispute, it was a dispute about Ecclesiastes.[6]

The dispute recorded in the *Mishnah* was whether Ecclesiastes and the Song of Songs were divinely inspired, and hence Holy Writings, or merely the human wisdom of their authors. Both works were problematic. Ecclesiastes seems to preach cynicism, and the Song of Songs is set as a secular love duet. By the time of R. Akiva, second century CE, the Song of Songs had been accepted by some groups as an allegory of the love between Israel and God, hence R. Akiva's extremely defensive stance. Ecclesiastes too was eventually interpreted in a manner which made it acceptable as Scripture.[7] A similar problem arose about the character of the Book of Esther, which is written in an overtly secular manner, until it was finally accepted as the product of divine inspiration.[8]

The second issue, that of allowing the free circulation of certain divinely inspired texts, comes out in reference to the prophecies of Ezekiel. Although Ezekiel was assumed to be one of the Holy Writings, certain of its teachings were apparently in contradiction to Jewish teaching, and the sages wished to put it into *genizah*, i.e. to take it out of circulation. It was only the efforts of Chananiah ben Chizkiah, a leader of the Shammaite faction in the first century who interpreted the controversial passages to fit in with accepted views, that guaranteed the inclusion of Ezekiel in the canon.[9] In a similar vein the contradictory nature of different verses in the Book of Proverbs threatened for a time to have that work placed in a *genizah*.[10]

The Jewish canon, then, was defined by two considerations. The first was whether or not a certain work was considered to be written under the influence of divine inspiration, and the second was whether such an inspired work should be allowed to circulate or be withdrawn lest it be misunderstood. The need for a strictly delineated canon, rather than a more loosely-knit collection of sacred, semi-sacred and secular texts is determined by the prevailing circumstances. When there are works in circulation which propound heretical ideas and claim scriptural status then it becomes necessary to draw the boundary between inspired scripture and extraneous works. When works, which are accepted as inspired, lend themselves to interpretations which are at variance with the tradition then the further step of removing the works from the area of practical reference has to be considered. By the end of the second century both these considerations had run their course and Judaism had fixed the biblical canon in the final form which it has retained to the present time.

Bible Study and Bible Commentary

Though the Hebrew Bible is the basic and most important component of the Jewish literary heritage, it is rarely read by Jews as a straight text. Instead it is studied with the help of the classical commentaries, since it is not the text as such which is holy but the text as interpreted by the Jewish tradition of rabbinic exegesis. The Pentateuch is the best known section, read in its entirety in a yearly cycle in traditional synagogues Sabbath after Sabbath. Progressive communities either follow the same cycle, though they are likely to select a portion of the weekly reading rather than the whole which may be considered overlong for public recitation, or use a triennial Pentateuchal cycle. Since the traditional reading of the Pentateuch is in Hebrew, sung or chanted according to a special cantillation, congregants will usually follow it from a text having the Hebrew plus a translation and often also a brief vernacular commentary.

Apart from the Pentateuch certain sections of the Prophets would be known to Jews as they form the concluding portion (*haftarah*) of the weekly reading. These, however, only represent a small proportion of biblical literature. Other biblical books are read on special occasions, such as the five scrolls (*megillot*), Song of Songs, Ruth, Lamentations, Ecclesiastes and Esther, and the Book of Jonah. Many selections from other books of the Hebrew Bible are included in the liturgy, interwoven with prayers, the Book of Psalms being the outstanding example of this genre.

Large sections of the Bible would be virtually unknown to the majority of Jews, even those who regularly attend synagogue services. Many will have been taught some biblical history, and perhaps studied selective texts in the preparation for their *bar mitzvah* or *bat mitzvah* ceremonies, for boys and girls respectively, which take place at the onset of puberty. Others will attend adult study groups which may take a biblical text as a subject of study, but usually from the Pentateuch rather than say Kings or Isaiah. Modern Jews who continue their religious education into adult life are, anyhow the exception not the rule.

Even more traditionalist Jews, who take the commandment to study the *Torah* as a religious duty devolving on young and old alike, will devote only a small proportion of their time to biblical books other than the Pentateuch. The curriculum of the *yeshivah*, which is the main educational institution of the traditionalist, reflects this situation acutely. The overwhelming percentage of *yeshivah* studies are concentrated on the *Babylonian Talmud* and its commentaries. A certain amount of free time may be set aside for the student to devote to the weekly Pentateuchal reading, but there are no public lectures on the Bible and no place is made available in the timetable for private study of it. While it is true that the *Talmud* refers on occasion to many biblical verses, it is concerned more with the Pentateuch than with say the prophetic message or the historical books of the Bible. There is a well-known Jewish joke about the *yeshivah* student who knows of a biblical verse because he knows on which page of the *Talmud* it is mentioned.

These features of traditional Jewish life bring out the centrality of traditional commentary and exegesis in the Jewish approach to Scripture. The sage has primacy over the prophet[11] because he interprets and integrates the divinely inspired message into the life of the people. Without the stabilizing effect of the traditional understanding of the Bible, the teachings of the latter are open to interpretations which would break up the cultural diversity-in-unity of the Jewish people. Certain sections of Scripture are more important to the traditional perspective, and these would be better known to Jews than the rest of the Bible. None of this, of course, justifies the avoidance of Bible study among Jews, and Jewish educationalists themselves have on occasion protested at this neglect of the basic text of Jewish religion. The *Mishnah* lays down a balanced educational programme:

> At five a boy [should be taught] Scripture, at ten *Mishnah* . . . at fifteen *Talmud*.[12]

Non-traditionalist groups in the last century or so have tried to rectify the situation, for instance Zionist educational institutions in Israel teach the Bible, biblical history and biblical poetry as an essential part of their curriculum, and Reform Judaism has also shifted the emphasis of its Jewish education from talmudic to biblical studies. The effect of all this has not, as yet, substantially changed the situation either among traditionalists or among the average synagogue-going Jews of the Diaspora.

Since it is the Bible seen through the eyes of tradition which is all-important for Judaism, a brief word is necessary on the main components of this traditional perspective. The process of commentary on the sacred text is presumably as old as the text itself. This process is implicit in the biblical account of how Ezra the Scribe read the book of the *Torah* of Moses to the people gathered in Jerusalem. He had with him the Levites and a number of prominent individuals who explained what was being read to the masses, so that they should understand its import.[13] In the course of time, when Aramaic rather than Hebrew became the *lingua franca* of the Jews, Aramaic translations-cum-commentaries arose which sought to incorporate rabbinic exegesis into their explanations of the scriptural text. These Aramaic versions are known as *targumim* (singular *targum*), and the public recitation of the *Torah* would be accompanied by a *targum*, or 'translation', in mishnaic times.[14] Eventually standardized Aramaic *targumim* were written down, though their origins and dates have not been established except tentatively, and much remains obscure about the circumstances of their composition.

The best known, and most popular, of the *targumim* is the *Targum Onkelos* on the Pentateuch. This is ascribed by Jewish tradition to a convert to Judaism who composed his *targum* under the supervision of two leading rabbis of the second century.[15] Most scholars regard this ascription as doubtful, and the consequence of confusion between *Onkelos* and a Greek translation of the Bible by Aquilas. Whatever its true origins *Onkelos* came to be accepted as an inspired version, and the ninth-century Babylonian sage Sar Shalom Gaon writes of it:

> Other *targumim* do not have the same sanctity as this *targum*. I have heard from the sages of old that the Holy One, blessed be He, performed a great thing for the convert *Onkelos* in that this *targum* came about through his agency.[16]

Onkelos provides a very restrained translation of the text, sticking closely to the Hebrew original and not introducing too many aggadic asides. A characteristic feature of *Onkelos* is the avoidance of overtly anthropomorphic expressions when referring to God, such biblical anthropomorphisms being neutralized in the Aramaic paraphrase. In most printed editions of the Pentateuch the *Targum Onkelos* is included side by side with the Hebrew text, although its importance for the modern Jew has receded, and been replaced by the commentary of R. Solomon Yitzchaki (1040–1105), known as Rashi. Whereas the *Talmud* recommends that the individual Jew should read over the scriptural portion of the week twice, and the *targum* to it once,[17] the fourteenth-century halakhist R. Jacob ben Asher says in his code:

> If someone has studied the scriptural portion with Rashi's commentary, that is as good as the *targum*. For the only purpose of the *targum* is to make the subject matter comprehensible.[18]

Other authorities disagreed with this ruling because they felt that *Onkelos* was in a class of its own, it was even said that the Aramaic version of *Onkelos* was revealed at Sinai. Nevertheless since Jews ceased to understand Aramaic the custom of using an alternative translation/commentary became widespread.

Of the other *targumim* to various sections of the Bible the most important are the various versions of *Targum Yerushalmi*, the Jerusalem or Palestinian *targum*, to the Pentateuch. Though this *targum* never attained the semi-canonical status conferred on *Onkelos* it is of major importance in understanding early rabbinic exegesis of Scripture. *Targum Yerushalmi*, which is written in Galilean Aramaic and thus contrasts with the Babylonian language of *Onkelos*, contains a great deal of midrashic material and is thus a commentary to, rather than merely a translation of, the text. In 1956 a complete manuscript of *Targum Yerushalmi* was discovered in the Vatican where it had been wrongly catalogued as a version of *Onkelos*. This manuscript, known as *Neofiti 1*, has added greatly to our understanding of many areas in the development of Jewish theology and Bible interpretation. Its importance has been recognized as second only to the discovery of the Qumran library, and a leading scholar of traditional Jewish exegesis says that the discovery of the manuscript of *Targum Yerushalmi* on the Pentateuch is the most important discovery, both in quantity and in quality, among Hebrew manuscripts relating to *Torah* subjects which have been uncovered in the world in recent times.[19]

Medieval and Modern Bible Commentary

In the medieval period we see the beginning of Bible commentary *per se*. The incentive came from the need to explain the text and to negate contemporary views about particular passages which were not in accord with orthodox rabbinic teaching. The Bible commentaries of Saadiah Gaon (ninth to tenth centuries), for instance, were concerned with polemics against Karaite schismatics and with defending traditional interpretations. The most important medieval commentator is Rashi, who lived in northern France in the eleventh century. Unlike the exegesis found in midrashic literature, which is not tied closely to the text but wanders far from its literal meaning, Rashi's commentary preserves rabbinic interpretations of Scripture while attempting a near literal exposition of the plain meaning of the Bible.

Interspersed in Rashi's commentary are grammatical explanations, criticisms of other commentators, translations of difficult terms into old French, anti-Christian polemics, and selected midrashic comments. The *midrashim* which Rashi quotes became the common heritage of the ordinary Jew who knew of them from his acquaintanceship with Rashi rather than from any contact with midrashic literature. Traditional Jewish Bible study was invariably accompanied by Rashi's commentary, which attained an almost sacrosanct status, and was commented on in turn by literally hundreds of super-commentaries. Rashi also influenced Christian students of the Bible in the Middle Ages.

Two other medieval commentaries attained the status of classics, and were in turn the subject of many super-commentaries, though neither supplanted Rashi as the standard expositor of the Bible. They were the commentary of Abraham Ibn Ezra (1089–1164), a peripatetic Spanish scholar, and that of Moses ben Nachman (1194–1270), known as Ramban or Nachmanides, who was a Spanish mystic and talmudist. Ibn Ezra was a man of many parts: poet, grammarian, astronomer, astrologer, mathematician and philosopher, and his Bible commentary reflects his various interests. The demands which Ibn Ezra makes on even the more sophisticated user of his commentary were such as to exclude popular access to his work, which had none of the homely character of Rashi's writings. He also possessed a sharp critical faculty and an independence of mind which led him to reject many of the traditional interpretations, even those proffered by the talmudic sages. For this he was severely criticized by later scholars, and pietists were wary of using his commentary, despite the fact that Jewish legend depicts him as a wonder-working mystic who at one point created a *golem*, or artificial man.

Nachmanides' commentary is closer to rabbinic orthodoxy than that of Ibn Ezra, and on occasion he takes the latter to task for his heterodox views. Nachmanides says in the introduction to his commentary that he has for Ibn Ezra 'a secret love but an open criticism'. He also argues against the allegorizing tendencies of Jewish philosophers who denied the reality of biblical accounts of angels or miracles. Nachmanides refers at certain points of his commentary to the mystical interpretation of the text which he believed was the true meaning of Scripture, but he never develops kabbalistic ideas at any length. He does, however, expand on certain theological themes, in contrast to Rashi whose comments are invariably brief.

Throughout the Middle Ages, and from then until modern times, Jewish scholars produced a great variety of biblical commentaries reflecting the theological, philosophical, homiletic and exegetical interests of each period. Some are genuine commentaries, others use the commentary form to clothe their ideas and diverge markedly from the text they are interpreting. Since the ordinary, unscholarly, Jew was most likely to absorb his knowledge of Jewish thought from study of the Pentateuch plus commentary, this was the surest medium for the transmittal of new ideas to the Jewish masses. It is no accident that when the Jews began to emerge from their physical and cultural ghetto, in the eighteenth and early nineteenth centuries, the ideology of the Jewish enlightenment should find expression in a new form of biblical exegesis.

The first work conveying this ideology was the commentary to the whole Hebrew Bible, known as the *Biur*, produced by Moses Mendelssohn (1729–86) and his colleagues. The *Biur* seeks to present the literal meaning of the text of the Bible in the spirit of the rabbinic tradition, but avoiding *midrash* or rabbinic dialectics. Accompanying the *Biur* was a translation of the Bible into German, written in Hebrew characters, which Mendelssohn hoped would educate the Jews in the language of their gentile cultural environment, and end their use of Yiddish, a Judaeo-German dialect. Another of Mendelssohn's aims was to reintroduce the poetry, beauty of expression, and moral values of the Bible to the Jewish populace who he felt were spiritually unprepared for the European world outside the ghetto.

Even the traditionalists, who opposed what they took to be the excesses of the Enlightenment, used scriptural exegesis as a primary medium of counter-reformation. Thus R. Samson Raphael Hirsch (1808–88), the father of German Neo-Orthodoxy, wrote a long German commentary on the Pentateuch in which the traditional interpretations of the Jewish past are defended against modernist ideas, but at the same time the tradition itself is reinterpreted in the sophisticated concepts of nineteenth-century thought.

4

The Origins and Growth
of Jewish Thought

Early Movements and Sects in Judaism

All forms of modern Judaism, Orthodox, Conservative, Reconstructionist and Reform, are developments of Pharisaic religion as it has come down to us in talmudic literature. The Pharisees and their interpretation of the religion of Israel dominated Jewish life in the period after the destruction of the Temple in 70 CE. The movements and sects which existed side by side with Pharisaism in the first century CE., such as the aristocratic, cult-centred Sadducees, the ascetic, monastic groups of Essenes, and the Jewish Christians who were the original followers of Jesus, fell into decline after the destruction of the Temple. They were unable to adapt to the challenges facing a Judaism bereft of a cultic centre.

The Sadducees did not accept Pharisaic methods of biblical interpretation which enabled the latter movement to develop both their doctrine and their rituals in a very flexible way. The Sadducees adopted a conservative literalistic approach to the biblical text. Thus they understood the injunction of 'an eye for an eye, a tooth for a tooth'[1] to mean precisely what it says, while the majority of the Pharisees interpreted it to refer to monetary compensation. It was this inflexible literalism, coupled with the importance of the sacrificial Temple ritual for the Sadducees, who were mainly priests, which prevented Sadducee religion from recovering after the trauma of 70 CE.

The Essenes were sectarians who kept to themselves and did not participate in the turbulent currents of Jewish life in Palestine in the pre-Christian and immediate post-Christian period. This may well explain why they are nowhere mentioned either in the New Testament or in rabbinic literature. We know of their existence, and something about their beliefs and way of life, from the works of the first-century Jewish historian Josephus, from non-Jewish authors such as Pliny the Elder, from Philo of Alexandria, and most importantly from the writings first discovered in 1947 in the Wadi Qumran area near the Dead Sea. There are discrepancies in the various accounts of the sect preserved in different sources, and it is therefore reasonable to assume that a number of Essene subgroups existed in the two centuries prior to the destruction of the Temple. Some Essenes lived in strict monastic communities like that at Qumran, while others formed sub-communities in towns and villages. While celibacy seems to have been common among the members of the sect, we have reports of Essenes marrying, and indeed the graves of four women and a child were found in the ancient cemetery of Qumran.

The Essenes, whose name probably means 'healers'[2] had much in common with Pharisaic Judaism in the area of *halakhah*[3] but were stricter in their interpretation of halakhic rules, particularly in their attitude to ritual purity and impurity. They differed from the Pharisees on a number of matters of belief, the Qumran sectarians, for example, considered themselves to be 'sons of light' who would fight against the ruling majority, the 'sons of darkness', in the messianic struggle which they believed was imminent. There is considerable scholarly dispute, however, about whether the literature found at Qumran all actually belonged to the Essenes, or whether many of the texts were deposited at Qumran by other sectarian groups for safekeeping.

The various Jewish-Christian groups in first – and second-century Palestine seem to have shared the general Pharisaic outlook. They differed from the Pharisees in their claim that Jesus was the Messiah, a claim which the Pharisees disputed. The doctrine of the Incarnation, namely that Jesus was the incarnate son of God, was not subscribed to by the early Jewish-Christians in Palestine and therefore did not act as the kind of theological barrier between Jews and Christians which it was to become at a late date. Jewish-Christian ritual was essentially Pharisaic, and there is some evidence of close contact between Jewish-Christians and Pharisees in the early period of the Jewish-Christian Church. Rabbinic literature tells how a leading rabbi of the first-second centuries, Eliezer ben Hyrcanus, learnt a Jewish-Christian *halakhah* from a pupil of Jesus, and was pleased by it.[4] Eventually, however, the rabbis severed their contacts with the sect, declaring them heretical and burning their writings. A prayer was even introduced into the daily liturgy against them.[5] With the spread of gentile Christianity, which differed from Jewish Christianity both in its attitudes to halakhic ritual and in its Christology, and with the shift away from Jerusalem as the centre of the fledgling Church after the destruction of the Temple, Jewish-Christians gradually disappeared from the scene.

In keeping with rabbinic dislike of disputation with sectarian groups the rabbis avoided direct theological confrontation with Christians after they had outlawed Jewish-Christian groups.[6] They did, however, polemicize against gentile Christian belief that God had a son,[7] or that Christianity was the New Israel.[8]

The Pharisees

The Pharisaic group within Judaism of the first century CE was one of the largest factions in Palestine. Although Josephus estimates their number during the reign of Herod the Great as 6,000,[9] he is possibly counting only those who were members of the Pharisaic inner community, the *chavurah*. To belong to this inner community a member, or *chaver*, had to undertake to follow special precepts of ritual purity and to be scrupulous about tithing procedures.

The Pharisees (*perushim*) began as a distinct movement sometime in the early Hasmonean period, i.e. after 160 BCE. The name could well mean 'separators', and may have been applied to them in the period of John Hyrcanus (second century BCE) when the Sadducees took control of the supreme religious council, the *Sanhedrin*. Those who separated themselves from the Sadducee dominated *Sanhedrin*, and refused to participate in its deliberations, would then have been referred to as Pharisees. Several other possible derivations of the name have been suggested, e.g. those who separate themselves from ritually unclean things, or, using a different etymology of the name, those who were 'interpreters' of the *Torah*.

The Pharisees appear together with the Sadducees in the New Testament as the opponents of Jesus, and the Christian polemics against them depict them in a very negative manner. Talmudic literature itself recognizes the besetting sins of Pharisaism[10] among which are numbered religious ostentation, false humility, and exaggerated chastity. The Pharisaic 'hypocrites' of the New Testament[11] may well represent real Pharisaic types, but are hardly typical of Pharisaic piety in general.

The Pharisees saw themselves as the true heirs of biblical religion, preserving ancient traditions which had been handed down orally, and at the same time developing Judaism through the Pharisaic methods of biblical exegesis. It was Pharisaism alone out of all the factions within first-century Judaism which was able to rebuild Jewish life after the destruction of the Temple. Most of the basic ideas, practices and religious terminology of Judaism during the last one and a half millennia are already found in the different forms of Pharisaic teaching preserved and expanded in talmudic literature of the first five centuries of the common era. These teachings were first given definitive form by the councils of sages at Yavneh, post 70 CE, and at Usha in the second century CE.

While it is impossible to summarize Pharisaic religion, and continual reference back to talmudic ideas is necessary for any understanding of developments in medieval and modern Judaism, it is helpful to characterize briefly the main features of Pharisaic belief. As it is expressed through the matrix of the *Talmud* Pharisaic Judaism is centrally concerned with the unity of God, His relationship to the People of Israel whom He has chosen to give His *Torah*, or divinely inspired teaching, in the form of the written *Torah* (the Bible) and the oral *Torah* (the tradition). The details of this teaching affecting belief, attitudes, ritual, ethics, social life, indeed every aspect of the life of the Jew, are the main subject of reflection for the talmudic thinker and the guide for action of scholar and layman alike. The belief, and hope, in a messianic redemption to be inaugurated by a personal Messiah and accompanied by the resurrection of the dead rounds off the picture.

The above features of talmudic Judaism were not expounded systematically, as they might have been had the culture of classical Greece had more influence on rabbinic thought. Instead they emerge from a mode of expression which is self-consciously concrete, parabolic, and diffuse. It was only in the Middle Ages when there was cross-fertilization between Greek philosophy and rabbinic *aggadah* that attempts were made to give systematic coherence to Jewish theology. Rabbinic thought in its early period of formulation belongs to the general category of *midrash*, a category not found outside

Judaism but one which is common to Pharisaism, the Dead Sea
Sect, and New Testament literature.

Midrashic Thought-forms

Midrash literally means the 'searching out' or 'investigation' of
Scripture. A text, any text, needs to be expanded and interpreted
if it is to serve as a basis for formalized religious life. A body of
canonical Scripture raises the further problem of reconciling and
explaining different texts in the light of each other. In Judaism
these tasks represent the midrashic enterprise.

The earliest extant midrashic works date back to the second century CE, and they are mainly concerned with the halakhic portions
of the Pentateuch. They explain how the various rabbinic traditions
were derived from, or based on, the scriptural text and how the
hermeneutic rules were used to develop these traditions to confront
new situations. Only occasionally in the older midrashic works
do we find theological comments which were presumably used
as material for sermons addressed to a wider audience of Jews.
Later midrashic collections are replete with ethical and theological
teaching, some of which is closely related to textual exegesis but
much of which diverges very far from the textual subject-matter.
Different sages, and different schools of thought, interpreted the
texts and developed their halakhic and aggadic consequences in a
great variety of ways.

Some of the midrashic interpretations were taken up by the edi-
tors of the *Babylonian Talmud*, and because of the central role played
by that work in medieval Judaism they assumed a semi-doctrinal
status for subsequent Jewish belief. Nevertheless even the *Talmud*
usually cites several divergent views on a subject, and unless some
practical consequence was at stake it does not come down in favour
of any of them. This meant that the doctrinal content of rabbinic
aggadah remained in a very fluid condition, allowing for a variety of
positions to be adopted, all of them orthodox. The Spanish scholar,
Samuel Ha-Nagid, writes in the tenth century in his *Introduction to
the Talmud*:

> *Aggadah* is every explanation which comes in the *Talmud* on any
> subject which is not actually a commandment . . . you do not have
> to learn from it except what seems reasonable . . . What the sages
> explained in the scriptural verses, each one did so as it occurred

to him, and as he perceived it in his mind. Therefore what seems reasonable among these interpretations one may study, and as for the rest – one does not rely on them.

More conservative scholars found Samuel's somewhat nonchalant approach to *aggadah* destructive and likely to open the gates to all manner of doctrinal positions and heterodox opinions. They insisted on the divinely revealed quality of *aggadah*. 'We have to believe in all that is said in the *aggadah* of the sages,'[12] writes a nineteenth-century Palestinian scholar, R. Chaim Medini. It is of course impossible to accept all of *aggadah* as doctrinally binding because different and often contrary views are expressed within it. The conservative approach would be to try to minimize the contradictions by reconciling the different views wherever possible. The more liberal viewpoint, akin to that expressed by Samuel Ha-Nagid, is less troubled by the divergence of aggadic opinions. It sees the *aggadah* as reflecting the outlook of the age in which the sages lived, and feels free to re-interpret aggadic theology.[13]

The above difference of approach to *aggadah* is found throughout the medieval period and has continued to the present day in Orthodox Jewish circles. Modern pietistically inclined Jews insist on the inerrancy of rabbinic thought, and some even insist on the literal truth of many midrashic teachings. Others adopt a more sophisticated position which interprets *aggadah* as giving symbolic expression to truths of a psychological, ethical, or theological nature. Others again see rabbinic thought as permeated by the 'scientific' and cosmological views of the first five centuries and not binding, at least as far as its details are concerned, for modern Jewish theology. This latter position within contemporary Orthodox Judaism is close to the Progressive viewpoint which generally does not hold the beliefs of the past as sacrosanct.

Encounter with Philosophy

Biblical and rabbinic teachings were not conceived of as problematic as long as Judaism was content to work entirely within the framework of *aggadah*. The Greek-speaking Jews of Alexandria in Egypt were the first to be forced into a self-conscious evaluation of their religion in the light of philosophical concepts. The writings of Philo of Alexandria (circa 20 BCE to 50 CE), who is also known as Philo Judaeus, are testimony to the tensions and conflicts involved in this evaluation and the attempts to resolve them. Philo, writing both for Greek-speaking Jews and for gentiles, had to grapple with biblical anthropomorphisms, with the spiritual meaning of the seemingly crude Bible stories and of Jewish rituals, and with the nature and content of Jewish beliefs. His acquaintance with midrashic traditions is apparent in his biblical exegesis, and it is generally assumed that he knew Hebrew, although there were considerable differences between the Hellenistic Judaism of Egypt and the rabbinic Judaism of Palestine in the first century CE. From the Philonic corpus a Jewish philosophical religion emerges which is a synthesis between Stoic and Platonic philosophy and the religion of Israel. Since he wrote in Greek Philo's particular version of the Greek-Hebrew synthesis had no overall effect on the development of Judaism, though it was an important influence on the thinking of the early Christian Church.

The main line of Jewish philosophical thought began in the Moslem world among Jews who became acquainted with Greek philosophical works in Arabic translations. As Islamic theology absorbed Greek influence, Jewish thinkers, who until that time had remained within an aggadic framework, began to broaden their theological horizons. The first major Jewish philosopher-theologian was Saadiah Gaon (852–942) who, unlike Philo, was deeply rooted in the literature and thought-forms of talmudic Judaism. Apart from his theological writings Saadiah wrote extensively on rabbinic topics and occupied a senior position in the Jewish world as head of the Sura academy in Babylon.

Saadiah sets out on his theological venture with the assumption that Jewish religion and philosophical inquiry are two paths to the same goal, and that though one can arrive at truth through philosophical speculation religious tradition is needed for the non-philosophically minded. His main philosophical work *The Book of Beliefs and Opinions* is thus a rational presentation of Jewish teaching, shorn of its aggadic clothing and given coherence and systematic expression. It is apparent from the polemical tone of much of Saadiah's discussion that his primary purpose as a theologian was to defend Judaism against the claims of both Christianity and Islam, and to defend the particular tradition of rabbinical Judaism against sectarian movements within Judaism.

The major sectarian schism threatening Judaism in the period when Saadiah was writing was that of Karaism. It had begun in 767 CE when after a leadership dispute among Babylonian Jewry for the position of exilarch, or head of Diaspora Jewry, the losing candidate Anan ben David broke away from rabbinic Judaism. He founded a sect which later came to be known as Karaite Judaism, the name in Hebrew meaning 'Men of Scripture'. Anan attracted to himself members of small sectarian groups who had in common with him an opposition to the talmudic interpretation of the Bible. The Ananites, and the Karaite movement which developed from them, understood the biblical text more literally than rabbinic Judaism, and were stricter in many of their ritual practices.

Saadiah was faced by the problem of not only showing that Jewish teaching about the nature of God and man was superior to Christian and Moslem doctrines on these subjects, he also had to justify the methods of rabbinic tradition in its interpretation of Scripture. Saadiah is not content merely to defend rabbinic Judaism against the criticisms of the Karaites, he also attacks Karaite doctrine where this diverges from the talmudic tradition. Thus he discusses the belief in the transmigration of souls, which was subscribed to either by Anan or by some Karaites, and shows that it is warranted neither by reason nor by Scripture. Despite Saadiah's rejection of the belief it became a cornerstone of medieval Jewish mysticism.

As a contribution to pure philosophy there is little that is new in Saadiah. As a work of Jewish theology, however, Saadiah's *magnum opus* represents an important breakthrough. He sets up rational inquiry as an alternative to revelation and tradition in the search for religious truth, and though he believes there is no conflict between them he in fact re-interprets Jewish tradition to bring it into accord with rational analysis. The seeds are sown by Saadiah for the conflict between philosophical knowledge and traditional teachings which was to occupy the leading Jewish theologians in the centuries which followed. Saadiah was eventually superseded and eclipsed by thinkers of greater philosophical stature, nevertheless his work remained popular among Jewish pietists who regarded philosophy, generally speaking, as anathema. His popularity was enhanced by the legend of Saadiah's proficiency in kabbalistic magic through the aid of which he is reputed to have created a *golem*, or artificial man. The legend presumably arose from the ascription to him of a commentary on the mystical work *Sefer Yetzirah*. The genuine commentary of Saadiah on this work is of a very different nature. In the thirteenth century, when the controversies surrounding the permissibility of Jews studying and using gentile philosophy in the formulation of Jewish theology were at their height, a number of thinkers were severely critical of Saadiah and his pioneering efforts, one usually broad-minded talmudist even claiming that pious men should not follow sections of *The Book of Beliefs and Opinions* since they were not acceptable to Judaism.[14]

Judah Halevi

A new development took place in the early part of the twelfth century with the appearance of Judah Halevi's *Kuzari*. Halevi (before 1075–1141) is best known as a Hebrew poet, a number of his religious poems having been incorporated into the liturgy, and is remembered for the yearning for the return of the Jews to Zion expressed in some of his more popular hymns. Indeed Jewish legend tells of how Halevi himself left his native Spain and after many wanderings made his way to the Holy Land. On arrival in Jerusalem he bent down to kiss the earth which had been the subject of his poetic longings and was trampled to death by an Arab horseman. In fact, however, Halevi does not seem to have reached the Promised Land and he died in Egypt on his way to his beloved Zion.

Halevi's theological work the *Kuzari* was originally written in Arabic and entitled *The Book of Argument and Proof in Defence of the Despised Faith*. It is set in the form of a dialogue between the representatives of several faiths in the presence of the king of the Khazars, a Turkic people settled in the Volga-Caucasus region, the leading families of which converted to Judaism in the eighth century. The king wishes to find out which is the true faith and most of Halevi's book is taken up with the views of the Jewish sage and his answers to the king's questions.

Unlike previous works of Jewish theology the *Kuzari* is not an attempt at synthesis between Judaism and Greek philosophy, rather it is a book which defends Jewish traditionalism and attacks philosophy. In Halevi's dialogue the Khazar king comes to realize that both Christianity and Islam are based on Judaism and so decides to explore the mother faith. The Jewish sage, in whose mouth Halevi puts his own theology of Jewish existence, explains to the king that religious insights not only differ from, but are superior to, the truths of philosophical speculation. Knowledge of God can only come through prophecy, a gift which is the sole property of the people of Israel, and cannot be attained by purely human endeavours. Religious experience takes man into a realm which is beyond the reaches of philosophy. The latter is valid but limited in its scope. The religion of Israel is guaranteed as a genuine religion of prophetic revelation because the theophany at Sinai was witnessed by the Israelite masses assembled at the mountain. The same claim cannot be made either by Christianity or by Islam, and therefore the teachings and practices of Judaism have greater claim to be the authentic message of prophecy than other religions.

The polemical character of the *Kuzari* is apparent, since it seeks to show not only that Judaism is superior to its two daughter faiths, Christianity and Islam, but also to Karaism and to philosophically based theology. Halevi is aware of the danger to Jewish tradition once philosophy is allowed to sit in judgment on its teachings, for revelation will eventually give way to reason and the precepts of the *Torah* will lose their binding character. He thus uses philosophical argument to show the incoherences and inconsistencies in philosophy itself, and to undermine its status as a threat to traditional Judaism.

Halevi's stance on the limitations of philosophy and the uniqueness of the religion of Israel is representative of much of conservative Jewish theology from the Middle Ages to the present day. Elijah the Gaon of Vilna, the foremost talmudist of the eighteenth century, who was totally opposed to philosophy, though he advocated secular studies as an aid to an understanding of the *Talmud*, said of Halevi:

> The *Kuzari* is holy and pure, the fundamental principles of the faith of Israel and the *Torah* depend on it.[15]

Moses Maimonides

Despite the attempt of Judah Halevi to negate the value of philosophy for Jewish religious thought, the twelfth century saw the high point of medieval Jewish philosophizing. Aristotelianism became the predominant influence on Jewish theology, and out of the co-mingling of the streams of rabbinic *aggadah* and the Greek Peripatetic school Maimonides produced his *Guide for the Perplexed*, the most brilliant monument to the attempt at Hebrew-Greek synthesis.

Moses ben Maimon (1136–1204), commonly known as Rambam or Maimonides, was not only the outstanding figure of medieval Jewish thought, he was also a talmudist whose codification of *halakhah* the *Mishneh Torah* (or *Yad Ha-Chazakah*) was a major, some would say the major, contribution to the field of Jewish law. Maimonides considered philosophical investigation to be an integral part of Jewish religion, and he devotes most of the first book of his legal code to matters of faith and doctrine. Although he tries to express himself in the *Yad* (as his code is often referred to for short) in a manner suitable for the general, non-scholarly, reader the theological parts of the *Yad* make considerable demands on the intellect, and presuppose a certain level of sophistication. The inclusion of philosophically oriented theology in his code had a profound effect on subsequent Jewish thought, more so perhaps than the *Guide* itself. The code was used extensively by generations of talmudists who had little understanding of, and no sympathy for, Greek philosophy. Even those talmudic purists who shunned the overtly philosophical teachings of the *Yad* could not avoid the philosophical asides which Maimonides introduced into his discussion of purely ritual matters, nor the assumptions which underlie the order and presentation of Jewish law by one steeped in Aristotelian thought.

Maimonides believed that Judaism unenlightened by philosophical reflection was likely to contain heretical ideas. This is apparent from his attitude to the corporeal descriptions of God found throughout the Bible and *Talmud*, which he explains away as anthropomorphisms. In his code he classifies as a heretic 'one who says that there is one Lord, but that He is corporeal and can be pictorially depicted.'[16] It is necessary, therefore, to have attained a minimum of philosophical sophistication to avoid holding heretical beliefs, since these beliefs are implicit in a literalistic interpretation of the tradition itself. One of Maimonides' most consistent critics, the mystic and talmudist R. Abraham of Posquieres (circa 1125–98), takes him to task for this attitude and comments on the above ruling:

> Why does he call this person a heretic? For several greater and better men than he have followed such a line of thinking, according to the way they understood Scripture, and even more from their understanding of the words of the *aggadah* which confuse the mind.[17]

R. Abraham is not disagreeing with Maimonides' claim that God is indeed incorporeal, but he is defending popular piety with its naive view of God from the strictures of the intellectual, philosophically-minded, theologian.

The *Guide for the Perplexed*, Maimonides' philosophical *magnum opus*, was written in Arabic towards the end of his life, circa 1190, while he was living in Egypt where he had fled from the anti-Jewish persecution of a fanatical Moslem movement in Spain. As its title indicates it was meant as an attempt to help those Jews, including Maimonides' own pupils, who had become perplexed by the teachings of Greek philosophy and did not know how to reconcile them with Judaism. It should not be imagined, however, that Maimonides himself saw the need for a philosophical interpretation of Judaism merely as an exercise in apologetics to win perplexed intellectuals back into the fold. He may have been motivated to write the *Guide* to satisfy such a need, but in it he expresses his mature views on Jewish theology, and the firmly held belief that without philosophy the teachings of Judaism cannot become the self-conscious possession of the believer.

To believe in Judaism without investigating one's beliefs is, for Maimonides, to believe only in a superficial and mechanical way. Towards the end of the *Guide* he uses an image to illustrate this point. There is a prince who lives in a castle and who has different kinds of subjects. There are those who do not even live within the prince's domain. These are human beings who have no religion, and live an animal-like existence. A second group live in the kingdom but they have turned their backs on the castle. They are people holding false religious beliefs. A third group seek the castle, but they have not yet even seen the walls. They are the ignorant Jewish masses who nevertheless keep the commandments. A fourth group has arrived at the castle but they wander around the walls seeking the entrance. They are Jews who are learned in traditional Jewish lore and have accepted the correct beliefs and practices, but have never investigated their faith philosophically. It is only the fifth group who enter the castle courtyard, and they are Jews who investigate the philosophical basis of their religious belief.[18]

This image, or allegory, shocked conservative talmudists, for it depicted them as standing outside God's domain unable to find the entrance. It seemed to elevate the teachings of Aristotle above the spiritual traditions of the Jewish sages. Some denied that the great Maimonides could have written the controversial passage in question, others said that if he did write it it should be censored.[19]

Many other passages from the *Guide* were the subject of profound criticism from anti-philosophical conservatives. For instance Maimonides explicitly declares a willingness to re-interpret rabbinic and even biblical teachings so that they conform to the truths of reason. Concerning the doctrine of the creation of the world Maimonides states:

We do not avoid the view of the eternity of the world merely because the *Torah* states that the world was created. For the verses teaching the creation of the world are not more numerous than those that teach the corporeality of God. The gates of interpretation are not closed before us, nor are we prevented from using this method in the case of the creation of the world. We could have explained away these verses as we did in negating the corporeality of God.[20]

He concludes his discussion of one philosophical theory of creation:

Since this theory does not contradict the basis of Jewish religion . . . it would be possible to re-interpret Scripture according to this view . . . But it has not been proven.[21]

It is apparent from the above that within certain limitations, namely those determined by fundamentals of Jewish belief, Maimonides is willing to allow his interpretation of Jewish texts to be dictated by the findings of philosophical investigation. This was considered almost sacrilegious by some of Maimonides' anti-philosophical critics.

Another feature of the *Guide* which proved unacceptable, even to some of Maimonides' more sympathetic opponents, was the attempt in it to give the *mitzvot*, the commandments of the *Torah*, a rational and historical basis. Maimonides sees the *mitzvot* as having three basic purposes: (a) to provide for social stability, (b) to enhance the moral development of the individual, and (c) to inculcate correct religious ideas which lead man to a knowledge of God. While many of the more obviously ethical commandments have the first two purposes, the highly ritualized ones have the third purpose as their goal.[22] Thus he explains the biblical laws of ritual purity as having the function of restricting the Jew's contact with the Temple, since the ritually impure were forbidden from entering its precincts or from participating in the sacrificial rituals. This restricting effect generates reverence and awe for the service of God, and leads a man to a sense of humility. Maimonides adds that laws of ritual impurity were common among idolatrous people in ancient times, and the restrictions were far more extensive. The Bible was, therefore, using an established practice of the times, but giving it a new ethico-religious direction.[23]

The sacrificial ritual itself is seen by Maimonides as a concession to the forms of worship and the rites known to the Israelites from their contact with idolatrous cults. In order to wean them away from the idolatrous focus of such cults they were commanded to bring sacrifices, but only to God, and only in ways which would eradicate the idolatrous tenets of these cults.[24] Though this idea is already adumbrated in a *midrash*,[25] it was bitterly criticized for seeming to relegate the whole sacrificial system, the sphere of the holy in ancient Judaism, to the mundane level of an educational policy. Indeed one of Maimonides' later critics, the eighteenth century kabbalist and scholar R. Jacob Emden, was even led to deny that Maimonides was the real author of the *Guide* because of statements of this nature.[26]

It was precisely the audacity of Maimonides' theology which made it a focus both for those who believed in the ongoing process of synthesis between Greek and Jewish thought, and those who opposed the whole enterprise. Maimonides was not working in a vacuum, he wrote in an intellectual milieu in which Jews absorbed gentile culture and were unsure of how to relate its conclusions to their own traditional beliefs.

His attempt to establish thirteen principles of Jewish doctrine was a response to the challenges to Judaism contained in Islamic, Christian and Karaite thought. For all the strictures of his critics his philosophical interpretation of Judaism enabled it to survive the intellectual turbulence of the period. When he first arrived in Egypt he found the state of traditional knowledge among the Jews of that country at a very low ebb. The Karaites were a powerful movement there whose influence needed to be neutralized by showing the value and validity of the rabbinical tradition. This he achieved, and by the end of his life he was the object of adulation among Jews as far away as the Yemen. He even tried to win Karaite schismatics back to talmudic Judaism by adopting a tolerant attitude towards them. They were not to be looked on as in rebellion against Judaism, but as people who knew no better.[27] In one of his responsa he writes of them:

> For these Karaites . . . it is fitting to apportion them honour. To draw near to them with straightforward action, and to behave towards them with humility and the way of truth and peace.

Post-Maimonidean Developments

A controversy raged in the Jewish world in the post-Maimonidean period about the potential and actual evil caused to Judaism by the study of philosophy. Apart from the subjects mentioned above Maimonides was attacked for his views on miracles, prophecy, angels, the nature and destiny of the soul, and his denial of astrology and superstition. His views on all of these topics were influenced by his philosophical approach, and in some cases he was in conflict with the accepted understanding of traditional Jewish teachings. His whole conception of Judaism was criticized as permeated by philosophical elitism, denying religious value to the unsophisticated, but pious and God-fearing, Jew.

Ultimately his opponents were victorious and a ban was proclaimed in 1304 forbidding the study of philosophy, and indeed of all Greek wisdom excluding medicine, till a person had reached the age of 25. The heyday of medieval Jewish theology was past, and though in the subsequent centuries philosophical works were written and there was much discussion of the doctrinal principles of Judaism based on Maimonides' pioneering formulation, it was the turn of other movements of thought to influence the direction which Judaism was to take. Kabbalistic views spread from the small esoteric circles of Jewish mystics, and began to infiltrate all areas of Jewish life. The flowering of Kabbalah owed much to the reaction against rationalism which was brought about if not by Maimonides himself, then by the excesses of some of his followers and admirers.

The period between the great creative period of medieval Jewish philosophy, which tapered off in the late fourteenth and early fifteenth centuries, and the new philosophical upsurge which began with the eighteenth-century Enlightenment, produced only two major attempts to work out a systematically based structure of thought. The first was that of Judah Loeb of Prague (circa 1525–1609), known as the Maharal of Prague, and the second that of Baruch (Benedikt) Spinoza (1632–77) who was excommunicated by the Amsterdam rabbinate for propounding heretical views. Judah Loeb was a highly original thinker who developed his own philosophical terminology in systematically re-interpreting kabbalistic and aggadic ideas. Unlike other philosophically minded mystics who synthesized the two disciplines, Judah Loeb rarely mentions Kabbalah by name, at most he hints at the profound mysteries underlying his theology. Some scholars were misled by his reticence into denying that he was ever seriously involved with Kabbalah, while the popular imagination, by contrast, saw him as one of the great practitioners of kabbalistic magic and told legends about the *golem*, or artificial man which he created.

Like Judah Halevi before him Judah Loeb believed in the unique role and destiny of the Jewish people, and tried to give expression to this belief in theological terms. The Jews are the 'form' of mankind while the gentile nations represent its 'matter'. Israel's chosenness and ability to rise above the constraints of the natural order through the *Torah*, makes them the foundation of human reality and indeed of all reality. The gentile nations, lacking this ability to transcend the world provided by the study of *Torah* and the fulfilment of the *mitzvot*, are subject to the natural order. Jewish history, however, is not subject to the rules and laws of human history, it is meta-natural because determined by Israel's connection with God.

Underlying Judah Loeb's conception of man and the world is his idea of the ordered harmony of all creation. Existence is defined by the relationship of each creature and object to this harmony, and departure from this harmony entails the lack of existence or reality. The *Torah* is the general order of harmonious existence, the underlying blueprint for the chain of being which interlinks all levels of creation. Man can attain his highest mode of existence by obedience to the *Torah*, hence the difference between Israel and the gentiles, the former 'existing' in a different way from the latter. Existence or reality is provided by the divine within everything, for by itself nothing besides God exists. The actualization of the divine sub-stratum, and mode of existence attained, is dependent on attachment to the *Torah*. Though Judah Loeb's theology is difficult to understand, and often unnecessarily prolix and repetitive, his insights were taken up and incorporated into the writings of many subsequent Jewish thinkers. Some indeed regarded his work as the most distinctly Jewish theological system, although he had no successors who developed his general theological approach. His reputation as a kabbalistic wonder-worker ensured that his philosophical ideas were surrounded by an aura of respectability, if not sanctity, even among anti-philosophical pietists.

Spinoza

Spinoza belongs to the philosophical tradition of Europe more than to the history of Jewish ideas. His importance for Judaism, however, lies in the fact that his critique of Judaism overshadows the thinking of Jewish theologians in the eighteenth and nineteenth centuries, who were forced to define their own positions in response to his strictures. Spinoza came to philosophy via the works of the medieval Jewish thinkers, indeed he received a traditional education and was thought of as a promising candidate for the rabbinate. At the age of 24, however, he was excommunicated, put in *cherem*, by the rabbis of Amsterdam for his heretical views and his 'evil' acts. This step was only taken after various rabbis, including his own teacher R. Saul Morteira, had tried to talk him out of his opinions or at least to gain a public recantation of them. This policy had worked with other free-thinking Amsterdam Jews, but Spinoza's love of truth would not permit him to put expediency first. The views of Spinoza were almost as damaging to Christian piety as to Judaism, and they threatened to undermine the somewhat precarious standing of the affluent Jewish community in Amsterdam. The Jewish authorities were, therefore, forced to take the ultimate step of dissociating the Jewish community from his views and from their author, thereby also neutralizing his influence on potential radicals in their own ranks.

With the publication of Spinoza's *Tractatus Theologico-Politicus* in 1670 his critical views moved firmly from the private to the public domain. The standing which Spinoza eventually attained within the European intellectual community, perhaps more from his purely philosophical work, the *Ethics*, and the fact that he wrote as an informed, educated, if un-orthodox, Jew meant that subsequent Jewish thinkers had to take issue with the thoroughgoing critique of traditional Judaism contained in the *Tractatus*. Whether they knew it or not they were carrying on an implicit dialogue with the God-intoxicated heretic of Amsterdam, even if they avoided direct reference to him. The *cherem* against Spinoza has never been lifted, and many traditional Jews today will not participate in any of the celebrations or commemorations associated with his birth or death.

Spinoza's main criticisms of Judaism, as they are set out in the *Tractatus*, may be summarized as follows:

(a) *Revelation*. The prophets received their revelation through their powerful imagination rather than through their intellect or ability for abstract reasoning. The biblical prophecies therefore vary according to the opinions and prejudices of the prophets themselves, and the latter were mistaken about many matters of fact.[28]

(b) *Israel*. The Israelites were by no means different from, or superior to other peoples. The Mosaic law was given to them to suit their special social organization, it is valid for them alone because of the constitution of their society, and applies to their independent life in their own land. Israelite ideas about God were quite ordinary, and their virtues on a par with those of the gentiles who had their own prophets.[29]

(c) *The Law*. Natural divine law is common to all men and arises from the perception of God's decrees as eternal truths. It does not demand ceremonial acts. Moses had a limited perception of divine law, he did not perceive it in terms of its absolute necessity, and he laid down what was relatively the best policy for the Israelites. In this he differs from Jesus who may be described as the mouthpiece of God. Ceremonial laws are human, not divine, and those in the Bible relate to the stability and tranquillity of the Jewish kingdom in Palestine. Similarly belief in the veracity of the biblical stories, though necessary for the masses, has nothing to do with the divine law. Someone who rejects these stories but knows of God's existence through natural reason, and has a true plan of life, is more blessed than the common herd of believers.[30]

(d) *Miracles*. The common masses imagine that God is inactive as long as nature works normally, and that God only acts through uncommon occurrences which they term miracles. A miracle, in fact, is a contradiction in terms since the universal laws of nature are divine decrees, eternally necessary and true. Events for which the cause is unknown are referred to as miracles, and all the miracles of the Bible are to be explained naturalistically.[31]

(e) *Interpretation of Scripture*. Theological interpretations of Scripture read teachings into it which are merely in the minds of the interpreters themselves. True interpretation must be based on historical perspective and the knowledge of the language and situation of the author of a text. One must also be on the look-out for interpolations. Claims to the aid of the Holy Spirit in interpretation are unsupportable since the results of such interpretation are human through and through.[32]

(f) *Authorship of biblical books*. Traditions about the history and authorship of the Bible are unsound, and the Pharisaic idea that Moses wrote the whole Pentateuch was even doubted by the orthodox scholar Abraham ibn Ezra, though he expressed himself cryptically for fear of censure. From Scripture itself it can be shown that the author of the Pentateuch was not Moses, and those of other biblical books were not the authors mentioned in Jewish tradition. The majority of the biblical corpus was most probably written down by Ezra, with some of the post-Ezra books added later. The text as we now have it is corrupt due to scribal errors and emendations.[33]

In his discussion of these issues Spinoza supports his arguments by copious scriptural quotations as well as by reason. His approach to Christianity is, in general, more sympathetic than his approach to Judaism, though he by no means adopts an uncritical attitude to the former. The *Tractatus* was not merely a theological work but was also a political one in which Spinoza argues for a liberal, tolerant, state where freedom of thought is allowed. It is no wonder that the first edition of the *Tractatus* was published anonymously with a false title page. It aroused the ire of conservatives, Jewish and Christian alike. Its effect on Jewish thought was felt most fully when the ghetto walls began to crumble in the mid-eighteenth century, but Spinoza's ideas were seen as paradigmatic of the dangers of gentile culture, the new spirit of heresy, long before that time.

The fear of contamination by Spinozism is brought out in the following incident. In 1704 a rabbi of the Spanish Jewish community in London, David Nieto, preached a sermon in which he denied deist notions about God's transcendence and lack of involvement with the natural world. In so doing the rabbi identified nature with God, or so it seemed to some of his congregants. This led to a storm of protest and Nieto was accused of Spinozist leanings, since Spinoza had made the pantheistic identification of God and nature in his *Ethics*. The synagogue authorities wrote for a ruling about the matter to R. Tzvi Ashkenazi in Altona. The latter's reply has been preserved in his collection of responsa.[34] There he fully supports Nieto's views, explaining that what he actually meant was not to preach pantheism but to point out that the natural order was controlled by God and part of divine providence.

5

The Growth of Modern Jewish Thought

Moses Mendelssohn

Jewish thought from the late eighteenth to the early twentieth century was dominated by a group of problems associated with the cultural, political and social emancipation of the European Jew. This process of emancipation to full citizenship rights was a gradual one. Begun in the wake of the egalitarian ideas of the French Revolution, it only found its culmination in the mid-nineteenth century. Long before the Jews were granted political recognition, however, they had begun to acculturalize to the language and lifestyle of European society, moving from the medieval world of the ghetto into the intellectual life of the eighteenth and early nineteenth centuries. The man who stood at the beginning of this acculturalization, and whose life and work dominated the direction which it took, was Moses Mendelssohn (1729–86).

He was born in Dessau, northern Germany, where his father, Menachem Mendel, was a minor synagogue official. Mendelssohn, who is known in Jewish literature as Moses of Dessau, Ben Menachem or Rambaman, received a traditional Jewish education till the age of 14, although he already evinced an interest in philosophy, studying Maimonides in his spare time. In later life he half-jokingly ascribed his hunch-backed condition to the time spent poring over Maimonides' *Guide*, adding that he thought it was worth it. In 1743 his teacher left Dessau and was eventually appointed chief rabbi of Berlin. The young Moses soon followed his teacher there and though Berlin was a centre of traditional Judaism he discovered a new world of ideas and culture which had been unavailable in his home town. In Berlin, with the aid of Jewish intellectuals who had mastered aspects of European culture, he learnt German, Latin, French and English. He was thus prepared to read and assimilate the new world of literature and philosophy which was closed to the Jewish scholar who knew only Hebrew, Aramaic and Yiddish. From this point on Mendelssohn straddled two worlds, that of traditional Judaism and that of eighteenth-century *belle lettres*.

In 1755 Mendelssohn met Gotthold Lessing for the first time, and a life-long friendship developed which was to have considerable effect on both thinkers. Lessing's tolerant attitude to Judaism was an important feature of their relationship, since Berlin society was still impregnated by a form of Christianity which saw Jews, at best, as potential converts to the one true religion. Together they studied the works of Spinoza, and it was Lessing who encouraged Mendelssohn to launch himself as a German writer, and who introduced him to kindred spirits of the Enlightenment. Mendelssohn's early work was of a philosophical and literary nature in which his Jewishness, regarded by him as a private matter, does not figure. In this way he was able to participate fully in the problems and issues common to his circle of associates without having to confront the main difference which separated him from them, namely that he was a believing Jew.

In his private life Mendelssohn remained an Orthodox Jew who preserved even the detailed customs of the community. He allowed his hair and beard to grow during periods of public mourning in the Jewish ritual year, and his wife covered her hair as is customary with Orthodox women after marriage. The significance of these features of his personal life will be realized when considered against the background of the social milieu in which he mixed. Though Mendelssohn did not flaunt his Judaism he was only prepared to make limited concessions to his non-Jewish environment.

The harmonious relationship between Mendelssohn the Jew and Mendelssohn the German intellectual came to an abrupt end in 1769. Till that time he had not expressed himself publicly as a Jewish philosopher explaining and defending his Jewish belief. This had led some of his more zealous Christian acquaintances to believe that he was really a secret Christian, and that his Judaism was only skin deep. In 1769 J. C. Lavater, a Swiss pastor who had met Mendelssohn on a number of occasions and to whom Mendelssohn had expressed qualified appreciation of the ethics of Jesus on the understanding that it remain confidential, issued a challenge to the 'Jew of Berlin'. This was contained in Lavater's introduction to his translation of a French work 'proving' the truth of Christianity. There he asked Mendelssohn to read the book and either to refute its arguments or to adopt Christianity openly. Such a public challenge could not be ignored and Mendelssohn, who was clearly upset by Lavater's challenge as well as by the publication of his privately expressed views on Jesus, originally intended to counter the arguments for Christianity presented in the book. On second thoughts he adopted a much less aggressive stance, realizing that harm could ensue from a religious controversy in which a Jew was seen to be attacking Christianity.

The challenge attracted considerable interest and people waited to see how Mendelssohn would respond. In Mendelssohn's reply to Lavater he explained why he would not accept the terms of the challenge, and why he would not engage in religious disputation. As a Jew he had examined his religion carefully, and was convinced of its truth. Had he found any other religion to be true he would have no hesitation in adopting it. Certainly it was not fear of his fellow Jews or intellectual laziness which made him remain a Jew. He did not feel the need to justify his belief in Judaism publicly, since as a Jew he was committed to religious tolerance and Judaism could respect the value of other religions, not seeking to convert their adherents to its own traditions. Mendelssohn concludes by remarking that as a member of an oppressed people, who owe a great debt to the country that they reside in, it would be unsuitable for him to criticise Christian belief.

The 'Lavater Affair' did not end with Mendelssohn's reply, it continued for some time both in print and in the exchange of letters between Mendelssohn and various German intellectuals. The whole controversy brought home to Mendelssohn how fragile his position as a Jew in an essentially Christian environment was, and how much of the old anti-Semitism lay beneath the Enlightenment veneer. Soon after this crack appeared in the fabric of Mendelssohn's two worlds, a new development occurred which was symptomatic of the strains within his own relationship with Jewish orthodoxy.

In 1772 the Jewish community of Schwerin were forbidden to bury their dead before three days had elapsed from the time of death to ensure that no one still living was buried by mistake. Since this was against the accepted Jewish practice of immediate burial the community turned for advice and aid to R. Jacob Emden, a renowned German talmudist, and to Moses Mendelssohn, without informing either of the other's involvement. Mendelssohn submitted a German text to be forwarded to Duke Friedrich, who had issued the original decree, explaining the difficulties involved in the three-day rule and suggesting an alternative. He also included a letter to the leadership of the Schwerin Jewish community, setting out his private views on the subject, in which he quoted talmudic precedents for delaying burial and suggested that contemporary medical evidence about mistaken burial made the three-day rule desirable for Jews to adopt. Though this letter was couched in traditional terms it aroused the ire of both R. Jacob Emden and the rabbi of Schwerin, since it seemed to make light of a time-hallowed Jewish custom. Mendelssohn was preferring the views of gentile doctors over that of the rabbinic tradition as to how death should or should not be determined. His traditionalist critics saw such a stance as undermining halakhic authority, while Mendelssohn had a different perspective on the matter through his contact with European philosophy and science.

In the nineteenth century this difference of approach to the *halakhah*, represented by Mendelssohn and his rabbinic critics, was one of the fundamental issues which split European Jewry into two camps. All of the Reforming movements, both moderate and radical, took Mendelssohn's position to its logical conclusion in reassessing the tradition of the past in the light of present knowledge. Some Orthodox groups, though unwilling to follow the Reformers in the extent of their innovations into ritual and doctrine, nevertheless accepted Mendelssohn's position in principle. The majority of the Orthodox leadership adopted a conservative stance, maintaining the sanctity of tradition and rejecting novelty and change except where these were products of the internal dynamic of the *halakhah* itself.

A project of Mendelssohn's which had an important effect on the emancipation of German Jewry, and aroused opposition and censure from leading rabbis, was his translation of the Bible into German. In 1770 he began to translate the Book of Psalms, and a few years later he started his translation of the Pentateuch. The incentive came from the need for an accurate, well-written translation for young students of the Bible, Mendelssohn's own children included. It was also Mendelssohn's intention to ensure that German Jews had a proper grasp of their native tongue, instead of their Yiddish dialect which served as a Jewish *lingua franca*, and that they were inculcated with biblical values. The translation, which was written in Hebrew characters, was accompanied by a commentary, the *Biur*, which Mendelssohn wrote in collaboration with a number of Jewish scholars. Though some rabbis gave Mendelssohn their qualified support, others opposed the whole project believing that it would lead to students concentrating on the improvement of their German to the neglect of their religious studies.

Mendelssohn's views on ecclesiastical power both within Judaism, and within society in general, were in accord with the tolerance and pluralism of Enlightenment thought. He himself suffered at the hands of the Jewish authorities, and he saw Jewish emancipation as dependent on the granting of full religious freedom. His mature thoughts on these subjects were brought together in his *Jerusalem*, which bore the alternative title 'On Religious Power and Judaism' published in 1783. There he argued for a non-coercive, voluntaristic relationship between the individual and a religious group. The latter has no power to demand man's conformity to its norms, whereas society as such is structured out of this very power. Society, however, can only demand conformity in action, it can make no such demands in the sphere of beliefs. The ideal form of religious association is provided by the rational persuasion exerted by that religion over its adherents, rather than by coercive force. This would apply to Judaism no less than to Christianity.

In the second part of his *Jerusalem* Mendelssohn argued that Judaism was a divine legislation, not a system of doctrine. The doctrines of Judaism were those of the universal religion of reason, available to all men through reflection, and not dependent on revelation. To assume otherwise would be to deny a saving knowledge of eternal truths to large portions of mankind, since the divine revelation is unknown to them. This conception of Judaism is already found in Spinoza's *Tractatus*, though Mendelssohn does not accept Spinoza's further claim that the legislative part of Judaism had long been superseded. The laws prescribed within Judaism are based on, and exemplify, the truths of rational religion, and are thus of continuing validity. Mendelssohn ends his *Jerusalem* with a plea for full emancipation of the Jews, but not at the cost of having to renounce their Judaism. Jews would prefer to decline the offer of civil liberties if that were dependent on the loss of their identity as Jews. On the other hand the religious commitment of Jews need be no obstacle to their emancipation, and full integration into the kind of pluralistic society which Mendelssohn had argued for in the first part of the work.

Mendelssohn's life and work were to determine the direction which German Jewry took in the century after his death. Judaism outside the ghetto in the nineteenth century bears the imprint of Mendelssohn and his circle, although he would certainly not have approved of many of its developments. It was particularly his ideas on education, which were implemented by his disciples, which introduced radical change into accepted patterns of Jewish life. He opposed the almost exclusive emphasis on talmudic scholarship, and especially on talmudic casuistry known as *pilpul*. In its place he proposed the study of the Hebrew language, the Bible, and Jewish cultural values, plus a grounding in secular subjects and the acquisition of vocational skills.

The synthesis between Judaism and the culture of the Enlightenment, to which Mendelssohn's own life is itself a monument, proved to be an uneasy one. Mendelssohn intended to open the gates of emancipation to Jews who would be able to preserve their Judaism intact. In fact he succeeded in opening the way to the total assimilation of Jews to the dominant Christian religion, since this was the simplest way of achieving emancipation and acceptance by gentile society. Leading members of the Berlin Jewish intelligentsia converted to Christianity, including Mendelssohn's own children and grandchildren. His advocacy of religious tolerance, belief in a universal doctrinal religion, educational reforms, and wholehearted acceptance of European ideas and values were at least partly, and inadvertently, responsible for the attitudes which made such conversion to Christianity possible.

Movements of Thought in the Nineteenth Century

The late eighteenth and the nineteenth centuries were times of considerable intellectual ferment in Judaism. They saw the beginnings of the Reform and Conservative movements, the rise of Zionism, and within Orthodoxy the spread of Chasidic teachings, the *Musar* movement, and German Neo-Orthodoxy. In different ways they represent the response of European Jews to the strains and tensions of emancipation. Some were a direct consequence of the breakdown of ghetto life, while others began independently but were soon caught up in the challenges to traditionalism inherent in the confrontation between secular culture and religious self-identity. The Jewish thinkers of the Enlightenment who followed Mendelssohn were mainly concerned with re-assessing Jewish life and customary behaviour. Their situation as men straddling two worlds involved them with educational reform, changes to the synagogue service, and modification in Jewish ritual. These may be seen as attempts to alleviate some of the worst incongruities facing the Jew who was, at the same time, trying to be accepted by a gentile environment to which he passionately wished to belong. Justification from within Judaism was sought for many innovations, but the majority of traditionalists were unsympathetic and often openly antagonistic even to moderate reforms. In its early stages the approach of the innovators was essentially pragmatic, and not as yet ideological. For someone who had stepped outside the ghetto both physically and culturally accommodation with the new ideas and mores was imperative, while for those still within the ghetto walls, culturally at least, such accommodation seemed a negation of Jewish values.

The first major theologian of the post-Mendelssohn era was Nachman Krochmal (1785–1840) who was born in Brody, northern Galicia, where he received his early education. Like Mendelssohn he acquired his knowledge of secular subjects mainly through his own efforts, his formal education having been a traditional one of biblical and talmudic studies. For most of his life he was of independent means and devoted his time to study, and to writing his *Guide for the Perplexed of the Time* which was published posthumously.

Krochmal's main interest was in the philosophy of history and he sought to arrive at a theological understanding of Judaism in the light of this interest. Because historical research was virtually unknown among Jewish scholars, Krochmal acted as a pioneer opening up new areas through historical investigation. Having established a historical framework for the subject he was able to show the overall structure of the evolution of Judaism and the various forms it had taken on at different periods. As a theological interpreter of this evolution he saw Israel's religious vocation as the guiding genius of Jewish history, the spiritual encounter with God was there at the inception and continued to operate on all developments within Judaism thereafter. Krochmal, however, was not a system-builder, nor did his philosophy of Judaism found a school. His importance lies in the fruitfulness of his ideas, and the historical dimension which he introduced and which was to dominate much of the nineteenth-century Jewish intellectual life. This emphasis on historical research became the main platform of the Science of Judaism movement which was initiated by a series of brilliant scholars who had come under Krochmal's influence, directly or indirectly. Some of those who followed his lead were traditionalists who brought secular studies and historical perspective to bear on talmudic and medieval material. Others, like Leopold Zunz and Zacharias Frankel, advocated moderate reforms in line with their researches into the history and development of Jewish ideas and practices. The so-called Historical School that they founded was the forerunner of the modern Conservative movement. Others, like Abraham Geiger and Samuel Holdheim, were in favour of more radical reforms, once again basing themselves on an ideology of historical development which saw the Jewish tradition, and the Bible itself, as part of an organically developing phenomenon. In the modern age the tradition had to be brought up to date, just as it was continually being revised in the past. Their work, and the organizations which they created became the basis for the Reform movement.

The progress of Jewish life and the writings of Jewish intellectuals once the ghetto walls had fallen were looked upon with consternation by the Orthodox leadership. Though they recognized that some of the Enlightenment Jewish scholars were themselves scrupulously observant of traditional rituals, they saw the new blend of Jewish and secular learning as responsible for the cataclysmic upheavals undermining whole Jewish communities. They considered Mendelssohn and Krochmal as ultimately responsible even for the more radical views expressed by later thinkers, and forbade their works to be read. As to the leaders of Reform Judaism, they were considered as worse than idolaters, as false prophets who were leading the masses astray and who had to be fought at every turn. The distance between the Orthodox rabbinate, steeped in talmudic studies, and those Jews who had absorbed something of European culture was growing and threatened to become an unbridgeable gulf. The polarization of the Jewish world into traditionalists and modernists left little place for those Jews who were acquainted with secular culture, but who nevertheless wished to remain faithful to the practice and beliefs of pre-Enlightenment Judaism. They could not communicate with the old-style rabbis, and they did not share the reforming zeal of the modernist rabbis who had undergone university training.

It was in response to this polarization that R. Samson Raphael Hirsch (1808–88), the founder of German Neo-Orthodoxy, attempted to create a new synthesis between Jewish religion and secular culture. At first Hirsch found himself in a spiritual no-man's-land, too orthodox for the reformers, and too modern, too secular, for the traditionalists. He eventually built up a community in Frankfurt-on-Main of Jews who felt themselves in the limbo generated by the polarization of attitudes, and for whom Hirsch provided an ideology of modernist orthodoxy. He rejected the historical understanding of Judaism, which originated with Krochmal and was developed by both moderate and radical reformers, and instead characterized Judaism as a symbolic system whose structure remained constant from its biblical origins despite the variety of forms it had taken. The revelation of old had, therefore, lost none of its validity in the cultural milieu of nineteenth-century Germany, for the symbolic structure underlying it was as relevant then as in antiquity. Indeed for Hirsch the task of the Jew was precisely to interpret the eternal truths of Judaism in terms of the secular culture of his age. To do so, however, was not to change or reform Judaism but to affirm its traditional meaning. The halakhic rituals encapsulating the Jewish symbolic world were sacrosanct, and Hirsch regarded the alteration of these to bring them into line with modern behaviour as a threat to the very fabric of Judaism. He therefore refused all co-operation with the Reform movement and insisted that Orthodoxy had to go its separate way.

The second half of the nineteenth century saw the beginning of new attempts to deal with the problem of Jewish emancipation. Whereas Mendelssohn, the Reform movement and Hirschian Neo-Orthodoxy were all concerned with the continuing validity of Jewish religion, whether in its traditional or updated form, in a non-Jewish cultural environment Zionist thinkers were concerned primarily with Jewish existence in its national guise. Jewish nationhood had been de-emphasized, if not positively rejected, by those interested in persuading the authorities that Jews were deserving of emancipation, and could be regarded as loyal citizens of their countries of residence. Zionism threatened such claims by working for Jewish national revival, and by its denial that Jews could simply be regarded as Germans or Frenchmen who subscribed to Jewish religion. What was common to early Zionist thinkers was a much less optimistic assessment of the willingness, or ability, of gentile society to absorb its Jewish members as fully equal citizens. Anti-Semitism would not simply fade away, but would continue to influence European civilization where it was endemic. The only solution to the Jewish problem under such circumstances was to create a homeland for Jews where their emancipation could take place away from the shadow of centuries of Christian prejudice against Jews.

Most of the Zionist leaders and ideologues were secularists, to whom the problems of religion and modernity were irrelevant. Their vision of Jewish national autonomy was one where Judaism, whether of the ghetto or post-ghetto variety, had no place. Judaism was a useful cementing force for Jewish life in exile, in scattered communities trying to preserve their ethnic identity in the face of a non-Jewish host society. Once that exile was at an end religion became anachronistic, backward-looking and a reactionary force. The exceptions to this generally held attitude among nineteenth-century Zionists were either messianic Zionists like R. Judah Alkalai or R. Tzvi Hirsch Kalisher, whose ideas were relatively without significance in the early Zionist movement, or those foresighted leaders like Theodor Herzl (1860–1904), the father of political Zionism, who saw the need for support from the rabbinate in order to give the movement a base among the traditionally inclined masses. The cultural Zionists, led by Asher Ginzburg (1856–1927) writing under the pen-name *Achad Ha-am* ('One of the people'), wished to see a cultural revival of the Jewish people rather than a purely national rebirth, but even they did not conceive of this cultural revival in religious terms. Ginzburg himself came to be known as the 'agnostic rabbi'.

The socialist Zionists were the most antagonistic to Jewish religion, they saw a Jewish homeland as a place where their ideas on social justice could be implemented, and they shared the general socialist suspicion of religious opiates. It is due to this latter group, which was instrumental in resettling Palestine and determining the nature of Jewish life there, that some of the more deep-seated conflicts between religion and state in modern Israel have proved so intractable, as well of course due to traditionalist opposition to Zionism.

The Twentieth Century

The two streams of thought which were separate in nineteenth-century responses to emancipation, namely those of religious and national revival, ran together in the work of R. Abraham I. Kook (1865–1935) and Martin Buber (1878–1965), major figures in Judaism of the early twentieth century. R. Kook was educated in the great *yeshivot* of Lithuania where he received his rabbinic ordination. Inclined to a mystically-based religious Zionism, he moved to Palestine in 1904 to become rabbi of Haifa. His involvement with the life of the *yishuv*, the old established Jewish community in Palestine, and his efforts on behalf of the non-religious Zionist settlers brought him into open conflict with more conservative members of the rabbinate. After his return from an enforced absence in London during the First World War he was appointed Chief Rabbi of Jerusalem, and in 1922 the first Ashkenazi Chief Rabbi of the Holy Land. Till his death in 1935 he was a key figure in the religious and political life of Palestine, using his halakhic authority to help solve the many problems associated with the application of traditional Jewish norms to modern life.

Apart from his considerable halakhic output R. Kook also wrote poetry, essays, commentaries, letters on ethical and social issues, and works of mystical theology. His writings, which are still being edited, are not presented in systematic form since he wrote, according to his own account, under the pressure of an inner urge. The words seemed to well up in an unstoppable flow, and once set down on paper he rarely corrected the text. In one of his letters he says that he does not write because he has the power to write, but because he does not have the power to remain silent.[1] R. Kook was steeped in the kabbalistic tradition and this, coupled with his reading of the works of Henri Bergson, inclined him to see an evolutionary component underlying the progress of history and human development. Every aspect of such development can be seen as a component of evolution leading to the messianic goal. The return of the Jewish people to their ancient homeland is, for R. Kook, a central feature of their role as catalysts of the messianic process. Even the rejection of religion by the secular Zionists, in the name of socialist ideals, is viewed by him as an advance on the negation of Judaism in the past which was motivated by a desire for self-indulgence in fertility cults.

The growth of secular knowledge and of science is bringing man to a clearer perception of the divine light within all creation, and thus to a higher form of perfection. It is the people of Israel, however, whose historical task is the uncovering of the sacred substratum contained within the seemingly profane overlay of mundane existence. Kook therefore saw the goal of Zionism to be not merely some national revival, but the expression of the divine teachings inherent in the *Torah* which will in turn aid the gentile nations to further their own spiritual potential. For the Jew love of his own people must, if unadulterated by impure motives, overflow into the love of all creatures, and R. Kook demanded that the Zionist settlers should show a sense of responsibility to the Palestinian Arabs dwelling in the Holy Land.

Martin Buber, unlike R. Kook, came to Judaism as a Western educated intellectual who had studied philosophy in Austrian and German universities. He gained his first-hand knowledge of the world of traditional Judaism from the time he spent with his grandfather, Solomon Buber, who was a scholar of midrashic literature living in Galicia. As a young man he became interested in Zionism, attending the Third Zionist Congress in 1899, but his emphasis on Zionism as a movement of cultural revival meant that he belonged to a minority sub-group among the Zionist factions. Unlike the leader of the cultural Zionists, *Achad Ha-am*, who was a professed agnostic, Buber centred all his writings about Judaism from its biblical origins to the Chasidic movement of the eighteenth and nineteenth centuries on the reality of a living God and the encounter with Him. This encounter between man and God is at the heart of Buber's analysis of man's two modes of being I–Thou and I–It, in the former of which God, the Eternal Thou, is revealed.

Whereas God can only be the subject of an I–Thou encounter, any attempt to talk about God rather than to relate to Him being to falsify Him, man can be the subject of both I–Thou and I–It modes. True life between man and man involves I–Thou relationship, the 'I' of I–Thou being differently structured than that of I–It. In the latter the object of the relationship is treated as a thing to be used and manipulated, not to be entered into open dialogue with. For the purposes of technological development man must relate to his environment functionally, in an I–It manner. Values, however, are dependent on I–Thou modes and it is these which, by themselves, can generate all existential values. Formalized religion is merely an attempt to concretize values arising out of I–Thou encounter between man and God, but since this relational experience is repeated in each age and for each individual there is no need for adherence to a religion. Indeed Buber goes further in claiming that religion may act as a block to the living, revelatory, quality of I–Thou encounter and thus have a deadening effect on man's ability to hear God's voice in the here and now.

All of Buber's writings are variations on this one theme of

dialogue-relationship-encounter. His basic ideas are most clearly expressed in his book *I and Thou*, but his interpretation of the message of the Bible, his understanding of the Chasidic movement, his views on education, his contrast between the faith of Israel and Christian belief, his attitude to Zionism involving work for a bi-national Arab-Jewish state in Palestine, and his new translation of the Hebrew Bible into German which tried to give fresh meaning for the modern European to age-old Hebrew thought forms, all are structured around his basic insight into the two modes of relationship. In his turn Buber has been criticized on various counts. His understanding of the Chasidic movement, which focuses on its sense of fellowship and its living relationship with God, is seen by scholars of Jewish mysticism[2] as ignoring the doctrinal beliefs of the various Chasidic groups. His anti-chauvinistic views on Jewish nationalism have been criticized as unworldly and irrelevant to the goals of political Zionism, and his antinomian rejection of the *halakhah* and of Jewish ritual has led to the accusation of religious anarchism. He has been most influential among Christian thinkers, and among Jews alienated from the Jewish tradition for whom Buber's interpretations of the Jewish past have provided a perspective unavailable in the writings of more traditionally-minded savants.

Another thinker who exerted considerable influence on Jewish theology in the early part of the twentieth century, and whose importance is still recognized today, was Franz Rosenzweig (1886–1929) a younger contemporary of Buber's and a collaborator with the latter in his Bible translation project. Rosenzweig grew up in an assimilated, though proudly Jewish, Berlin family. While pursuing a university career he contemplated conversion to Christianity, finding Judaism a shallow religious alternative. He decided, however, that he would come to Christianity as a Jew, and so he wished to attend the High Holiday services for what he thought was the last time in 1913. He spent the Day of Atonement in a small Orthodox synagogue in Berlin and was so moved by the intensity of prayer and the fervour of the congregants, which contrasted sharply with the form of assimilated Jewish service known to him till then, that he decided to remain a Jew. He retained a sympathetic understanding of Christianity for the rest of his life, maintaining that there were two valid paths to God, Judaism for the Jews and Christianity for the gentiles.

During the First World War Rosenzweig was stationed as a

soldier in eastern Europe and was impressed by the piety and religious vitality of the Jews in that area, as Buber had been before him. He began his *magnum opus* in the form of postcards to his mother while serving at the front. On his demobilization he wrote up the postcard notes into a book, *The Star of Redemption*, which was published in 1921. Rosenzweig's theology is based on the premise that man can only relate to God in response to God's self-revelation to man, and that man's relationship to his fellow, and to the world at large, is not prior to but a consequence of that divine self-revealing. Being a Jew, for Rosenzweig, means being open to the central message of God's loving revelation of himself contained within the Jewish tradition. It is possible for the gentile to be open to such a message through Christian teaching, and Rosenzweig discusses the religions of India and China in order to show that they have an inadequate grasp of this message. Only Judaism and Christianity have understood the basic structure of the divine-human relationship, and they represent two alternative covenants of man with God.

Though Rosenzweig's thought shows a dependence on Buber's existential theology, he was closer to the traditional Jewish position than his mentor. In his essays and letters he adopts a position mid-way between Buber's rejection of all religious legalism and the traditional demand that halakhic norms are binding on the Jew. He accepts a personal, subjective, element in the individual Jew's approach to the *halakhah* allowing for the existential meaning which must be found in a particular commandment before it can be adopted into the Jew's life-style. Whereas Buber considered ritual as opaque, and a block to encounter with God, Rosenzweig saw it as something which could become transparent and a vehicle for that very encounter, provided that it was integrated into the existential situation of the individual.

Rosenzweig's thought has continued to exert a growing influence on contemporary Jewish theology, especially with the English trans-lation of *The Star of Redemption* in 1970. It is not merely Rosenzweig's writings which are of import, it is also the details of his life. He spent his last years in a struggle against the creeping paraly-sis which eventually killed him. During this phase of his life he manifested extraordinary courage, and continued to write even when he had lost the use of his limbs. Since Rosenzweig himself always emphasized the connection between life and thought, it is fitting that Rosenzweig the man, as well as Rosenzweig the thinker, should be the subject of contemporary theological reflection.

Modern Jewish Thought

Two recent events in Jewish life have left an indelible mark on modern Jewish theology and will, no doubt, continue to determine its direction for some time to come. They are the destruction of the Jewish communities of Europe during the Nazi era, and the founding of an independent Jewish state in the Holy Land in 1948. The consequences of both events for Jewish consciousness and self-identity are enormous, and have eclipsed much of the thinking about Judaism current up to the Second World War. The Nazi-inspired Holocaust, by the sheer enormity of its persecutions, massacres, death camps and overall inhumanity, has made the optimism of pre-Holocaust Jewish theology seem facile. It has reawakened a sense of the reality of evil, the isolation of the Jewish people, the distrust of impotent liberalism and of gentile attitudes towards Jews. The establishment of the State of Israel has meant that Jewish ethnicity, and national identity, are situated in the forefront of Jewish existence both for Jews who are actively Zionist and for non-Zionists as well. Until the 1940s Jewish thinkers mostly in the USA and Western Europe were still grappling with the problems that emerged with Jewish emancipation. This is seen clearly from the work of Mordecai Kaplan (1881–1983), one of the most original Jewish theologians on the North American continent during this period. Kaplan broke away from the Conservative movement to found Reconstructionism, the ideology of which he set out in his most important work *Judaism as a Civilization*, first published in 1934. There Kaplan interprets Jewish experience as the total cultural expression of the Jewish people evolving through time and projecting its highest ideals as 'God'. Both the religious and secular features of this culture are integral parts of Jewish civilization, which in its totality manifests the changing patterns of the Jew's search for meaning and purpose. Kaplan advocates the adjustment of Jewish rituals to modern conditions, and plays down the supernatural and metaphysical side of Judaism, preferring to see Jewish life in terms of the group dynamics of an ethnic culture. In so doing he attempts to bring Jewish tradition into the scientific age, to overcome the strains and tensions implicit in the struggle between tradition and modernity, and between traditional beliefs and the scientific understanding.

Another influential Jewish thinker in the USA, one who did not actually found a specific movement around his ideas but was regarded by many American Jews as the most enlightened sage of his times, was Abraham J. Heschel (1907–72). Although Heschel's English writings only date from after his arrival in America in 1940 as a refugee from Nazi Europe, he soon established himself as a major theologian and interpreter of eastern European piety. Heschel had grown up in the highly traditional atmosphere of Polish Chasidism, and had subsequently studied at the University of Berlin where he produced a work on the nature of biblical prophecy. He thus combined within himself the worlds of intense Jewish traditionalism, with its strong roots in kabbalistic mysticism, and that of modern academic approaches to Jewish subjects. His philosophy of Judaism emphasizes the sense of awe and wonder, of radical amazement in the face of a mysterious universe, which lies behind the down-to-earth and everyday religion of the Jew. Judaism is structured round an awareness of a concerned and loving God who seeks man out and addresses him. Something of that awareness, and the awe it entails, is necessary for modern man to experience the inner world of Jewish experience. In effect Heschel provides an insight into, and an interpretation of, the thought and life-style of a pre-modern Judaism for the Jew who has grown up and completely absorbed the secular culture of the Western world.

Kaplan and Heschel, though both of them wrote in the post-Holocaust era and both produced works about Israel and Zionism are thinkers whose mature views on Judaism were formed prior to the over-shadowing events of Auschwitz and the State of Israel, the cataclysmic symbols of destruction and rebirth, of death and resurrection, for the modern Jewish mind. Some Jewish religious leaders have taken the attitude that an over-concentration on the terrors of the Nazi era is inimical to the work of rebuilding and recreating Jewish life, and that the important task is not to find meaning in the seemingly absurd events of the Holocaust but to re-invigorate traditional Jewish life among the remnants who have survived. Other thinkers have remained silent because the sheer enormity of what took place in Nazi Europe is beyond the power of theological expression, and the lack of distance from the events prevents the groundswell of emotions, fear, rage, despair, numbness and mute grief from overtaking rational discussion.

It is perhaps for this reason that most of the Jewish response to the Holocaust has taken the form of literature rather than theology. A host of novels, essays, poems and personal reminiscences have appeared, often written by people who lived through the concentration camps. Perhaps the most impressive writer of this genre is the novelist Elie Wiesel who writes not so much of the atrocities but of the response of the victims. In so far as one can find a message in Wiesel's work it is one of defiance, the defiance of a God who died at Auschwitz. For, argues Wiesel, if at that most momentous period of Jewish history God did not choose to intervene in man's inhumanity to man then He cannot, or what is worse He does not wish to, be concerned with humanity.[3] Though others have tried to describe this divine inactivity as God hiding His face, an eclipse of God in Buber's phrase, Wiesel sees it in paradoxical terms. God has died, and men must take up a stance of defiance against the God who has failed them.

The Holocaust's message of the death of God is brought out more clearly, if with less artistry than in Wiesel, in the writings of the American theologian Richard Rubinstein. Rubinstein, a one-time Reform rabbi, is one of the thinkers who has taken a renewed interest in the reality of evil as a consequence of the Holocaust. In his closely argued book *After Auschwitz* he maintains that the only conclusion which can be drawn, without violating our sense of justice, is that atheism is the theology of post-Auschwitz Judaism. Rubinstein builds upon images taken from the Kabbalah in which the Godhead is described as the infinite nothing. The nothingness of God has important implications for man in an indifferent universe, for it means that man has to shape his own destiny, invest the world with meaning, and take responsibility for his actions. Judaism, for Rubinstein, is a meaning-giving pattern the rituals of which have psychological and social value. An atheistic Judaism à la Rubinstein has seemed too anomalous to win many adherents, since the logical conclusion of such a mode of thinking is closer to existential humanism than to the religion of the Covenant.

Another Reform theologian who has written extensively about the Holocaust is Emil Fackenheim, an ex-rabbi and professor of philosophy. Fackenheim sees the message which emerges from the Holocaust, what he calls the 'commanding voice of Auschwitz' as the prohibition on Jews to give Hitler posthumous victories. In his book *God's Presence in History* and in a number of impassioned essays, he has argued that the primary Jewish duty of the post-Holocaust era is Jewish survival. This duty, he believes, underlies the dogged determination with which Israeli Jews have fought to ensure the survival of their fledgling state. Fackenheim sees an integral connection between the destruction suffered by the Jewish people and their resurgence into history as a nation reborn. The duty of survival also entails retelling the story of Nazi atrocities to a world that would prefer to forget, and for the religious Jew it further involves a posture of protest against God in the name of God's own values for what has been allowed to happen. Just as the Patriarch Abraham argued with God over the justice of the destruction of Sodom and Gomorrah, so the post-Auschwitz Jew must affirm in faith and action the traditional witness to Jewish values, even if God Himself seems to have forsaken them.

The paradoxical nature of the responses of Wiesel, Rubinstein and Fackenheim to the Holocaust is apparent. Defying a God who has died, perpetuating a religious atheism, and saving a God from his own powerlessness are new, and revolutionary, theological positions as far as Judaism is concerned. Other more generalized attitudes are found. Thus Zionists, both religious and secular, interpret the Holocaust as a consequence of, or a divine punishment for, the unwillingness of European Jewry to leave the Diaspora and make *aliyah* ('ascension', i.e. migration) to Palestine when they had the opportunity early in the twentieth century. Some ultra-Orthodox Jews see it as the result of Jewish assimilation, adoption of gentile ways, and the wholesale rejection of Jewish tradition. The anti-Zionist *Neturei Karta*, comprising a small minority of ultra-Orthodox zealots, view the Nazi atrocities as divine retribution for Zionist attempts to bring about the ingathering of the exiles to the Holy Land, rather than wait for God to send the Messiah. One of the spiritual leaders of the *Neturei Karta*, R. Joel Teitelbaum the Satmar Rebbe, wrote extensively on this subject adducing arguments from the *Talmud* about the catastrophe which would ensue if Jews tried to return *en masse* to the Holy Land.

A more reasoned approach to Holocaust theology by an Orthodox thinker is found in Eliezer Berkovits' *Faith after the Holocaust*. Berkovits tries to set the Holocaust within the wider perspective of Jewish history and experience, of martyrdom and persecution. It is different in degree from anti-Jewish measures of the past, but not different in kind. While the enormity of Nazi atrocities makes it impossible to view them as a form of divine punishment for human sins, it is possible to interpret the Holocaust in terms of God hiding His face from man. When God hides Himself He gives man an opportunity to act maturely as a responsible, moral being but He also allows man to act immorally and to shun his responsibilities. In his analysis of the factors which made the wholesale annihilation of Jewish communities possible Berkovits isolates Christian antagonism to Jews and Judaism as an important component. Like other thinkers he sees the rebirth of the State of Israel as a manifestation of the divine involvement with history, a revealing of God's face once again. The very survival of the Jews is an anomaly and their return to their ancestral land after such a long exile is absurd. But these phenomena cannot be judged by the normal standards of human history, for here we are dealing with the history of Israel and its special role in the creation of the kingdom of God on earth. Because the history of Israel can be anomalous and absurd, because that history is integral to the messianic process, the Jewish people can be reborn in Zion. Precisely for the same reason, however, Israel can experience an Auschwitz, a Treblinka, a Belsen, which are also of the nature of the absurd.

Discussions about the meaning of the Holocaust, and whether Judaism needs to change radically in response to it, continue within Judaism today. Although the Holocaust is a problem of the past the literature about it has been growing exponentially over the last few years, after a period of silence in the immediate aftermath of the Second World War. One of the reasons for this is that as Holocaust survivors enter old age the memories of their early life tend to dominate their minds. Indeed the incidence of suicide among Holocaust survivors is indicative of the hold which distant suffering still has over them. Primo Levi, the great Italian Jewish writer of Holocaust tales, killed himself (1987) as did Bruno Bettelheim (1990), whose psycho-analytical studies of Holocaust experience have become classics. Another reason is that some of the younger generation, the grandchildren of the survivor generation, seem obsessed with the Holocaust almost as if they feel guilty at their own good fortune in surviving physically unscathed.

The nature and significance of the State of Israel is also a subject which has consequences for the future of Jewish life in all its aspects. There are ongoing disagreements among Jews about the significance of the State of Israel. Whether or not it is the beginning of the messianic era or simply an aberrant interruption of Diaspora experience. In Israel itself groups of religious Zionists, imbued with a sense of the messianic status of the new state, are determined to turn their religious views into political realities. These groups originated with the *Gush Emunim* movement, founded after the 1967 war when all of the Holy Land came under Israeli control. *Gush Emunim* was led by R. Tzvi Yehudah Kook, the son of R. Abraham I. Kook, who opposed the return of any of the ancient territory of the Holy Land to Arab control on both halakhic and messianic grounds. Mundane considerations of bargaining for peace count for naught in an atmosphere filled with expectations of a new dawn, a new millennium, approaching. It is this ideology which underlies Jewish settlement on the West Bank, and the virulent opposition to the peace agreement between Israel and the Palestinians. It also led to the assassination of Prime Minister Yitzchak Rabin in 1995 by Yigal Amir, a religious Zionist student who sympathized with the West Bank settlers.

Some Diaspora leaders have supported the stance of not giving up land for peace. Thus R. Menachem Schneerson, the late Lubavitcher Rebbe, came out strongly against one inch of the Holy Land being given up in exchange for peace. Most Diaspora rabbinic authorities, whether Orthodox, Conservative or Reform, take a more pragmatic and less messianic view of the matter. The spiritual head of Modern Orthodoxy in the USA, R. Joseph D. Soloveitchik, advocated a flexible attitude to the whole issue, although he stressed the centrality of Israel for the religious Jew of today. Similarly R. Immanuel Jakobovits, a former British Chief Rabbi, angered right-wing Zionists by coming out publicly against allowing messianic considerations to intrude on the search for a political settlement between Israel and her Arab neighbours.

6

The Jewish Mystical Tradition

Introduction

Judaism is not, in essence, a mystical religion. It does not depend on the enlightening mystical experience of a founder who subsequently interprets his insights to a group of disciples. Biblical prophecy may be construed as distinct from mystical experience, though sufficiently similar to be confused with it particularly by mystics themselves. The difference between them may be expressed as follows. Whereas in mysticism man experiences himself as breaking through to a level of reality beyond the ordinary world of forms and objects, in prophecy the prophet experiences a greater reality breaking through to the level of the everyday. The norms of rabbinic Judaism prevented Jewish mysticism from withdrawing too far into its own inner world, but these norms in their turn were shaped by the attitudes and beliefs of the Kabbalah, as medieval Jewish mysticism is known, and esoteric teachings often passed into the consciousness and behaviour of ordinary Jews.

The Origin and Development of Jewish Mysticism

The first references to Jewish mysticism in rabbinic literature appear in the mishnaic corpus which was redacted in the late second century CE. The *Mishnah* issues the following warning:

> One does not explain the *Maaseh Bereshit* [Creation Mysteries] to two students at the same time. Nor the *Merkabah* [Mysteries of Ezekiel's vision of the divine Chariot] to a single student unless he is wise and understands from his own knowledge. He who contemplates four things, it were better had he not come into the world: What is above, what is below, what is before, and what is after.[1]

Though the statement of the *Mishnah* is terse and cryptic, it pre-supposes an established teaching concerning two esoteric doctrines, Creation Mysteries and Mysteries of the Chariot. The former may be taught but only in the one-to-one situation of contact between master and pupil. The latter may not be generally taught, unless the pupil is suitable material for instruction having first-hand contact with mystical experience. The continuation of the *Mishnah*, 'what is above, what is below', etc., presumably refers to these two esoteric doctrines. From the talmudic discussion of this text it emerges that the *Merkabah* tradition involved a series of techniques and practices whereby the mystic explored the spiritual space between the human world and that of the Chariot of God, the goal of which was a vision of God seated on His heavenly throne.

It is unclear whether there was opposition to *Merkabah* theology, or whether it was simply believed that esoteric teachings of this nature should remain the preserve of the mystics themselves. Certainly a number of warnings were issued against dabbling in such matters unless one was ready, the most famous being the story of the four sages who undertook the mystical trip to Paradise.

> Four entered Paradise. They are Ben Azai, Ben Zoma, Acher (Elisha ben Avuyah), and R. Akiva. R. Akiva said to them: When you reach the stones of pure marble be careful not to say 'water, water', since Scripture says 'A speaker of lies cannot stand before My face' (Psalm 101). Ben Azai gazed and died. Ben Zoma gazed and was mentally disturbed. Acher cut the plants, and R. Akiva came out in peace.[2]

This tale indicates the extremely dangerous nature of the enterprise. We are almost presented with a typology of the three possible consequences of a malfunction in the mystical journey: death, madness and heresy (i.e. cutting the plants of Paradise).

A whole literature of *Merkabah* mysticism is extant, dating most probably from the late talmudic period. From these literary remains, and from the references in talmudic sources, we can put together a picture of the techniques used by the mystic in preparation for his journey to a vision of the divine throne. These comprised fasting, ritual bathing for purificatory purposes, sitting in a special posture with the head between the knees, chanting hymns and mystical names of the angels or of God, prayers, and the use of a contemplative technique of gazing the exact nature of which is obscure. The mystical traveller had to pass through a series of seven halls, *heikhalot*, each of which was guarded by an angel and the door of which was impassable except to those possessing the correct mystical password, or formula. Any mistake in the latter could be fatal, as could a lack of the necessary preparation prior to undertaking the journey. The *Heikhalot* texts, as this *Merkabah* literature is known, abound in angelic names and formulae to be used by the adept as well as in descriptions from the two pseudepigraphic heroes of these works, R. Ishmael and R. Akiva, describing their mystical journeys and encounters. A prominent figure in these texts is the angel Metatron, the steward of the angelic hosts, who acts as a kind of intermediary between God and man. Metatron is depicted as the transfigured biblical character Enoch who was taken up to heaven from the midst of a sinful generation[3] and transformed into an angel. The heresy of Acher (Elisha ben Avuyah), one of the four sages who entered Paradise, is explained as mistaking Metatron for a second deity and thus believing in dualism.

It has been speculated that the catastrophes which beset Judaism during the early rabbinic period, namely the destruction of the Temple in 70 CE and the defeat of the Bar Kokhba rebellion against Rome in 135 CE, created a religious environment where God was felt to have withdrawn from any involvement with the mundane world to His celestial kingdom. God's transcendence, His distance from man, is certainly a major theme of *Merkabah* teaching and it may well be that the situation of Palestinian Jewry fostered this form of mysticism among some of the leading rabbis of the period.

The other mystical tradition, *Maaseh Bereshit* or Mysteries of Creation, would seem to have been concerned with the creative power of Hebrew letter combinations, presumably of the type found in the *Sefer Yetzirah* or Book of Formation. This work is ascribed to the Patriarch Abraham, perhaps indicating that it represents a tradition stemming from outside the Sinaitic revelation. The *Sefer Yetzirah* indeed ends with an account of how Abraham mastered the mystical techniques which led to the covenant between him and God. The *Sefer Yetzirah* opens with the 32 paths of wonderful wisdom through which God created the world. These are made up of the ten *sefirot*, possibly numbers or dimensions, which are described as *belimah*, without substance, plus the twenty-two letters of the Hebrew alphabet. Much of the book is taken up with a discussion of the classification of the letters into various groupings and the significance of each group. A parallelism is set up between the elements of a threefold division: the world (space), the year (time), and the soul (man). The creative power of letter combinations is brought out in talmudic stories associated with the *Maaseh Bereshit* traditions: Rava created a man and sent him before R. Zeira who spoke to him, but the man did not answer. He then said: You are from the sages (or alternatively 'from the magicians'), return to your dust. R. Chanina and R. Oshaya would sit every Friday and engage in the study of the *Sefer Yetzirah* (or 'the laws of *Yetzirah*'), and created a three-year-old calf which they ate.[4]

It will be obvious that *Maaseh Bereshit* mysticism is closely associated with magic, but this should cause no surprise considering the close relationship between mysticism and magic in other mystical traditions. Even the clearly contemplative mysticism of the *Heikhalot* texts guarantees the adept an insight into the inner workings of the world, a knowledge of the future, and great power.

> Sometimes he [the *Merkabah* mystic] stands before the Lord God of Israel to see all that they do before the throne of His Glory, and to know all that will come to pass in the world: who will be brought low, and who raised up, who will be weakened and who strengthened, who impoverished and who enriched. He sees and recognizes all the deeds which men do even in the interior of their homes, whether they are good or evil deeds. Anyone who lifts his hand against him and smites him is covered in plague boils.[5]

Some of the main features of later Jewish mysticism, particularly of medieval Kabbalah, are present in the terse formulae of the *Sefer Yetzirah*, which may date back to the third century CE although the present form of the work contains a number of later additions. One of these features is the idea of man as a microcosm of the universe, implicit in the parallelism between the soul, the world and yearly time. This doctrine is central to the mystical exploration of man's inner nature as a means of unravelling the workings of the cosmos. Another feature is the embryonic theory of emanation contained in the teachings of the *Sefer Yetzirah* about the *sefirot*. Although nothing is said explicitly about the emanation of the *sefirot* from God, the nine lower *sefirot* seem to emerge from the first *sefirah*, the Holy Spirit of God. Since the *sefirot* constitute created reality, and together with the letters of the alphabet are the means whereby God forms the world, it was natural for the later Kabbalah to understand them as stages in the emanation of the lower levels of existence from the divine substance. This differs from traditional Jewish teachings about *creatio ex nihilo*.

Some time during the talmudic period the centre of Jewish

mysticism shifted from Palestine to Babylonia, which was becoming the main focus of Jewish life both culturally and economically. During the Geonic period (seventh to eleventh centuries) Babylonian Jews preserved the mystical traditions which they had inherited from the past, but these same traditions grew in their new setting, at least partly from contact with native esoteric movements. A well authenticated story tells how a Babylonian mystic and wonderworker, Abu Aaron of Baghdad, brought mystical teachings from the East to Italy in the ninth century. The Italian mystics were already conversant with the *Merkabah* traditions, and presumably Abu Aaron added to them the developments which had taken place in Babylonia. From Italy the new features travelled north to Germany, carried by a student of Abu Aaron's, where they helped to inaugurate the era of German-Jewish mysticism associated with the *Chasidei Ashkenaz*, or German Pietists. An important work of European mysticism, the *Sefer Ha-Bahir*, was edited in Provence in the twelfth century from teachings emanating from the East. This work is the earliest mystical text to put forward the notion of the transmigration of souls, a doctrine already found among the early Karaite sectarians in eighth-century Babylonia. Like the sectarian use of the doctrine, the *Sefer Ha-Bahir* introduces it as a solution to the problem of the suffering of the righteous who are being punished for sins committed in a previous life. The *sefirah* teachings of the *Sefer Yetzirah* are found in a more developed form in the *Bahir*, where they are described in a highly colourful symbolic language as attributes or powers of God, or depicted in the form of a tree linking heaven and earth. The lowest *sefirah* is the *Shekhinah*, the divine indwelling of God in the world, which the *Bahir* often refers to as the daughter of the king. One outstanding feature of the theory of the *sefirot* found here is the identification of evil with the *sefirah* of *Din*, or Judgment, thus implying that it is part of the divine structure itself, and not something extraneous to God.

Medieval Jewish Mysticism in Germany

The *Merkabah* tradition, modified by the developments it had undergone in Babylonia which were transmitted to Europe by Abu Aaron and later by the *Bahir* sources, led to two main undercurrents of mystical thought in the Middle Ages. The first was in Germany and is exemplified by the *Chasidei Ashkenaz* movement, and the second took place further west in the Iberian peninsula and in southern France and saw the beginning of the kabbalistic movement. The German Jewish pietists of the eleventh and twelfth centuries were characterized by their asceticism, their strong emphasis on ethical as well as ritual behaviour, their magical practices and beliefs, their isolation from the Christians among whom they dwelt and who nevertheless influenced their thought, and their mystical theology. At the centre of this mysticism was the idea of the *Kavod*, or Divine Glory, which was an emanation from the Godhead and could be contemplated by the mystic at the end of his journey through the *heikhalot*. This *Kavod*, which is also referred to as the *Shekhinah*, is seen in mystical vision seated on the divine throne. The speculations on the immense dimensions of the body of God, known as *Shiur Komah*, which were an embarrassment to philosophically minded Jewish theologians, were understood by the *Chasidei Ashkenaz* as referring to the *Kavod*. The unknowable Godhead, not amenable to mystic vision, was not thought of as withdrawn from the workings of the world. On the contrary it was conceived as immanent in all creation, an immanence verging on pantheism. In a well-known hymn cycle written in these pietist circles, and still used today in some versions of the synagogue liturgy, we find the following stanza: You were before all creatures. Alone, needing nothing. The beginning and the end are ordered by Your hand. You are in them, and they are bound with Your spirit.[6]

This hymn cycle, known as *Shir Ha-Yichud*, or Song of Unity, is full of a lofty spirituality reflecting the mystical theology of the *Chasidei Ashkenaz*. Nevertheless its pantheistic strain was considered too heterodox by some rabbis, who tried to forbid its inclusion in the liturgy. The criticism focused on phrases such as 'Everything is in You, and You are in everything', 'Surrounding all things and filling all things, when everything comes to be You are in everything' 'Before the all, You were the all, and once all was, You fill the all'. What might seem objectionable to rational theology, however, can seem innocuous to the mystic.

The mysticism of the *Chasidei Ashkenaz* remained the preserve of an elitist circle, although the movement as such was influential among a broad spectrum of German Jewry which absorbed many of its secondary features. The anti-intellectualism, emphasis on ethical character, centrality of prayer, magical beliefs and practices, indulgence in asceticism and penitential acts, and belief that sin must be atoned for by the self-imposed sufferings of the sinner, all left an indelible mark on central and eastern European Jewry long after the movement itself had disintegrated. These ideas permeated through the one major literary work outside the halakhic sphere produced by the *Chasidei Ashkenaz*. This was the *Sefer Chasidim* edited from the teachings of R. Judah the Pietist (1150–1217) and members of his circle. R. Judah was a member of the Kalonymus family which had migrated from Italy to Germany in the ninth century, bringing with it mystical traditions.

The German pietists were committed to halakhic norms, and though they initiated a number of new customs their mystical views were generally not allowed to override the traditions of the *halakhah*. The nearest the movement came to a conflict between mysticism and the halakhic process was the use, by at least one of the pietists, of mysticism to solve halakhic problems through heavenly revelation in dreams. Such an attempt is extant in the work *She'elot U-Teshuvot Min Ha-Shamayim* ('Questions and Answers from Heaven') by Jacob Ha-Levi of Marvège (twelfth to thirteenth centuries). Jacob posed the questions by going into seclusion, praying, and uttering divine names. His answers would be given in a dream, often incorporated in biblical verses which could be interpreted as conveying a message relevant to the problem. Such a procedure runs counter to a well-established tradition that the *halakhah* was not to be decided by prophecy, but by the majority decision of the sages after discussion and analysis of the issues involved. Nevertheless Jacob's solutions were accepted and quoted in subsequent halakhic literature.

The Kabbalah in Provence and Spain

The developments which took place among the Jewish mystics of south-western Europe in the twelfth and thirteenth centuries were very different from those which characterized the German pietistical movement. Provence, where medieval Kabbalah originated, was a centre of Jewish intellectual activity and the place where many of the philosophical texts written in Arabic were translated into Hebrew. The mystical theology which emerged in such an environment was more speculative than its German counterpart, it was more interested in exploring the structure and dynamism of the divine nature, and is therefore often referred to as theosophy. The leader of the circle of mystics in Provence in the twelfth century was R.

Abraham ben David, known as the Rabad, whose written legacy deals purely with halakhic, and not mystical, issues. His esoteric teachings were handed down orally, and continued by his son Isaac the Blind (circa 1160–1235) who has been called the 'father of the Kabbalah'.[7] Isaac based his teaching on the *Bahir*, but developed the doctrine of the *sefirot* still further, seeing them as stages of the divine emanation to which the mystic passes in meditational prayer. It is to Isaac that we owe the description of the unknown and unknowable Godhead as *Ein Sof*, the Infinite or Limitless. This distinction between the unknown Godhead and the aspect of God known in and through the *sefirot*, is central to Isaac's school of mysticism, and becomes even more pronounced in the work of his Spanish disciples.

The spread of kabbalistic ideas to nearby Spain, and their acceptance among wide circles of Jews, was enhanced by the fact that the leading rabbinic authority of Spanish Jewry of that period, R. Moses ben Nachman (Nachmanides, 1194–1270), was himself a kabbalist. Although he does not expound his kabbalistic ideas at any great length in his popular writings, the many hints he gives of the mystical interpretation of Scripture in his commentary on the Pentateuch gave the nascent Kabbalah an aura of respectability. Many later kabbalists talk of him with great respect, and his mystically based theology was a much more acceptable alternative to Jewish conservatives who viewed the medieval Jewish philosophers and their philosophical theology with deep suspicion. The ideas of the Kabbalah about God and the world may have been new, and at times radical in a monotheistic framework, but unlike the philosophers the kabbalistic mystics maintained an absolute commitment to the details of the *halakhah*.

By far the most important work of Spanish Kabbalah was the *Sefer Ha-Zohar* ('The Book of Splendour'), which appeared in mysterious circumstances circa 1280–86. It was circulated by the kabbalist Moses de Leon as being a copy of an ancient mystical manuscript recording the teachings of R. Simeon bar Yochai and his disciples in second-century Palestine. It is interesting that one explanation of the appearance of the work which was current at the time was that it had been sent to Spain by Nachmanides who had emigrated to Palestine. The attempt to authenticate the *Zohar* by associating it with Nachmanides shows the high regard in which he was held by all those involved with Kabbalah. R. Isaac of Acre, a contemporary of Moses de Leon, has left us a long account of his efforts to verify the antiquity of the Zoharic text. One of the views which R. Isaac came across was that Moses de Leon only ascribed the work to the great sage R. Simeon bar Yochai in order to charge more for his copies of the manuscript. In fact, however, he wrote it himself through the possession of a 'magical writing name', i.e. a technique of automatic writing where the author composes under the influence of an angelic or heavenly force. Moses de Leon swore on oath to R. Isaac that he had the original, ancient, manuscript in his house and invited him to come and see it. Unfortunately Moses died before the offer could be taken up.

Modern scholars of the Kabbalah generally accept the view, reported by Isaac of Acre in the name of Moses de Leon's widow, that the *Zohar* was composed by Moses de Leon himself and that various other authors subsequently added their own contributions which today make up the Zoharic corpus. Kabbalists, and more traditional scholars, deny that the *Zohar* is a pseudepigraphic work since they cannot accept that Moses de Leon was a forger, and the riches and depth of the *Zohar*'s teaching could only have come from a sage of the standing of R. Simeon bar Yochai. Even the critically-minded kabbalist, R. Jacob Emden, who pointed out that certain passages of the *Zohar* clearly reflected the conditions of thirteenth-century Spain and could thus not have been written in second-century Palestine, still believed that the main body of the *Zohar* was of ancient provenance. His motives for showing up the obviously late additions to the work, as he thought of them, even though this angered conservative kabbalists, were associated with the use made of the more radical teachings of the *Zohar* by the Shabbatean sect.

The Teachings of the Zohar

The *Zohar* is not a systematic treatise on Jewish mysticism. It is written in the form of a *midrash*, or homiletic commentary on the Pentateuch and other biblical books. In its various sections, and sometimes within one section, the same theme may be treated in a number of different ways, using a series of symbolic descriptions. Many of the streams of thought in Kabbalah are taken up, and developed at great length, in the *Zohar*. At the same time at least one kabbalistic doctrine is played down, if not ignored altogether. This is the teaching about *shemittot*, or world cycles, which maintained that at different periods a different one of the seven lower *sefirot* dominated the world, and that a specific aspect of the *Torah* and specific norms were in operation. The idea of changing norms, of a new *Torah* applying to each new age, has obvious antinomian connotations, and this may explain the *Zohar*'s reticence on the subject.

The mystical doctrine of the *Zohar* focuses primarily on the structure and workings of the divine sub-stratum, which underlies reality as we know it. Central to this divine structure is the unity-in-complexity of the ten *sefirot*, the matrices which have emanated from the Godhead and by which reality is formed and controlled. The symbols used of the *sefirot* have strong mythological overtones. They are the branches of a tree with its roots in heaven, connecting heaven and earth. They are the organs of the body of *Adam Kadmon*, Primal Man, the archetype of every human individual. They are the faces of the divine King, the garments of God, divine names, the basic features of all language, etc. In a sense they are the body of the Godhead, which is itself the soul of the *sefirot*. They are divided into male and female, two principles which constitute all reality, and individual *sefirot* are known as Father, Mother, Son, Daughter, Husband and Wife. A sub-section of the *sefirot* constitutes the world of evil, a subject to which the *Zohar* devotes considerable space. This world of evil is known as the *Sitra Achra* ('Other Side'), and the *sefirot* of evil, which have also emanated from the Godhead, are known as the Forces of Impurity. These Forces, led by Samael and his female consort Lilith, are ranged against the other *sefirot* which are the Forces of Holiness. The mythological element in the *Zohar*'s descriptions of evil and its battle against holiness are pronounced. Evil is present not merely in the human sphere, but in the divine as well, though it has no life of its own and must attach itself parasitically to holiness in order to draw vitality from there. The *Sitra Achra* is of the nature of waste matter, a shell (*kelipah*) around the living kernel of things, or around the divine light within all reality. It is man's action which plays a crucial role in the operation of the *Sitra Achra*, for through sin he feeds the Forces of Impurity with the life-providing elements which they cannot generate of themselves. By keeping the laws and prescriptions of the *Torah* the Jew can help to keep the *Sitra Achra* in check, and maintain harmony in the universe. This balance or harmony also necessitates acts favourable to the Forces of Impurity, a kind of religious bribery of evil. In general the sins of Israel not only provide vitality for the

Sitra Achra, they allow Samael, the male aspect of the demonic, to take control over the *Shekhinah*, the female aspect of the *sefirot* of holiness. When this happens the *Shekhinah* is separated from her true husband, *Tiferet* the male aspect of the *sefirot*, and cannot act as the womb through which the divine power flows down to earth. Suffering and calamity ensue for man and for the world. The keeping of the *mitzvot* by the Jew, and the avoidance of sin, are seen by the *Zohar* as of great consequence for the human and divine worlds.

This whole panorama with its strong mythological, gnostic, and even dualistic overtones paints a theological picture of great symbolic power. It is at the same time at variance with many aspects of non-kabbalistic Jewish teaching. Though the strange and some what unusual Aramaic in which most of the *Zohar* is written made it incomprehensible to the non-scholarly, its ideas soon filtered through to all levels of popular religion. Its teachings on the nature of the *sefirot*, the demonological powers, the structure of the soul, the role of the *mitzvot* within the cosmic drama of the struggle between good and evil, the theory of transmigration of souls on which it elaborates at considerable length, and its many innovations in Jewish practice, all became common currency among medieval Jewry. A clash was inevitable between the Judaism of the *Zohar* and that of the exoteric rabbinic tradition, the former basing itself on the authority of mystical inspiration and the latter on the discussion of talmudic texts and halakhic reasoning. If the clashes which emerged were only mild ones, that is because even the kabbalists gave public precedence to talmudic *halakhah*, although in private they followed the *Zohar* in cases where the two conflicted. Thus R. Joseph Caro, the author of the standard sixteenth-century code the *Shulchan Arukh* and himself a mystic, states explicitly that halakhic rulings should follow talmudic tradition rather than the *Zohar* when it offered a contrary view.[8] The many kabbalistic practices advocated by the *Zohar* which were not contradicted by the *Talmud* were taken up by halakhists and eventually incorporated as normative Jewish law in the codes. Jewish life thus underwent a transformation as it absorbed the ideas and attitudes of the Kabbalah.

The Mystics of Safed and Lurianic Kabbalah

From the fourteenth to the mid-sixteenth centuries, though there was considerable creativity in mystical circles, no work emerged which seriously challenged the central place occupied by the *Zohar*, the 'Bible' of the Kabbalah. The traumatic and dislocating consequences of the expulsion of the Jews from Spain in 1492, undertaken at the instigation of the Inquisition to prevent Jews influencing their co-religionists who had been forcibly converted to Christianity, acted as a catalyst in the development of new forms of Kabbalah. A circle of mystics of Spanish origin formed in Safed, a town in the Upper Galilee region of northern Palestine, inspired by a renewed messianism to return to the Holy Land and await the Redemption. It was among these kabbalists that the Kabbalah of the *Zohar* reached its zenith in the encyclopedic writings of Moses Cordovero (1522–70). Cordovero's work is essentially an attempt at systematizing the Kabbalah, setting out and reconciling the different tendencies of the various mystical sub-traditions. In his major book the *Pardes Rimonim* there is hardly a theme of any importance in the writings of his predecessors which he does not analyse. The only topic on which he is silent is the doctrine of *shemittot*, or world cycles, which the *Zohar* itself plays down. At the end of the first chapter of the *Pardes Rimonim* Cordovero discusses the attitude of kabbalists to Jews who are not involved with the mystical tradition. He distinguishes between those who are ignorant of the *sefirot* doctrine, and those who consciously reject it. The former type of Jew cannot be accused of heresy, 'nevertheless he has not merited to see the light in his lifetime nor tasted of the sweetness of the *Torah*, he dies without wisdom and has not seen [true] goodness.' The latter deny the mystical doctrine 'because they have become habituated to external [i.e. philosophic] wisdom. They are to be called heretics, since they deny the oral traditions of *Torah* interpretation.'

During the last year of Cordovero's life he was a teacher to Isaac Luria (Ashkenazi), who had recently arrived in Safed from Egypt. Luria was then only 35 years old, and had spent some time as a recluse studying Kabbalah on an island of the Nile. After Cordovero's death, and even perhaps while he was still alive, Luria drew to himself a circle of disciples whom he instructed in what later came to be known as Lurianic Kabbalah. His teachings were transmitted orally, and recorded in note form by his pupils, because they flowed from Luria under the pressure of inspiration which made it impossible for him to record them himself. The most important presentation of Lurianic Kabbalah is contained in the work *Etz Chaim* of Chaim Vital (Calabrese) (1542–1620), who was Luria's closest disciple from the time he arrived in Safed to his death in 1572. Vital explains, in his introduction to the *Etz Chaim*, how he was first drawn to the study of Kabbalah. He was, at 30 years old, greatly perturbed by the fact that the messianic age seemed no closer, and that the long exile of the Jewish people had already extended for more than one and a half millennia. He then found a passage[9] in Zoharic literature, which stated that a major factor in delaying the Messiah was the neglect of kabbalistic study. From that time he became a kabbalist. This messianic motif was not restricted to Vital, the whole mystical circle in Safed was imbued with a yearning for the Redemption and Isaac Luria himself seems to have believed that he had a central role in the messianic process.

Lurianic Kabbalah, although seeing itself as an extension of the teachings of the *Zohar*, introduces a series of new symbols to explain the relationship of God to the world, which give a novel direction to Jewish mystical theology. The initial act of God in the cosmogonic process, according to Luria, is one of *tzimtzum*, contraction or self – withdrawal. This is necessary so that a vacuum is formed in which the world can come into being, for without such a vacuum the Godhead, *Ein Sof*, is everywhere and there can be no world.

> Know that before the emanations were emanated, and the created beings created, the undifferentiated upper light filled all existence and there was no vacant space. When it was His undifferentiated will to create the worlds *Ein Sof* contracted Himself into a central point in the middle of which was His very light, and He contracted that light and withdrew into the sides around the central point. Then a vacant place, and space, and an empty volume was left.[10]

This doctrine of *tzimtzum*, the withdrawal of God into Himself, became a powerful and suggestive symbol for subsequent kabbalists. In the Lurianic system it is an act which is repeated at each stage of the creative process, but Luria's disciples warn against taking it literally. *Tzimzum* refers to a symbolic truth, nevertheless it was interpreted as implying a real division between the infinite God and the finite world. The Kabbalah of the *Zohar* had pantheistic overtones since it taught that the world had emanated out of God's substance, while a literal interpretation of *tzimtzum* was a re-affirmation of theism and in a sense a denial that a perfect God could be part of an imperfect world. R. Jacob Emden, writing two centuries after Luria, maintains that the doctrine of *tzimtzum* is a rational necessity without which no thinker could conceive of the creation unless he postulated a finite God.[11]

There were other kabbalists who saw *tzimtzum* not as a literal statement, since it is an act prior to the creation of space and any contraction or withdrawal of God must be metaphoric, but as expressing a symbolic truth. Israel Baal Shem Tov (1700–60), originator of Chasidic mysticism, in particular wished to emphasize the immanence of God in all creation which a literal interpretation of *tzimtzum* would negate. He, and the Chasidic mystics who followed him, interpreted the self-withdrawal of God as meaning that God had hidden Himself within the created world. In the Chabad/Lubavitch school of Chasidism this was sometimes understood to mean that God had simply allowed man to perceive a world which from God's point of view did not actually exist at all, while the mystics of the Braslav branch of Chasidism saw the *tzimtzum* doctrine as teaching that at the heart of reality lies a paradox that cannot be grasped by rational thought, but only by faith. This paradox involves the empty space generated by the *tzimtzum*. On the one hand God must be absent from the space for the world to be formed in it, on the other hand if God is indeed absent there could not be a world since nothing can exist without the continuing sustenance of God. The immanence and transcendence of God, though contradictory, must both be affirmed of Him.

After the initial self-contraction of God the creative process begins with the projection of the divine light into the empty space, the light having the structure of *Adam Kadmon*, Primeval Man. According to Luria the undifferentiated light needed vessels, *kelim*, to individualize and to separate out into its various forms. The vessels of the lower *sefirot* lights were unable to contain the divine light flowing into them, and they broke, trapping the light sparks in the broken shards. A new light of rectification had to be projected in order for the creative process to continue, involving a new configuration of the *sefirot*. This rectification, *tikkun*, was not complete and it is up to man to complete the *tikkun* of raising the sparks trapped in the shards by performing the *mitzvot* with the correct mystical intention. When every individual has fulfilled his own task of *tikkun* the world will attain a state of cosmic harmony and the messianic age will dawn. In so far as a man fails in his task of rectification he will be reincarnated after death, to continue the work of *tikkun*.

The themes of Lurianic Kabbalah gave expression to the feelings of crisis and catastrophe following on the expulsion from Spain and

Portugal and also provided a theology of potency for the hapless
Jew who in all other respects seemed anything but in control of his
destiny.

Post-Lurianic Messianism

Lurianic Kabbalah, which was in essence an elitist esoteric teaching,
spread rapidly throughout the Jewish world and helped to generate
a fever pitch of messianic expectation. This messianism was aided
by the distressed condition of European Jewry following on the Cos-
sack revolt against Polish rule, which led to the terrible Chmielnicki
massacres of 1648. When the news reached far-flung Jewish communities that a messianic figure, Shabbatai Tzvi (1626–76), had
appeared among the Jews of the Levant it was greeted with great
excitement. The propagandists of Shabbatai's messianic status were
imbued with Lurianic ideas about mystical eschatology. Even after
Shabbatai Tzvi's forced conversion to Islam in 1666 the faithful
among his followers continued to believe he was the Messiah,
and interpreted his apostasy as a stage in the process of *tikkun*.
The Messiah had to descend into the depths of the powers of evil
in order to release the last remaining sparks trapped there. Lurianic
Kabbalah in the hands of its Shabbatean interpreters proved a
powerful source of heterodox theology, and with the waning of
the Shabbatean movement following on the Messiah's apostasy a
reaction set in among more orthodox sections of the Jewish world.
They saw it as a challenge to the whole halakhic structure of ritual
and morals. The implicit tensions between esoteric and exoteric
Judaism had become explicit, and strong pressure was applied
to restrict Kabbalah to small circles of mystical contemplatives to
prevent it constituting a danger to the very fabric of traditional
Judaism.

These profound misgivings about the heterodox potential of
Lurianic ideas were strengthened by the activities of the movement
begun by Jacob Frank (1726–91), in the wake of the Shabbatean
débâcle. The Frankist movement in Poland and eastern Europe
adopted many of the practices of the more extreme Shabbatean
sects. They used ritualized antinomian behaviour, particularly in
infringement of halakhic sexual restrictions, as part of their cult,
and they taught a doctrine of the Messiah as a deified man, a
status claimed by Frank himself, which was anathema to Jewish

belief. After persecution from the orthodox Jewish leadership, still reeling from the inroads of Shabbatean heresy, the Frankists sought the protection of the Catholic Church by converting to Christianity. They made it clear that though they were against the teachings of the *Talmud*, and were willing to subscribe to Christianity, they wished to retain the *Zohar* as a religious text even after conversion and thus to continue their practice of mystical Judaism.

The Chasidic Movement

It is against this background that we must view the activities and teachings of Israel ben Eliezer (1700–60), known as the Baal Shem Tov, or Besht. The Besht was an itinerant faith healer who wandered among the impoverished Jewish communities of the Ukraine and southern Poland. Those who came in contact with him were struck by his penetrating religious insight, and he eventually gathered round himself a following of both unlettered and scholarly Jews. The Besht received little formal education, and seems to have been mainly self-taught. He was, however, an ecstatic and his own mystical experience served as an alternative authority structure to the intellectually based one accepted by the eastern European rabbinic leadership, which emphasized talmudic scholarship.

Something of the Besht's ecstatic character is brought out in a letter which he wrote to his brother-in-law, R. Gershon of Kutov, who was then resident in the Holy Land. The Besht's disciple, R. Jacob Joseph of Polonnoye, was meant to deliver the letter but was unable to make the projected journey. The letter was eventually published at the end of his book *Ben Porat Yosef*, and it is an important document of the early phase of Chasidism, being an authentic statement of the Besht's own ideas unmediated by the interpretation of his disciples.

On the New Year festival 5507 [i.e. 1746] I performed a conjuration of soul ascension, as is known to you, and I saw wonderful things in a vision which I had not seen from the day my thought matured. . . . When I returned to the lower Garden of Eden, however, I saw there several souls of the living and the dead who were known to me – those not known to me were without number – moving to and fro in great joy to ascend from world to world through the pillar which is known to the mystics. . . . Because of the great joy which I beheld among them I agreed to ascend with them. And I saw in a vision that Samael[12] had gone up to make accusation against the great joy the likes of which had never been. He had performed his activities, decrees of destruction against a number of souls that they should die unnatural deaths. I was seized by trembling and I risked my life. I asked my teacher and master[13] to go with me, for it is a great danger to go and ascend to the higher worlds. I went up level after level until I entered the hall of the Messiah, where the Messiah studies *Torah* with all the *tannaim* (mishnaic rabbis) and *tzaddikim* (righteous ones) and also with the seven shepherds (of the Bible). I asked the Messiah directly: When is the master coming? He replied to me: By this you shall know. When your teaching becomes well publicized and revealed in the world, and the well-springs of what I have taught you, and you have grasped on your own, shall spread forth. When they will also be able to perform unifications and ascensions like you. Then all of the shells[14] will be finished, and it will be a time of divine good-will and salvation. I was amazed at this, and I experienced considerable anguish[15] at the great length of time when this might possibly be.

A number of the Besht's followers were greater scholars than he was in both esoteric and exoteric Judaism. Some of them, like R. Phineas Shapiro of Koretz (1726–91), never actually became disciples although they were clearly influenced by the master's teachings. Others, like R. Jacob Joseph of Polonnoye (d. 1782) and R. Dov Baer the Maggid of Mezeritch (d. 1772), had already attained scholarly and rabbinic status before they became disciples of the Besht. What attracted them to his teachings was not his ability to impart book knowledge, but his religious understanding. In the words of the later Chasidic tradition, the Besht's knowledge of Judaism had 'soul' whereas theirs lacked 'soul'. Thus, merely by telling them parables or fables, he enabled them to gain new understanding, particularly of Kabbalah, and to see its relevance for their own existential situations.

The encounter with the Besht changed the life and attitudes of his scholarly disciples. They took away a novel approach to Judaism from the Besht, and developed it each one in his own way. R. Jacob Joseph, who was the author of the first Beshtian work *Toldot Yaakov Yosef*, is our main source for the original teachings of the Besht since the latter wrote nothing himself. Although R. Jacob Joseph must be regarded as the most authentic interpreter of the master's ideas, it was R. Dov Baer who was acknowledged as the leader of the movement after the death of the Besht.

R. Dov Baer gathered round himself a group of young, enthusiastic, and highly gifted disciples who formed an elite circle to be entrusted with the propagation of the new doctrine. Dov Baer had deeper roots in the classical kabbalistic tradition than the Besht, and he gave form and structure to the ideology of the fledgling movement. He also had to bear the brunt of the savage attacks on the Chasidim launched by the *Mitnagdim*, literally 'opponents', who saw Chasidism as simply a resurgence of Shabbatean ideas. Chasidism constituted a serious challenge to the attempts of the mitnagdic rabbis to keep religious excitement to a minimum in the aftermath of mystical messianism.

During the lifetime of Dov Baer the Beshtian Kabbalah developed in two separate directions. Dov Baer who, unlike his master, was something of a recluse, taught his own, official, version of Chasidism to the inner circle of disciples at Mezeritch, and had little contact with the ordinary unlettered Jews outside. At the same time a variety of individual scholar mystics propagated their version of the Beshtian teachings which, though having much in common with that of Dov Baer, were not always in agreement with the direction he gave to the movement.

Chasidism in the nineteenth century is, in essence, a continuation of the Mezeritch stream rather than that of Dov Baer's rivals. After the death of the Maggid his pupils founded schools and dynasties of their own, and the movement became a series of sub-movements split up as much by national boundaries as by differences in theology, religious practice, and leadership. The only strand of Chasidism outside the tradition of the Maggid of Mezeritch which has survived into the present is that founded by R. Nachman of Braslav (1772–1811), the great-grandson of the Besht.

The original teaching of the Besht would seem to have turned around a number of central pivots. He emphasized the subjective side of religion, in opposition to the objectivist teachings of the eastern European rabbis. One can serve God not merely through the performance of the *mitzvot* but with all one's actions, for God is to be found everywhere. The important thing is the inner state of man, his intentions, and his joyful service of God. The key term for the Besht is, thus, *devekut* or devotion, rather than any of the concepts associated with the accumulation of *Torah* knowledge or the meticulous carrying out of the rituals. This idea of an alternative standard to the supreme value of halakhic meticulousness which was current in orthodox rabbinical circles, is implicit in the mystically justified anti-nomianism of the Shabbateans and Frankists. Beshtian teaching does not reject halakhic ritualism, however, it simply puts a different value at the centre of religious concern.

Every man has to find his own religious level and work from there.

The social consequences of his teaching were of enormous importance. The simple, almost illiterate, Jew who was looked down upon by the elitist scholar becomes, in the Beshtian scheme of things, an equal and possibly even a superior religious being. His value *qua* Jew depends not on the knowledge he has of the intricacies of talmudic law, but on his inner state. Since the divine sparks are trapped in the material world, and can only be freed by man, it is up to each individual Jew to free those sparks within his orbit by uniting each thought and action to its roots in the divine.

The egalitarian aspect of the Besht's teaching is only part of the story, however. There is a clearly delineated belief in the role of the great-souled man, the *tzaddik*, within Chasidism. This doctrine is already found in the medieval Kabbalah, was developed further by Lurianic teaching, and is also behind some of the claims made about the leaders of the Shabbatean and Frankist sects by their followers. The Chasidic version of the doctrine of the *tzaddik* takes many forms, and at its most extreme there is a very fine line between the adulation of the *tzaddik* and his powers and the belief that he is a semi-divine being. The Besht himself regarded the *tzaddik* as the point of contact between the human and divine worlds, the channel through which the divine energy can flow down from heaven to earth, and the means of raising the prayers of the multitude heavenwards where they can play their part in the process of *tikkun* or rectification.

In the period following the death of the Maggid, when Chasidism began to congeal round the absolute leadership of individual *tzaddikim*, the doctrine of the *tzaddik* itself underwent change. In the writings of R. Elimelech of Lyzansk (1717–87), a disciple of Dov Baer, we find the idea first adumbrated that the *tzaddik* has control over all things, both spiritual and material:

> The *tzaddik* through his holy deeds can annul all evil decrees against Israel. God fulfills his words . . . for He has made him a partner in the process of creation.[16]

Although there were protests even from among the early *tzaddikim* themselves against the idea that the *tzaddik* could and should control the success of his followers' livelihood, their wives' barrenness, and their recovery from sickness, these soon became accepted as part of the *tzaddik's* role. Some *tzaddikim* lived like lords, supported by donations from their chasidim, and wielding temporal and spiritual power over their often extensive community of followers.

The *Mitnagdim* were unhappy about many aspects of the Chasidic movement, they objected to the emphasis on song and dance, the use of alcohol and tobacco, the Chasidic neglect of *Torah* study, the non-observance of the correct times for prayers, and a host of small changes in the rituals introduced by various Chasidic leaders. They were even more perturbed by the status of the *tzaddik* as a kind of intermediary between man and God. R. Chaim of Volozhin (1749–1821) who is usually tolerant of Chasidism, though he was the main disciple of the spiritual head of the *Mitnagdim* Elijah of Vilna, writes:

> Even to make oneself subservient, and to cleave through a form of worship, to that aspect of the Holy Spirit in man, be he prophet or inspired by the Holy Spirit, that also is true idolatry.[17]

Chasidism, as a mystical movement, revived the flagging spirits of the eastern European Jewish masses. It also served as a matrix for Jewish creativity by developing the use of the short story or parable as a medium for teaching religious ideas. Among the more outstanding products of the movement were the systematic reinterpretation of Lurianic Kabbalah formulated by Schneur Zalman of Liadi; anti-intellectual ecstatics like Abraham of Kalisk; God intoxicated mystics like Levi Isaac of Berditchev; profound yet tragic figures like Nachman of Braslav who created his own genre of mystical fairy tales, or like Menachem Mendel of Kotsk whose search for absolute truth in himself and others led him to spend the last nineteen years of his life in total seclusion. The variety of theologies of Judaism generated by the movement in a short span of time is equally noteworthy. Perhaps the most extreme of these was the theology of Mordecai Joseph Leiner of Izbica, a one-time pupil of Kotsk but subsequently a bitter rival, who denied that man possessed free will, or that in reality there was such a thing as sin. God, for Leiner, was the source of all human action and it was only from our partial human viewpoint that good and evil are distinguished.

In the course of time the Chasidic movement became institutionalized and ceased to be a movement of protest and revolt. Today Chasidim are still distinguishable from other Orthodox Jews mostly by their dress, which is modelled on the garb wore by Poles before they adopted Western dress in the nineteenth century. Thus a Chasid, particularly on Sabbaths and festivals, wears a fur hat (*shtreimel*), a long black silken coat (*bekeshe* or *kapote*), and white socks into which he tucks his trousers. He also wears a black silken cord (*gartel*) wrapped round his waste as a belt for prayers to divide 'the heart from the genitals', i.e. between the higher and lower aspects of man. Despite this antiquated appearance Chasidim have come to be accepted by most Jews as an integral part of the Orthodox establishment, and share many of the same values as other ultra-orthodox sub-groups within Judaism. Even the study of Kabbalah is no more characteristic of contemporary Chasidism than it is of non-Chasidic Jews. The only Chasidic groups which still specifically emphasize mystical Judaism are the Chabad (or Lubavitch) Chasidim, who follow the ideology of their founder R. Schneur Zalman of Liadi, and the Braslav Chasidim who are known as the 'Dead Chasidim' because they appointed no successor to their first leader R. Nachman of Braslav, and continue to study his writings as a guide to their pattern of life.

The Musar Movement

The success of the Chasidic movement led to something of a Counter-Reformation among the *Mitnagdim*. This took the form of the *Musar* movement which, though not specifically mystical in orientation, emphasized the inwardness of religious life and the ethical side of all action. The new movement was initiated by Joseph Zundel of Salant (1786–1866), who was a pupil of R. Chaim of Volozhin the most important theologian of anti-Chasidic orthodoxy. Joseph Zundel kept out of the public eye, and consistently refused to accept rabbinic office, preferring anonymity. His pietistical ways influenced his pupil Israel Lipkin Salanter (1810–83), who learned techniques of self-scrutiny from his master, and a new discipline of self-perfection in the service of God. Behind the ideas of both Joseph Zundel and Israel Lipkin was the teaching of R. Chaim that a Jew has to participate to the utmost of his being in the sufferings of his fellow and to aid him.

It was Salanter who actually founded the *Musar* movement, spending much of his mature life wandering among Jewish communities and spreading *musar* ideals. He preached a renewal of the ethical side of Judaism, consideration for the duties man owes to his fellow which tended to be overshadowed by purely ritual considerations, and the necessity for self-perfection. His wanderings took him as far as Germany and France, but the main effect of his teachings was felt in his native Lithuania, particularly through the educational institutions which he established there. Salanter was very concerned about the spiritual welfare of his fellow Jews, and he instilled this concern into a number of gifted disciples who in turn created the educational means for training a new generation with *musar* values.

Salanter's views met with considerable opposition from conservatives among his rabbinical colleagues. While they recognized that Salanter was helping to stem the influence of the secularizing *Haskalah*, or eastern European enlightenment, on *yeshivah* students and adults, they believed that traditional talmudic studies were sufficient to inculcate all the *musar* necessary for the Jew. Salanter seemed to be setting up a standard of ethical purity as the central norm of Judaism in place of the older halakhic standards, much as the Chasidim had set up devotional religion there.

The *Musar* movement, while encouraging the study of the *Talmud* and the classical commentaries, believed that only through the intensive study of pietistical literature can man come to the true service of God. This literature should be read by the *musarnik* in a mournful tune and with great emotion, so that he is led to reflect on his own shortcomings. Group sessions were also encouraged during which the participants could explore their failings and subject each other to critical scrutiny.

After Salanter's death his pupils developed the movement in a number of different directions. R. Isaac Blaser (1837–1907) edited the first work of the new movement *Or Yisrael* which included a number of short letters from Salanter. He also set up elitist colleges for the teaching of the *musar* path, which included a *kolel* for married students in Kovno and a *yeshivah* in nearby Slobodka. Blaser encouraged his students to meditate on man's sinfulness and lowly status, and thus to come to true humility and to an all-pervasive sense of awe in the presence of God. This world is a testing ground in which man is free to choose, and through his exercise of choice for good to attain to his reward in the world of eternal life to come. Blaser himself practised a kind of penitential asceticism, and would undertake a vow of silence during the whole of the Hebrew month of *Elul* which precedes the Jewish New Year festival and the Day of Atonement.

A more extreme form of *musar* teaching is found in the sub-branch of the movement established by R. Joseph Yaizel Hurwitz (circa 1850–1919), who rejected any attempts at compromise between *musar* and ordinary life in the world. Hurwitz, before undertaking an active role in spreading his *musar* ideas, himself spent a number of years in total seclusion wrestling with his own soul. If the *musarnik* really believes in divine Providence, then he must live entirely by such a belief with complete trust in God alone. Hurwitz, and those of his pupils who were able to live up to the uncompromising demands of his teaching, travelled throughout Russia setting up a network of *yeshivot* where Navardok *musar*, as it came to be called, was taught. The Navardok followers thrived on the difficulties and obstacles which they met on every side. In this way they could put their trust in God to the test, and perfect their inner strength. Hurwitz advocated the relentless search for truth in the service of God, and is reported to have said: 'If I knew that there was someone in a distant land who could clarify the truth for me, I would leave everything I have in order to learn from him'.[18]

A somewhat more moderate form of *musar* was advocated by R. Simcha Zissel Broida of Kelme (1824–98). Broida believed in a pedagogic structure for the gradual education of the *musar* acolyte in self-reflection and continual thoughtfulness about all his actions. This was a life-long process of self-discipline, self-control, and above all of mindfulness over confused or hasty action.

The *Musar* movement, despite rabbinical opposition, spread rapidly among the ranks of the *Mitnagdim*. It came into an ideological vacuum, the challenges to rabbinical orthodoxy from the Chasidim on the one hand and from the secularizing *Haskalah* on the other hand had created the need for a new dynamic. R. Chaim of Volozhin had tried to fill the gap by providing a kabbalistic rationale for the central value of the *Mitnagdim*, namely the life of *Torah* study. But his work, *Nefesh Ha-Chaim*, presupposed a thorough acquaintance with Lurianic Kabbalah, and was beyond the horizons of talmudically educated intellectuals. *Musar*, by contrast, spoke in terms which everyone could understand whether or not they agreed with its basic premises. As the movement grew it infiltrated many of the eastern European *yeshivot* which introduced a compulsory half-hour study of *musar* texts as part of the daily curriculum, and appointed a *mashgiach*, or moral supervisor, whose task it was to care for the spiritual welfare of the students.

A by-product of *musar* was the renewed interest in Jewish theology, though it was not the philosophical theology of the Middle Ages but a theology which sought to explore the psychological dimensions of man's relationship to God, and his struggle to live a holy life. In a way this paralleled the Chasidic re-interpretation of Lurianic theosophy in psychological terms. The theological interests of the *musarniks* eventually led them to borrow ideas from classical Kabbalah and Chasidism, and to use them to explicate basic *musar* insights.

As the movement became institutionalized it lost its original charisma, and few followed its more extreme forms. The destruction of European Jewry during the Nazi era swept away the great *musar* centres, just as it eliminated the strongholds of Chasidic life, and today *musar* survives in an attenuated form in the *yeshivot*, a shadow of its former self.

The Halakhah

The Jewish Path

The religion of the Hebrew Bible is inextricably associated with the life of an agricultural people and their rites and symbols. During the Babylonian exile (sixth century BCE) the religious structures of the Land of Israel were interrupted and new forms of worship, including the institution of the synagogue as a local house of study and prayer, were substituted. It was only after the destruction of the Second Temple in 70 CE, however, that Judaism as it exists today began to develop the distinctive concepts and institutions which enabled it to survive without a sacrificial ritual and without a land.

The deliberation of the sages in Yavneh, which began after the destruction of Jerusalem and lasted till the outbreak of the Bar Kokhba revolt against Rome in 132 CE, created the framework for the new forms of Jewish religious life. While seeing themselves as faithful to pre-destruction Judaism the Yavneh sages gave an emphasis and direction to Jewish religion which allowed it to build novel structures and to create more adaptable institutions. The centre of gravity moved away from the ritual of the Temple to community-based and home-based rituals.

The two central concepts of post-Yavneh Judaism are *Torah* and *mitzvah*. The *Torah* is not merely the word of God expressed in the Bible, it is the whole living, organic, tradition of Jewish teaching. The study of *Torah*, and search for new *Torah* insights, are among the highest of Jewish values.

> He who occupies himself with *Torah* and with deeds of loving kindness is forgiven all his sins.[1]

This emphasis on study guaranteed a process of growth within

Judaism, for although formal study inevitably leads to scholasticism, the demand to find new insights in *Torah* meant that an inner dialectic of change was inescapable. Great ingenuity and intellectual energy was expended by scholars who expanded the scope and application of the *Torah* concepts of the past in their search for new insights.

The notion of *mitzvah* too came to mean much more than its original sense of 'commandment'. A *mitzvah* was any precept of Judaism, ancient or modern, referring as much to charitable acts as to highly ritualized behaviour. United under the rubric of *mitzvah* was the total way of life of the Jew, for there were no specifically religious rites – all of the Jew's behaviour was an expression of the patterns for living commanded by God. Daily life itself becomes a sacrament, a participation with God in the continuing work of creation.

Halakhic Codification

The determination of the content of *mitzvah* led to a great body of Jewish legal writing on the subject of *halakhah*, which means the way or the path. The earliest example of this literature, outside of biblical references to legal issues, is the *Mishnah* which was given its final form by R. Judah the Prince and his circle at the beginning of the third century CE. The *Mishnah* is not a code, but a record of opinions expressed about halakhic issues. It was either written down, or arranged and memorized, as the standard halakhic source which all subsequent legal debate should take as its point of departure.[2] The high esteem in which R. Judah the Prince was held, and the conditions of turmoil in Palestine under hostile Roman rule which led to its final redaction, helped establish the *Mishnah* as the authoritative basis of rabbinic *halakhah*. Two other works emanating from mishnaic times were edited at a later date. They are the *Tosefta*, which follows the same order as the *Mishnah* but includes material not found in the latter, and the halakhic or tannaitic *midrashim* which are legal commentaries on the Pentateuch (excluding Genesis which contains no straightforward *halakhah*). The midrashic form was not widely used in the legal writing of later periods, for though it has the advantage of connecting *halakhah* with the biblical verses from which it may derive, it was too disjointed to serve practical legal purposes.

From the third to sixth centuries the material contained in the
Mishnah was studied, analysed and compared with other halakhic
collections preserved in oral form. The vast body of this new
matter was finally redacted in Palestine in the latter part of the
fourth century, when Jewish life began to deteriorate under Christian persecution, and came to be known as the *Jerusalem Talmud*
although it was not actually edited in Jerusalem. A century or so
later a separate redaction was made in Babylonia, the *Babylonian
Talmud*, presumably also in response to anti-Jewish legislation and
persecution which made the need for a well ordered, authoritative
text an urgent prerequisite. The two redactions differ in style,
techniques of legal inquiry, theology, and even in their decisions
about final halakhic rulings. For a time Palestinian Jewry followed
the *Jerusalem Talmud* while Babylonian Jewry followed the teachings
and conclusions of the *Babylonian Talmud*. A major split in Judaism
was averted because Jewish life in Palestine declined rapidly, while
Jewish life in Babylonia flourished in the centuries following on the
redaction of the two *Talmud*s. The text of the *Babylonian Talmud* was
worked over, re-edited, and added to by post-talmudic sages known
as *savoraim*. The *Jerusalem Talmud*, by contrast, was not subjected to
editorial refinement and eventually came to be regarded as of less
authority than its Babylonian counterpart. More than any other
work of Jewish literature, with the possible exception of the Bible,
the *Babylonian Talmud* has shaped the outlook, ways of thinking,
practice and theology of Judaism over the last fifteen hundred years.
To the Orthodox Jew it is the authoritative text of Judaism, and its
authority can only be denied at the risk of heresy.

From the close of the *Babylonian Talmud* till the eleventh century the centre of halakhic development was among the sages of
Babylonia, known as *geonim* (singular *gaon*). This title, meaning
'exalted one(s)' was given to the heads of the main Babylonian
academies who saw themselves as the guardians of the traditions
of the *Babylonian Talmud*. Questions were addressed to them from
all over the Jewish world, many of which asked for clarification of
obscure talmudic passages. It was among the *geonim* that we find
the first attempts at codifying talmudic *halakhah*. The effect of this
codification was to standardize Jewish practice and to make the
halakhah available in ready-reference manner to those unable to
follow the intricacies of talmudic discussion. It in turn led to further
attempts at codification among Jews outside Babylonia, the most
important code being that of a North African rabbi, Isaac *Alfasi*,

known as the Rif, who extracted the halakhic (and some aggadic) material from the *Babylonian Talmud* in the eleventh century.

With the decline of Babylonia as the main centre of Jewish life in the eleventh and twelfth centuries new forms of halakhic creativity appear among the Jews of Europe and North Africa, who could not look for guidance to their co-religionists in the East. The best known halakhic work of this period is the great code of Maimonides, the Spanish philosopher-sage whose mature years were spent in Egypt as physician to the family of the Sultan. Maimonides' *Mishneh Torah*, or *Yad Ha-Chazakah* as it is alternatively known, attempted to marshall all of the *halakhah* found in rabbinic literature, whether or not it was applicable in the twelfth century, and to order it according to subject-matter. He did not give the sources for his decisions which he formulated in a clear, easily readable Hebrew and he explained the principles behind the *halakhah* as well as including material of a theological and doctrinal nature. In his introduction to the code he writes:

> I saw fit to compose matters . . . affecting what is forbidden and allowed, what is unclean and clean, together with the other laws of the *Torah*. All of them in a clear language and concise manner, so that the oral teaching should be available to everyone without question or difficulty. . . . In order that all the laws should be openly revealed to young and to old. . . . So that no one should need any other work in the world concerning the laws of Israel, but that this work should be a collection of the whole of the oral teaching. . . . Therefore I have called this work *Mishneh Torah* ('Second to the *Torah*') because a man first reads Scripture and afterwards reads this work . . . and does not need to read any work in between.

Maimonides' code, like his theological *magnum opus The Guide for the Perplexed*, was the subject of considerable controversy. He was criticized for not mentioning his sources, for not referring to dissenting opinions found in earlier literature, for including philosophical material, and for the neglect of talmudic study which use of his code would entail. The controversy generated a whole series of commentaries on the code, both defending and attacking the author. What Maimonides intended should be a simple and undisputed collection of halakhic rulings became, in the course of time, the centre of a casuistic literature of considerable proportions.

In order to counter the defects which his critics had found in Maimonides' code many scholars in the post-Maimonidean period reverted to the older form of halakhic summary, which followed the order and contents of the talmudic tractates. In the early fourteenth century such a code was compiled by R. Asher ben Yechiel, known as the Rosh, a German scholar who migrated to Spain. R. Asher included material from the Franco-German academies which was not found in codes emanating from the East, North Africa or Spain. He intended his work as a supplement to the *Talmud*, to be used by those conversant with the talmudic discussions who were seeking clarification of halakhic rulings. Indeed in one of his responsa he opposes the use of codes like Maimonides' by those who are unfamiliar with the talmudic text.

Although R. Asher's code was widely respected, it was the work of his son, R. Jacob ben Asher, which was instrumental in determining the code form taken as a paradigm by all subsequent halakhists. R. Jacob divided the subject matter of the *halakhah* into four categories which he called *Turim*, or rows, the whole of his code eventually being known as the *Arba'ah Turim*. The first category, *Tur Orach Chaim*, deals with the daily life of the Jew, and with the rituals associated with the Sabbath and festivals. The second, *Tur Yoreh Deah*, deals with dietary laws, idolatry, usury prohibitions, menstruation, oaths, education, circumcision, proselytes, etc. The third, *Tur Even Ha-Ezer*, deals with the relationship between the sexes, marriage and divorce. The fourth, *Tur Choshen Mishpat*, deals with matters affecting Jewish courts of law and the details of civil and criminal law. R. Jacob follows Maimonides in separating the codification of law from the discussions of the *Talmud* and in including theological material in his code, though the *Tur* reflects the views of the German pietist school rather than philosophy. He differs from Maimonides in quoting many divergent opinions on a particular subject before giving his own ruling, which often follows the ruling of his father R. Asher.

In the sixteenth century R. Joseph Caro wrote an extensive commentary on the *Tur* in which he subjected R. Jacob's halakhic conclusions to a wide-ranging critical analysis. Caro based his own conclusions on the rulings of his three most eminent predecessors, *Alfasi*, Maimonides, and R. Asher. Where there was disagreement he opted for the majority opinion among these three. From this commentary, called *Bet Yosef*, Caro extracted his conclusions which he wrote up as a separate work called the *Shulchan Arukh* or 'Prepared Table' in imitation of the *Tur*, with the same divisions and sub-divisions. Caro was of Spanish origin, and though his vast erudition meant he was conversant with the main works of

Ashkenazi scholars of Central and Eastern Europe, he emphasized the Sefardi approach to the *halakhah*. A Polish scholar, R. Moses Isserles, known as the Rema, sought to rectify this bias in Caro's work by adding his own glosses, the *Mappah* ('Tablecloth'), to Caro's *Shulchan Arukh* based on his own commentary to the *Tur*. The fact that the *Shulchan Arukh*, in its expanded form, contained the decisions of the two leading scholars of Sefardi and Ashkenazi Jewry gave it an acceptability unattained by previous codes. As a single work it became the most authoritative halakhic text, and with the exception of the Yemenite Jews who continued to follow Maimonides' rulings, it shaped the religious life and practice of every Jewish community. The art of printing, which was introduced in the fifteenth century, was also an important factor in enabling the *Shulchan Arukh* to be disseminated widely and quickly, and played a not inconsiderable role in its acceptance as the standard halakhic reference work. Although local custom, *minhag*, still prevailed in different communities and thus preserved diversity in halakhic detail, on most issues the rulings of the *Shulchan Arukh* generated considerable uniformity of practice.

Like other codes before it the *Shulchan Arukh* was fiercely opposed by a number of leading rabbis, who did not wish to see the *halakhah* fossilized in a legal textbook. One of its most virulent opponents, R. Judah Loeb of Prague, writes:

> It is more fitting, and better, that someone should arrive at a halakhic decision from his study of the *Talmud*. Even though there is reason to suppose that he will not proceed correctly, and will not decide correctly, for the ruling to be the right one. . . . Even though his understanding and wisdom lead him astray, nevertheless he is beloved of God when he rules according to the dictates of his mind. . . . That is better than someone who decides an issue out of a book, without knowing any of the reasons for the decision. The latter is like a blind man on the road.[3]

In the centuries following the publication of the *Shulchan Arukh* many commentaries were written explaining and justifying its rulings, or modifying them in the face of new circumstances. This process has continued into modern times, but the mass of material which has accumulated round the code has made it unwieldy for the layman to use and led to various attempts at simplification. The best known, and most popular, of these attempts is the *Kitzur Shulchan Arukh* ('Shortened *Shulchan Arukh*') by R.

Solomon Ganzfried (1808–86) which excludes halakhic material not relevant to the ordinary Jew, and even those matters which the author considered were so much part of Jewish life as not to need explicit formulation like many of the Sabbath laws.

With the renewal of Jewish life in Palestine, and the establishment of the Jewish State of Israel, there has been a spate of halakhic creativity in response to problems raised by mòdern technology, although no up-dated code on the lines of the *Shulchan Arukh* has emerged which has won general acceptance among Orthodox Jews. In the USA, however, Conservative Judaism has established a Committee on Jewish Law and Standards which has introduced innovations to bring the *halakhah* into line with prevailing Conservative attitudes to marriage, divorce, conversion, Sabbath observance, etc. These Conservative measures have been fiercely attacked by Orthodox rabbis who are very wary of any wholesale modernization of the *halakhah*.

Halakhic Responsa

Whereas the codification of *halakhah* led to its standardization, the main source of halakhic development in the post-talmudic period was the responsa literature. In Hebrew responsa are known as *she'elot u-teshuvot*, 'questions and answers', and they constitute the replies of rabbinic authorities to questions addressed to them often from thousands of miles away. Occasionally the responsa form is merely a literary device, the respondent concocting a question to which he has an interesting answer, but the vast majority of responsa originate in real-life problems about which the questioner seeks guidance from a halakhic expert. In style responsa range from simple answers of one or two sentences to long, keenly argued essays covering all aspects of the subject and quoting extracts from relevant sources. It is sometimes difficult, in the latter type of responsa, to find the respondent's answer which is qualified in the course of the casuistic exposition.

The qualities necessary for an outstanding respondent – a grasp of the issues involved in a problem, the ability to marshall arguments and counter-arguments, and ability to find creative solutions to difficult problems – were different from the qualities demanded by other branches of Jewish learning. An excellent codifier, or *Talmud* commentator, might make a poor respondent. Although the responsa literature is mostly concerned with technical issues of *halakhah*, it also deals on occasion with theological themes, sectarian movements within Judaism, historiography, medical and scientific matters, and the realia of Jewish life. As such it is a rich source of data for historical and sociological research, since the questions, and often the answers as well, reflect prevailing social conditions. Turbulent periods of Jewish history are characterized by the numerous responsa devoted to the status of wives whose husbands had disappeared in pogroms or during the expulsion of Jews from whole areas. These abandoned women, known as *agunot*, cannot remarry unless there are halakhic grounds for presuming their husbands dead. The respondents exercise considerable legal ingenuity in trying to find such grounds.

A responsum set a precedent in Jewish law which would be argued about by other scholars, criticized or supported in subsequent responsa, and eventually perhaps included in some future code as normative halakhic practice. Sometimes controversy raged for long periods over a respondent's innovation or interpretation of source material. This was the fate of a responsum of R. Tzvi Ashkenazi (1660–1718), no. 74 in his responsa collection *Chakham Tzvi*, where he replies to a question about a chicken in which no heart was found. Under normal circumstances the absence of a major organ of this kind would make an animal unfit as kosher food. Ashkenazi, however, allowed the chicken to be eaten on the grounds that the young girl who had opened the chicken to discard its innards to the house cat must have thrown away the heart as well, without noticing it. The chicken could not have lived at all without a heart, and since it was alive and well before being slaughtered there could be no other explanation of the missing heart. The fact that the girl denied she had removed the heart was of no account, according to Ashkenazi, since she was most probably not paying attention at the time. Ashkenazi's ruling was vigorously attacked by a number of leading rabbis so that he was forced to relinquish his rabbinical position in Germany, and move to the relative tranquillity of Amsterdam. The controversy was no doubt exacerbated by Ashkenazi's outspoken and uncompromising stand on public issues, which made him a difficult rabbinical colleague.

By penning a responsum in which a controversial ruling is put forward the respondent exposes his own reputation to the critical judgment of other rabbis. There has, therefore, been a tendency

to play safe on the part of many respondents, and to avoid lenient rulings which might earn the censure of 'holier than thou'
contemporaries. It is precisely the mark of a great respondent that
he shows originality in dealing with halakhic problems, and the
courage to publish any radical solutions he may have devised. One
modern rabbi, R. Moshe Feinstein (1895–1986), whose orthodoxy
and scholarship are beyond question, found himself the object of a
demonstration by Jewish zealots, who disagreed with a responsum
of his allowing artificial insemination under specific circumstances,
and were protesting publicly about the matter. The same rabbi, who
has ruled leniently about a number of questions of Jewish dietary
law, has been the butt of a joke among his detractors: 'If Rabbi
Feinstein says of a certain food that it is not kosher, then even a
non-Jew should not eat it.'

Technological advances have raised questions for Jewish practice
which were undreamt of in classical halakhic texts and codes, and
rabbis have found the responsum the quickest and most useful
medium for dealing with them. Thus, for instance, the classical codes all outline the various prohibitions associated with the
kindling of fire on Sabbaths and festivals. With the advent of
electricity the whole subject had to be re-opened for discussion,
and rabbis were forced to struggle to master an understanding of
the working of the electric light and its similarities or differences
from the candle or oil lamp. Naturally enough their comprehension
of the technical issues was sometimes incomplete, and rulings based
on such comprehension were overturned when halakhists attained
greater technical sophistication.

On many sensitive issues leading rabbis exchange responsa with
each other without allowing their views to be published. This is
particularly true when they wish to be lenient in a specific case and
either do not wish to face the ire of more conservative colleagues
and laymen, or are afraid that their leniency in one case will be
misconstrued as a general leniency applying to quite dissimilar
cases. One such sensitive issue is that of the *mamzer*, or child born
from an incestuous or adulterous relationship. Although the *mamzer*
has all the rights and responsibilities of his fellow Jews, he or she is
forbidden to marry anyone who is not either a *mamzer* as well or a
convert to Judaism. This imposes great hardship on the *mamzer*, who
is scarcely to be held responsible for the acts of his parents which led
to his special status. Rabbis try, wherever possible, to find means
whereby the *mamzer*'s status can be annulled, for instance in the case

of a child born from an adulterous union if the mother's marriage can be faulted on some technical grounds then her relations with the father of the child would not in fact be adulterous. Such attempts are rarely publicized because they might be misinterpreted as an encouragement to adultery, the couple concerned believing that any stigma attaching to a child of their union could simply be removed by the casuistry of a sympathetic rabbi.

When in 1972 R. Shlomoh Goren, one of Israel's two Chief Rabbis, published a lengthy responsum allowing a brother and sister, who had been declared *mamzerim*, to marry freely and removing the stigma from them he was attacked by many leading rabbinic authorities. The Langer Affair, as the case came to be known, was something of a *cause célèbre* in Israel, with the government putting pressure on the religious establishment to free the two siblings from the stigma of *mamzerut*. Goren's action was seen as giving in to this pressure, and his halakhic arguments were dismissed as invalid. Indeed ultra-Orthodox Jews in Jerusalem held a public meeting during which they rent their garments, and declared a public fast over what they took to be an act of sacrilege by the Chief Rabbi. This whole incident shows the problems faced by a respondent who may wish to put forward halakhic views which are of a controversial nature, and as we have already seen with the responsum about the chicken the problems are not entirely new. The determination of halakhic precedents through the use of responsa, though most widely found among Orthodox rabbis, is also used by Conservative and Reform rabbis but in the latter case the authority attaching to a particular responsum is of a less binding nature. A Reform responsum is not so much a decision by a halakhic expert as to how a Jew must behave in particular circumstances, but more in the nature of advice about such behaviour.

8

(1) The Ritual Lifetime: Childhood and Youth

Introduction

The highly complex patterns of Jewish ritual, which have grown up through the machinery of the *halakhah* and the variety of local custom (*minhag*), affect the life of the Jew at many points and on different levels. These ritual patterns determine behaviour, attitudes, family structure, and even the social institutions of the traditional Jew, and create a symbolic world around him relating him to his co-religionists, and differentiating him from the non-Jew. Jewish ritual can be most usefully analysed into three basic dimensions. There are first the linear time determinants which impinge upon the Jew at different stages of his life, from birth through the various turning points which see his role and status change, to death and its accompanying rituals. Within this linear model there is a second time dimension, made up of the cyclical determinants which divide his day, his week, his month and his year into ritually spaced particles of time. The third dimension is neither linear nor cyclical, but is made up of the atemporal demands made upon the Jew throughout his life.

This threefold division, although convenient, is by no means the only way of categorizing the ritual totality of Judaism. Halakhists developed their own schemata for legal purposes, while philosophers divided the *mitzvot* up into theological categories, e.g. those which were rational and those revelatory. The *Talmud* itself divides the 613 biblical commandments into the 248 positive and 365 negative *mitzvot*, as well as making a general distinction between demands owed to God and those owed to one's fellow man. Any schematic framework necessitates a measure of artificiality, and the advantage of the threefold schema used here is that it brings out the central role that time, as opposed to space, plays within Judaism. With the destruction of the Temple in 70 CE, though deeply attached to the sacred places of its tradition, Judaism functioned independently of sanctified locations. It hung its rituals on temporal co-ordinates which were more suitable to the experience of a religion in exile.

Linear Time Determinants: Childbirth

The birth of a child is an event charged with both ritual and folk customs within traditional Judaism. The dangers of childbirth to the mother, and the high rate of infant mortality, surrounded the process of parturition with magical rituals designed to protect the mother and the embryo from demons. Though these superstitious practices have their origin at the dawn of Judaism, the attitude of the rabbinic establishment to them has varied from period to period. The *Tosefta*, a work emanating from before the third century CE, says:

> He who stops up the window with thorns, or who ties iron to the legs of the bed of a woman in childbirth, or who sets the table before her, these are [forbidden] Amorite ways.[1]

while Maimonides (twelfth century), whose rationalistic opposition to magical practices earned the criticism of later authorities that he was 'drawn after the accursed teachings of philosophy',[2] writes:

> He whom a scorpion or snake has bitten, it is permitted to whisper an incantation over the place of the bite, even on the Sabbath. In order to put his mind at rest and to strengthen his heart. Even though such an activity has no effect, since the patient is in danger the rabbis allowed it to prevent him becoming distraught.[3]

In general there are many precedents in the *Talmud* for the use of magical cures and protective devices against destructive demons, based on the principle that 'Everything which is done for the sake of healing is not to be considered as [forbidden] Amorite ways.' Later halakhists accepted this as the standard of permissible behaviour.[4]

The woman in childbirth was thus surrounded by amulets, talismans and rituals of sympathetic magic, such as opening everything in the house to enable her womb to open easily, many of which were borrowed by Jews from their non-Jewish neighbours. Today most modern Jews would shy away from the more overtly superstitious practices of this kind, though they are still found in some traditional Jewish circles and particularly among Oriental Jews. The integration of kabbalistic ideas into the popular Jewish consciousness in the Middle Ages added greatly to the ordinary Jew's awareness of the demonic powers at work in the world. The process of parturition was depicted as the work of outside forces hostile to human pro-creation. This contrasts with the biblical ascription of the difficulties of labour to the curse of Eve, and to the mishnaic idea that women die in childbirth because they have been negligent of the three *mitzvot* which are specifically the preserve of the woman: sexual separation during menstruation, the gift of dough to the priest, and the kindling of the Sabbath lights.[5]

After giving birth the mother is considered a menstruant for the next seven days for a boy, or fourteen days for a girl, and is therefore in a state of ritual impurity. In ancient times she would wait a further thirty-three or sixty-six days respectively before bringing a burnt offering and a sin offering to the Temple, indicating that she was once again ritually pure. The *Talmud* in discussing the need for a sin offering, which seems out of place in this context, quotes the opinion of one sage that it was necessitated because while undergoing the pain of labour the woman swore never more to have sexual relations with her husband.[6] With the abolition of the sacrificial ritual, and the consequent down-grading of the laws of ritual impurity, the mother simply observes a seven-day period after post-natal bleeding has stopped before taking a ritual bath and being able to resume sexual relations. There are communities, however, where for the full forty or eighty days, for a boy or girl respectively, the husband and wife remain sexually separate, even though Maimonides says of such a practice:

> This is no custom, but is a mistake . . . and heresy. . . . For they have learnt this from the Sadducees (i.e. Karaites). It is a *mitzvah* to compel them to expunge this from their hearts.[7]

The Child

In the Bible and throughout rabbinic literature one finds a strong desire for sons, and there is clearly a distinction between the joy felt at the birth of a male and that felt at the birth of a female. The male will come to play social, economic and religious roles in the Jewish community not open to his female counterpart. An often repeated statement of the *Talmud* has it that:

> It impossible for there to be a world without males and females. Nevertheless happy is the man whose children are males, and woe to the man whose children are females.[8]

Although other, less one-sided, views are also found none deny the relative superiority of the male child. The differences are brought out in the rituals surrounding the birth of a son or a daughter. Whereas for the male a feast is prescribed on the first Friday night after birth, on the eighth day following the circumcision ceremony, and in the case of a first-born a month after birth, there are no such celebrations for the female. All that is customary is for her father to announce the child's name publicly in the synagogue, on the first Saturday after the birth, and to invite the congregants to a *kiddush*, a light celebratory repast, after the Sabbath services.

This inequality between the rituals associated with the different sexes has led some younger Jews in North America to seek more elaborate rituals associated with the birth of a daughter. The incentive has come from the overspill of women's liberation ideologies onto traditional Jews in the USA. Some attempts have been made to renew defunct rituals, such as the custom of planting a pine tree at the birth of a girl, the wood of which would later be used to build the canopy at her wedding.[9] A more radical innovation is the attempt to create a kind of female circumcision ritual, without any surgical operation, seeking to reduplicate the idea of the entry of the child into the Covenant of Abraham which is the central motif of male circumcision. To date there has been little support from the rabbinic establishment for such rituals.

Circumcision

The covenant of circumcision, *berit milah*, is a halakhic prescription devolving on the child's father. Originally the father himself performed the operation, removing the foreskin of his male child on the eighth day after birth, but today most people make use of the services of a professional circumciser, or *mohel*, who is not supposed to charge a fee since the performance of the operation is a *mitzvah*. The *mohel* need not be a doctor, although there are Jewish doctors who perform circumcision according to halakhic requirements, and one most frequently finds this role adopted by the ritual slaughterer who already has the necessary dexterity with the use of a knife. Theoretically a woman could also perform circumcision, we even find the wife of Moses doing so in the Bible, but since some halakhists were opposed to it the practice is discouraged.[10] Any adult male Jew who is not known to be a heretic is allowed to act as *mohel* and it is the custom for him to lead the prayers on the day of the circumcision. Another important participant in the ceremony is the *sandek* who holds the child on his lap during the operation. Once again this role may be played by a woman, and indeed this does occur in some Oriental Jewish communities, but Ashkenazi halakhists discourage it since they consider it immodest.[11] The *sandek* serves as a kind of godfather to the child, and it is considered a great honour to be asked to act in such a role. Although the whole notion of the *sandek* is post-talmudic, it has come to assume a major position in the ritual and was compared by one rabbi to the altar on which the incense was offered up. The *sandek* even takes precedence over the *mohel* for some ritual purposes.[12]

Apart from the parents, child, *mohel* and *sandek* the *dramatis personae* of the ceremony have increased with time. Elijah, the zealous prophet of the ninth century BCE who castigated Israel for not keeping the Covenant with God, is said by the *midrash*[13] to attend every circumcision, so a special chair is set aside for him.

In the Middle Ages other roles were created as part of the ceremony. Among these were the Ashkenazi *kvater* and *kvaterin*, a second godfather and a godmother, whose task it was to bring the child to the place of the circumcision. Often a couple was chosen who were themselves childless, in the belief that their participation was a *segulah*, or magically efficacious act, for procreation.

The circumcision takes place on the eighth day after birth, if the child is healthy, even if that day is a Sabbath or festival. The *mohel* will have examined the child beforehand to ensure that he is not suffering from jaundice or some other sickness which might delay the operation. On the Friday night before the circumcision relatives, friends and neighbours gather in the parents' house to eat light refreshments, including such traditional dishes for the occasion as chickpeas. The reasons for this gathering, known in some communities as *shalom zakhar*, 'peace of the male', are obscure and one opinion was even expressed that it was a mourning feast, held to mourn for the *Torah* which the child had learnt before birth and forgotten on coming into the world, chickpeas, in fact, being a dish eaten at mourning feasts in Judaism.

On the morning of the circumcision, after prayers have been said, the child is brought by the *kvaterin* into the room, the synagogue, or in Israel into a specially appointed hall in the hospital. Those assembled welcome the child who is taken by the *kvater* while various biblical verses are chanted by the father, the *mohel* and the guests. The child is placed momentarily on Elijah's chair and then on the lap of the *sandek*. The *mohel* adjusts the position of the child, with the *sandek* firmly holding both legs. He then either grasps the foreskin between his fingers, or uses a lyre-shaped shield to hold it fast, and makes a blessing. After the foreskin has been cut off the father makes a blessing which ends with the words 'who has commanded us to take him into the Covenant of our Father Abraham'. The *mohel* then tears back the inner lining of the foreskin with his fingernails so that the glans of the penis is fully exposed. This latter action is an integral part of the Jewish circumcision rite, though it is not found in non-Jewish forms of the operation, and without it the circumcision is considered incomplete.[14] The last part of the rite consists in the *mohel* sucking out the blood from the wound with his mouth, *metzitzah*. This was instituted as a therapeutic measure to ensure that the blood flows freely,[15] but it has increasingly become the subject of considerable controversy since it was realized that diseases can be transferred in this manner. While most ultra-orthodox groups insist on the traditional method of *metzitzah*, many modern rabbis allow the blood to be sucked out by the use of a glass tube and this is common practice. *Metzitzah* is not in any way part of the circumcision, and without it the operation is deemed complete. A *mohel* who did not practise it, however, was banned from performing circumcision altogether. After the operation is over the *mohel* publicly announces the name of the child for the first time: 'his name shall be called in Israel So-and-So the son of Such-and-Such'. This is usually preceded by the blessing over wine and a second blessing referring to the Covenant of God which He has placed in man's flesh. At the conclusion the wine is drunk and also given to the child. A festive meal then follows.

The Significance of Circumcision

There are many comments in Jewish literature about the meaning and purpose of circumcision, over and above its covenantal significance. It teaches man that he must perfect himself, serve God with every organ of his body, not be satisfied with his natural condition, not to allow himself to become submerged in the corruption of his environment but to become holy. It is seen as an atonement for Adam's sin, a sign of Israel's transcendence of nature, a distinguishing mark of the Jew. It was even interpreted as lessening sexual desire in the male. In modern times Jews have sought to explain and defend the practice on medical grounds, an idea first expressed by Philo Judaeus in the first century CE. Whatever the merits or demerits of circumcision from a medical point of view, and the value of such an explanation for understanding the significance of the circumcision rite for Jewish religion, many modern Jews continue the practice as much for reasons of health as for those of a purely religious nature.

The actual role played by the rite of circumcision, as far as the *halakhah* is concerned, is quite complex. Although every Jewish male must be circumcised, the uncircumcised Jew is, for all that, still a Jew and accepted as such by the community. Although the Bible threatens that the soul of the uncircumcised male shall be cut off from his people, this was understood by Judaism to mean that he would be punished by an untimely death and die childless.[16] It was not understood to mean that circumcision was a rite of initiation into the community of Israel. A Jewish child whose two older brothers had died after circumcision, perhaps through haemophilia, was not allowed to be circumcised until considered fit enough, yet his status as a Jew was not in doubt.[17] Although the importance of the rite is emphasized in rabbinic literature it is comparable to other central facets of Jewish life which do not have a particularly sacramental character, as is apparent from the greetings uttered at the circumcision ceremony, 'Just as he enters the Covenant, so may he enter into *Torah*, the wedding canopy, and deeds of loving kindness'.[18]

The situation is complicated by the fact that the gentile male convert to Judaism must undergo circumcision, or if already circumcised must undergo a symbolic re-circumcision by the shedding of a drop of blood from the penis, as a necessary condition of his conversion to Judaism. Without the ritual the would-be convert is not considered by the *halakhah* to be a Jew at all,[19] although there is a minority view in the *Talmud* which does not hold the rite to be a prerequisite of conversion. Since underlying conversion is the idea that the convert has been born again once he becomes a Jew,[20] circumcision does have overtones of initiation in this instance. A further complication is the custom of only publicly announcing the name of the child after circumcision has taken place. This name, the Hebrew name of the child which in the Diaspora may well differ from the name appearing on the birth certificate, is the one which will figure in all religious ceremonies and documents. Only if the Jew becomes seriously ill will the name be changed or added to, in the belief that the new name and therefore the person possessing this new name will be free of the evil decree afflicting the old name and its owner. At the Resurrection it will be through this Hebrew name that the Jew will be remembered and resurrected. For this reason there is a biblical verse beginning and ending with the first and last letters of his name which the Jew repeats each day in his prayers, in order that his name be not forgotten at the Resurrection. Similarly a child which dies before circumcision is circumcised at the graveside, and given a Hebrew name so that he will be resurrected.[21] The child is only ready to become a named individual, indeed a Jewish person, after he has been circumcised and this seems to contradict what we have outlined as the halakhic view of the matter, namely that circumcision does not effect a change in the status of the Jewish child. This initiatory view of circumcision is brought out strongly in kabbalistic literature. Thus R. Abraham Azulai, basing himself on a passage in the *Zohar*,[22] writes:

> Know that a man is not called by the name of man except through ritual circumcision. Without it he is called an evil spirit and not a man. . . . As long as the evil forces have a hold on the foreskin and uncleanliness of man, it is impossible for the higher soul to alight on him. Therefore he cannot be called an Israelite. For this reason we have the custom not to announce his name except after the circumcision, since then the foreskin and uncleanliness have been removed . . . then he may be called an Israelite man . . . Thus it has been explained that he is called an Israelite through the *mitzvah* of circumcision.[23]

In this case, as elsewhere in Judaism, it would seem that the Kabbalah and popular customs have preserved, or re-created, a more archaic level of Jewish practice in which circumcision is an initiatory pre-requisite of membership in the community, while the *halakhah* has spiritualized or rationalized the function of the rite and in the process de-sacramentalized it.

With the emergence of Jews into modern European culture, and the rise of Reform Judaism in the nineteenth century, there was a tendency to treat circumcision as a somewhat barbaric practice unbecoming the enlightened Jew. The radical wing of the Reform movement led by Samuel Holdheim (1808–60) argued that the uncircumcised Jew was a Jew in all respects, and that the actual operation should be abandoned. They sought to re-interpret the Covenant of Abraham in purely spiritual terms. Although today the majority of Reform Jews do have their sons circumcised this is often done not so much as a rite but as an hygienic measure. In the USA where Reform Judaism has its largest following, circumcision is almost a routine operation performed by doctors in gynaecological wards of hospitals on Jew and non-Jew alike. The barrier between the circumcised Jew and the un-circumcised Christian, which nineteenth-century Reform sought to remove with the abolition of circumcision, exists no more. The only ideological opposition to circumcision still to be found among Jews comes from the socialist Bund, which is devoted to the strengthening of Jewish, specifically Yiddish, culture, but objects to practices of a purely ritual or religious nature.

Redemption of the First-born

Unlike the rite of circumcision, which is still almost universally practised among Jews, the ceremony of redemption of the first-born male child, *pidyon ha-ben*, is only maintained by traditionalists. The under-lying idea is that a special holiness attaches to the first-born who should theoretically play a priestly role, except that this role has been transferred to the *kohen*, or priest, and the father therefore redeems the child by making a small payment to the priest.[24] The *pidyon ha-ben* takes place immediately after thirty days have passed since the birth of the child, who at that time is considered to be a viable baby. The ceremony is only necessary if neither the child's father or maternal grandfather is a *kohen* or a levite, and it takes place at a feast prepared by the child's parents to which they invite a *kohen*. After the guests have broken bread together the *kohen* holds the child and asks the father whether he prefers to have his first-born son, or the five silver coins needed to redeem him. The father replies that he wants his child. He then makes the appropriate blessings, following which he hands over the coins to the *kohen*, and the latter returns the child. Various additional verses and blessings are then recited, and the ceremony ends with the *kohen* blessing the child with the priestly blessing (Numbers 6:24–6).

Aside from having to undergo this ceremony the first-born son is only differentiated by the *halakhah* from other children on two issues. He has to fast on the day before the Passover festival, when the Egyptian first-born were slain and those of the Israelites saved. He also inherits a double portion of his father's estate. A daughter does not have the status of a first-born, and indeed she inherits no share of her father's estate if there are any male children or descendants.[25]

Educating the Child

There has always been a difference in attitude, within Judaism, between the way a young boy and a young girl are brought up, a difference reflected in the ceremonies surrounding their childhood and early youth. Till the age of 3 children are allowed to develop without distinction of sex. In some communities the boy's hair is not cut for the first three years, making him indistinguishable from his sisters. Once his hair is cut (*upsherinish*) he begins his training in his religious role as a male. The age of 3 was chosen as the child begins to talk around that time, and the *Talmud* recommends that the child be taught his first verses from the Bible then.[26] By cutting off his hair, but leaving the side-curls, *peot*, hanging over his ears, the child is introduced to the *mitzvah* of not cutting off the corners of one's hair as commanded in the Bible.[27] It is also customary to begin the wearing of the fringed undergarment, the *tallit katan*, at this age in accordance with another biblical precept,[28] and for the boy to wear a skull-cap (known as a *yarmulke*, *kappel*, or *kippah*) on his head.

Although the three-year-old girl does not undergo any ritual introduction to her future role as a Jewish female, she is considered to be sexually a female from this age. Thus the laws restricting men and women from being alone together in the privacy of a locked room or house, *yichud*, apply to a girl of three. They only apply to a boy from the age of 9, the rationale being that from these ages the female and the male are sufficiently sexually mature to be the objects of sexual desire. In the language of the *halakhah* they are fit for sexual intercourse.[29] These *yichud* restrictions cause considerable difficulties for the Orthodox Jew living within the complex structure of modern urban society. Progressive Judaism has simply shelved the whole concept of *yichud* as inapplicable to modern views of relations between the sexes.

In the *Mishnah*[30] we find a dispute about the advisability of educating Jewish girls, and later halakhists accepted the negative view, although they did recommend that girls be taught those parts of Jewish practice applying to females.[31] Despite this clear ruling, and the statement of the *Zohar* that the *Torah* was meant only to be given over to males,[32] the education of Jewish women in many branches of Jewish lore has become an established feature of modern Jewish life. In 1917 the Bet Yaakov Movement opened its first school for girls in eastern Europe under the auspices of the strictly orthodox Agudat Israel organization, and today runs a whole network of schools and seminaries for women. Stern College for Women in New York, an institution identified with the Modern Orthodox trend in Judaism, even has a programme of talmudic studies for girls. Other Orthodox groups, though they consider the *Talmud* an all-male preserve and the teaching of it to women too flagrantly in breach of halakhic prohibitions, do offer a wide-ranging curriculum in other areas of Jewish studies for females. This seeming *volte-face* in Orthodox attitudes to women's education may be explained in a number of ways. In part it is the consequence of Jewish emancipation, and a reflection of the more public role adopted by women in Jewish life. It is justified by the claim that the Jewish girl, under pressure from an environment hostile to Judaism, can only retain her traditional values if she is prepared educationally to face up to these challenges.[33] At the moment only Reform, Reconstructionist and Conservative Judaism have gone as far as opening their courses leading to rabbinic ordination to women.

One result of the growth in religious education for the female, which has disrupted the traditional family structure and pattern of authority, is that some women are now better educated in Judaism than their husbands. The curriculum for female education was devised to introduce the student to an all-round knowledge of Jewish thought, history and ritual. The curriculum for the male student in many institutions has remained with its main focus on talmudic studies to the exclusion of other areas. A number of prominent rabbis, both medieval and modern, have expressed their concern over the undue concentration on talmudic studies, and particularly over the manner in which the *Talmud* is taught in *yeshivot*, or academies of religious instruction. What they particularly found objectionable was the method of *pilpul* whereby a talmudic text and its commentaries were analysed so that contradictions were reconciled, and novel nuances of meaning were sought. It is reported of

R. Jacob Pollack, a great sixteenth-century advocate of *pilpul*, that he once delivered a lecture from a talmudic text from which his pupils had removed several pages. Not noticing the discontinuity R. Jacob simply continued with his lecture, associating the discussion on the page he had just been studying with the one several pages later.[34] The Jewish theologian R. Judah Loeb of Prague, who lived a generation after Pollack, said that those who studied *pilpul* wasted their time in lies, and were better off learning carpentry.[35]

The Beginnings of Adulthood

A new era begins for the Jewish child when he or she develops the secondary sexual characteristics associated with puberty, and in particular the growth of pubic hair. A girl after the age of 12 and a boy after the age of 13 who already have two pubic hairs are considered adults, and henceforth responsible for their actions in the religious sphere.[36] In the years preceding puberty the child is prepared for the religious and sexual role he or she will play as an adult, and from the time they can understand the notions of God and religious obligation children are encouraged to follow halakhic norms. Although theoretically pubic hair is necessary as a sign of adulthood, in practice the age factor suffices. The rabbis accepted the possibility that hair may have grown and fallen out, and therefore at the age of 12 or 13 a girl and a boy respectively must take upon themselves the 'yoke of the commandments'. The appearance of secondary sexual characteristics remains important in determining whether the girl or boy is genuinely to be regarded as sexually female or male, and thus halakhically permitted to marry a member of the opposite sex.

The distinction between a boy and a girl, already found in the rituals surrounding their birth and early childhood, is even more pronounced in their passage from childhood to adulthood. As soon as a boy passes his thirteenth birthday, according to the Hebrew calendar, his maturity is celebrated by a ceremony known as a *bar mitzvah*, or 'son of the commandment'. Although not found in talmudic literature this ceremony has become an integral part of Jewish life since at least the fourteenth century.[37] The usual custom is for the *bar mitzvah* boy to be called to the reading of the weekly scriptural portion chanted in the synagogue from the *Torah* scroll on Saturday mornings. Since a child would not be allowed to participate in the ritual, the boy's participation serves as an announcement to the community that he is now an adult. Family and invited guests attend the synagogue to witness the ceremony, and after the boy has said the concluding blessing his father thanks God for releasing him from his responsibilities for the boy's sins.[38] A *kiddush*, or light repast, provided by the parents of the boy follows the service, and congratulatory speeches are usually made. During the service the rabbi's sermon will contain words of exhortation and religious encouragement to the *bar mitzvah* boy, as well as dwelling on the merits of parents and grandparents for whom the *bar mitzvah* is an occasion of great family joy, known as *nachat* (in Yiddish *nachas*).

On the Sunday, or one of the weekdays, following the *bar mitzvah* the parents of the boy invite family, friends, and often close business acquaintances to a banquet which is a measure of the parents' status in the community. The social pressure on the parents to provide a *bar mitzvah* banquet equal to, if not more extravagant than, similar celebrations provided by their neighbours has meant that, among middle-class Jews in the Western world, the religious significance of the *bar mitzvah* is almost lost altogether. This situation has led to open protests, particularly from Orthodox rabbis in the USA. One of them, R. Moses Feinstein, writes in a responsum:

> If I had the power I would abolish the whole process of *bar mitzvah* for boys in this country. As is known this does not bring anyone closer to the *Torah* and the commandments, not even the *bar mitzvah* boy. On the contrary, in many places it leads to the desecration of the Sabbath and of other prohibitions.[39]

Unlike the celebrations surrounding the onset of maturity for the boy, the girl passes into adulthood with hardly a ripple of public acknowledgment in traditional circles. Adulthood for the boy entails public responsibility, he is now eligible to be counted in a *minyan*, or quorum of ten males, needed for certain prayers, he may be called up to the *Torah* reading, and he wears the *tefillin*, or phylacteries, during the morning service. The girl's life remains relatively unchanged after maturity, she simply has to fulfil the various religious laws which she has been trained in during the previous years, and there is therefore no call for public acknowledgment of her new status. In the early nineteenth century the *bar mitzvah* was replaced by a Confirmation ceremony for both boys and girls in certain German Reform congregations. It took the form of a collective graduation after a course of instruction in Jewish religion and ethics, and was often held when the child had reached the late teens. The festival of Pentecost, *Shavuot*, was eventually accepted as the most fitting occasion for holding the Confirmation. This innovation, despite the strong opposition of the Orthodox leadership, spread among Reform communities in western Europe and the USA, and is still found in places today although the more traditional *bar mitzvah* ceremony has been re-introduced. One of the distinctive features of the Confirmation is that it gives equal place to boys and girls, and a more recent development has been the introduction of a ceremony for girls to parallel the *bar mitzvah*. This is known as a *bat mitzvah*, literally 'daughter of the commandment' and has been adopted even in some Orthodox circles. Although no fixed procedure exists for the *bat mitzvah* it often takes the form of a ceremony for a group of girls in the synagogue, after they have passed their twelfth birthday according to the Hebrew calendar. It is possible that the pressure for a greater role for females in traditional Jewish life will make the *bat mitzvah* a permanent feature of the Jewish scene, despite rabbinical hesitation.

(2) The Ritual Lifetime: Sexual Behaviour, Marriage and Old Age

The Jewish Sex Ethic

The attitude of the *halakhah* towards the sexual behaviour of the Jew may be summarized as an encouragement of marital sexual relations, and a proscription of pre-marital, extra-marital and non-heterosexual activity. Maimonides formulates the *halakhah* as follows:

> Before the giving of the *Torah* a man would meet a woman in the market place. If they were both agreeable to marry he would take her into his house, have sexual intercourse with her in private, and she would be his wife. Once the *Torah* was given Israel was commanded that if a man wished to marry a woman he should acquire her before two witnesses. . . . If she wishes to be divorced she needs a *get* [i.e. a bill of divorce].[1]

In order to prevent prohibited sexual relations from taking place, whether of the more serious incestuous or adulterous kind, or of the less serious but also forbidden pre-marital kind, the *halakhah* greatly restricts social relations between the sexes. It encourages men to keep their distance from women, not to act with levity in their company, gaze on their beauty, smell their perfume, or walk behind them. It forbids a man to walk close by a brothel, listen to a woman singing, have a woman serve him in private, or hug and kiss a near relative with the exception of parents with their pre-pubescent children.[2] There is also the previously mentioned restriction on being alone in a locked room or house with a member of the opposite sex, known as *yichud*. This applies irrespective of whether or not one or both of the parties are married, and whether the other person is a Jew or gentile, the exceptions being parents with their children, husbands and wives, and an adult with a girl under three or a boy under nine. Similarly the appointment of a man to a position of responsibility over women is forbidden where this would give him an opportunity for familiarity. An extension of this prohibition is not to allow an unmarried man or woman to act as a teacher to young children, because they come into frequent contact with parents of the opposite sex when they come to pick up their children.[3]

Aside from these precautionary measures to prevent illicit heterosexual relations, on the assumption that no one can consider himself totally master of his sex drive, the *halakhah* also forbids male masturbation. Female masturbation is not explicitly forbidden in the halakhic codices because there was considerable dispute among medieval authorities about the subject. Thus R. Jacob ben Meir (twelfth century) allows female masturbation because the female 'seed' does not leave her body, unlike the seed of the man. Other early halakhists disagree and forbid masturbation for the female as well.[4] Concerning male masturbation the *Zohar* says:

> Of all the sins with which a man defiles himself in this world, this is the sin with which he is most defiled.[5]

A series of precautionary measures are laid down by the *halakhah* to prevent the possibility of masturbation. A man should not bring about a voluntary erection, think about sexual matters, sleep on his back, watch animals at sex-play, handle his genitals even while urinating, or wear tight pants.[6]

Although male homosexuality is explicitly forbidden on pain of death in the Bible, unlike masturbation which is not mentioned there at all, it does not figure prominently in the codes. Indeed the most important code, the *Shulchan Arukh*, does not directly mention the prohibition on homosexuality. It merely states, quoting the *Talmud*, that Jews were not suspected of homosexual practices and that a Jew was therefore allowed to be alone in private with another Jewish male. Nevertheless for good measure it is better to avoid this also. R. Joseph Caro, the author of the code, then adds the remark that in these generations when men of bad morals have increased one should keep far away from privacy with a fellow male. A later commentator explains that Caro made this statement because he lived in a Moslem country where homosexuality was common. In

Christian lands where it is uncommon there is no need for Jews to be too concerned about the matter.[7] Female homosexuality, though not explicitly prohibited in the Bible, is forbidden by the *halakhah* on the grounds that it is one of the 'deeds of the Land of Egypt' which Jews must avoid. Husbands are therefore warned not to let known lesbians associate with their wives.[8]

All of the above restrictions on sexual behaviour would be accepted as the ideal by strictly orthodox Jews, and, as far as is possible in such matters, would be implemented to the letter. Naturally enough a degree of compromise is demanded of those Jews who live in modern urban society, since the conflicts between the erotic flavour of advertising, the cinema, television and contemporary fashion, and the halakhic ideal generate considerable tension. Those traditional Jews who do compromise with halakhic demands justify their action on the grounds that what is prohibited as erotic varies from period to period, from society to society, and the *halakhah* of the *Shulchan Arukh* reflects a very different social ethos. Progressive Judaism has, in general, jettisoned many of the details of these halakhic sex norms, seeing them as representing a mixture of medieval and Victorian attitudes. The central idea of sexual relations being reserved for the married couple, and of fidelity in marriage, is still primary to Progressive Jewish thinkers.

Courtship and Marriage

It is a positive duty devolving on every Jewish male to marry and have children. This is based on the command to Adam and Eve (Genesis 1:22) and to Noah (Genesis 9:1,7). A Jew who does not attempt to procreate a family is considered as if he has shed blood, diminished the image of God in which every person is created, and caused God's presence to depart from Israel.[9] The usual age for marriage was 18 years, though from 13 a male is of marriageable status and in past generations the earlier age was preferred. At the latest one should not delay marriage beyond the age of 20, and the religious authorities used to put pressure on a bachelor, who had passed this age, to find himself a wife. The only acceptable reason for life-long celibacy is the desire to devote one's life to the study of *Torah*, if this is coupled with the assurance of being able to control one's sexual desire. Even in such a case, however, celibacy was discouraged, since there is a positive duty to have children, to 'be fruitful and multiply'. This duty is fulfilled once one has a son and a daughter, but children are considered a blessing from God and therefore a large family is both a religious ideal and a social reality among Orthodox Jews.[10] It is also considered salutary for a widower or a divorcee to remarry even though he may have children by a previous marriage.

The *mitzvah* of procreation does not apply directly to the Jewish woman, although some post-talmudic authorities maintain that she is indirectly duty-bound to marry and procreate based on the verse in Isaiah (45:18), that God did not create the world 'to be void, He formed it to be inhabited'. Another reason given is that a wife has to participate in the *mitzvah* of her husband, enabling him to have children.[11] Given the strict separation of the sexes in traditional Jewish communities, young Jews cannot meet their future marriage partners in the normal course of their social life. They are usually introduced to each other (*shiddukh*) by a third party whose knowledge of both families concerned enables him to suggest the match. A professional marriage-broker, or *shadkhan*, might also be used. The *shadkhan* was an integral part of Jewish life in the Middle Ages, and it is even mentioned in the *Talmud* that one of the sages would punish any man who betrothed a woman without an arranged marriage.[12] To indicate the difficulty of genuine matchmaking the rabbis relate that God, having created the world, spends his time arranging marriages, which He finds as difficult as dividing the Red Sea.[13]

An arranged marriage is not simply the coming together of two young individuals, it is the marriage of two families each of which will have some say in the suitability of the match. The features sought after by parents in any prospective match are good lineage (*yichus*), i.e. a family boasting illustrious forebears, a sound financial situation in the case of a daughter-in-law whose parents would be expected to help support the young couple, and most importantly that a future son-in-law should be a learned and God-fearing Jew. The young man and woman would meet for the first time in the house of someone who knows them both, and if this meeting is successful they will meet again a couple of times before being expected to make up their minds. On the whole such courtships are relatively brief, since the match is only suggested if there is sufficient compatibility between their respective backgrounds and attitudes to indicate that a positive response is likely. If they both consent, and there is no objection from either family, the next step is the arrangement of the *tenaim,* an engagement ceremony where both parties stipulate the conditions of the marriage, such as the dowry, and the penalty for breaking the engagement. Although the *tenaim* has no religious significance, it is accompanied by a celebratory feast at which the *tenaim* document is read aloud and an earthenware plate is broken. This latter act is explained to signify that even at moments of great joy the Jew should remember the destruction of Jerusalem in accordance with the 137th Psalm. It may also be a technique for warding off demons who are thought to be most active at times of joy and celebration.[14] A Jewish folk belief has it that any unmarried girl who takes home a piece of the plate is sure to be married within the year.

Although the *tenaim* may be broken off at any time prior to the actual marriage ceremony, subject only to the payment of the stipulated compensation, it was regarded by some sections of Jewry as a binding commitment. Thus both the followers of the Chasidic movement and those of Elijah of Vilna, who was the leading opponent of Chasidism, consider it better to go through with the marriage ritual and then divorce rather than break off the *tenaim.*[15] Among contemporary Jews the *tenaim* has given way to the secular engagement party, and is only found practised in traditionalist circles.

Marriage

The Jewish wedding ceremony has two components which were once separate but have come to be joined into one rite. First there is the *erusin* or *kiddushin,* a pre-marriage commitment which binds the couple in wedlock, necessitates a divorce to be dissolved, but does not allow the couple to live together as man and wife. Then there is the *chupah,* or canopy, which symbolizes the entry of the bride into the groom's house and which concludes the process of marriage. The accepted practice nowadays is for the *erusin* to take place under the wedding canopy immediately prior to the *chupah* ceremony.

The order of events preceding the ceremony proper are as follows. On the Sabbath before the wedding the groom is given an *aliyah* (i.e. called up) in the synagogue to read the *haftarah,* a section from the Prophets, or from the weekly portion of the Pentateuch. This is known among Ashkenazi Jews as an *aufruf.* When the groom has finished he is greeted with cries of *mazal tov*, 'good luck'. Hymns may also be recited requesting divine blessings for the couple. There is a custom in some communities not to allow the groom to go out unaccompanied from this point on. A variant form of the custom, mentioned in the *Shulchan Arukh*, forbids the groom from going out alone for the whole of the first week after the wedding. Behind these customs lies the fear that a demonic attack may take place against the groom, an attack which will not take place if someone else is with him. The *Talmud* enumerates three categories of person who need to be guarded against demons: a sick person, a bridegroom and a bride.[16]

The Wedding Day

It is customary for both bride and groom to fast on the day of their wedding, from dawn till the ceremony is over. During their prayers they will confess their sins and include special penitential passages.[17] The idea behind the fast is twofold. On the one hand Jewish tradition sees marriage as a completely new stage in a person's life, life begins anew and all sins are forgiven. The wedding day is like a personal Day of Atonement for them, therefore the couple repent and seek forgiveness for transgressions they may have committed. The second reason for the fast is of a more mundane nature. It is to prevent someone from entering the marriage ceremony while drunk.[18]

Before the wedding ceremony takes place the *ketubbah* document is prepared and signed by two witnesses. The *ketubbah* stipulates the maintenance to be paid by the husband should he divorce his wife and outlines the responsibilities of the husband within marriage. The married couple are not allowed to live as man and wife unless they possess a *ketubbah*, and if it is lost a new document must be drawn up. The groom then goes to the room where the bride is waiting and covers her face with a veil (*bedeken*), before being led away under the canopy by his parents, or by his father and father-in-law. Should either of the couple's parents be deceased or divorced then other relatives or friends may take on this role, which is considered a great *mitzvah*. Rabbinic literature tells how God and the ministering angels acted in this role for Adam and Eve on their wedding day.[19] The groom stands under the canopy facing Jerusalem and the rabbi and cantor stand opposite him. Ashkenazi

Jews use a *chupah* canopy which consists of embroidered cloth stretched over four wooden poles and set up under the open sky in the synagogue courtyard. Sefardi Jews may use a similar *chupah*, or a prayer shawl (*tallit*) held aloft by four men as a canopy, and their custom is to conduct the wedding indoors. Many Ashkenazi congregations, particularly those in colder climates, have adopted the Sefardi practice of holding the wedding inside the synagogue but this has not won the universal approval of the Ashkenazi rabbinate.[20]

The bride is brought to the canopy by her father, or by her mother and mother-in-law to be who sometimes carry lighted candles. Her entrance is accompanied by music and singing, and the guests go to meet her and walk with her to the *chupah* at traditional weddings. In some communities she walks round the groom seven times (or three times), before taking her place at his side. The cantor (*chazan*), who leads the congregation during public prayers sings a greeting to the bride and groom asking for God's blessing and the ceremony proper now begins. A cup of wine is poured out and the officiating rabbi chants the blessing over wine followed by the benediction for the *erusin* part of the ceremony. After the couple have tasted the wine the groom takes a plain wedding ring and in front of two previously designated witnesses he places it on the forefinger of the bride's right hand, saying: 'Behold you are sanctified to me with this ring, according to the law of Moses and of Israel.' The bride's acceptance of the ring signifies her willingness to enter into marriage with the groom. Orthodox practice does not allow an exchange of rings, since this might seem as if the bride were refusing the ring and returning it to the groom. The use of a ring for *erusin* is first mentioned in the geonic literature of tenth-century Babylonia and the current custom involving a plain wedding band is because a precious stone in the ring might mislead the bride about its real worth.[21] To ensure there are no problems about the validity of the marriage the groom is asked whether the ring is indeed his, and the two witnesses have to satisfy themselves that it is of the necessary minimum value and that there can be no mistake about its worth.

Following on the *erusin* the rabbi addresses the couple about the significance of marriage (sometimes this short sermon is delivered before the *erusin*). The *ketubbah* document is then read aloud in Aramaic, and in some Western communities a shortened English version is also read. The *ketubbah* is handed over to the bride, and the second part of the ceremony, the wedding proper, begins. The rabbi or cantor takes another cup of wine, makes the blessing over it and then chants the seven marriage benedictions which end with the words:

> Speedily, O Lord our God, may there be heard in the cities of Judah, and in the open places of Jerusalem, the sound of rejoicing and of gladness, the voice of the groom and the voice of the bride, the jubilant sound of bridegrooms from their wedding canopies and of youths from their feast of song. Blessed are You, O Lord, who gladdens the bridegroom with the bride.

The couple once again drink from the cup of wine, and then the groom breaks a glass with his foot to cries of *mazal tov* from the guests. The glass breaking, like the plate breaking of the *tenaim*, indicates a sense of mourning for the destruction of the Temple in Jerusalem even at a time of great happiness (Psalm 137), as well as being an anti-demonic prophylactic. The sense of mourning is also manifest in the custom of smearing the groom's forehead with ash prior to the ceremony.

Immediately following the *chupah* the bride and groom are led away to a room to be alone with each other (*yichud*). The two witnesses to the marriage ensure that they are indeed alone, signifying their newly wed status since *yichud* is normally forbidden. The couple usually take this opportunity to break their fast. According to some halakhic authorities *yichud* is an essential part of the wedding and without it the *chupah* is incomplete.[22] A festive meal or wedding banquet now follows, during which at Orthodox weddings the male guests dance round the bride and groom, and dance with the bride herself holding a kerchief between them. Light-hearted songs composed in honour of the couple are sung. Speeches are an integral part of most Jewish weddings – learned discourses, toasts and laudatory remarks about the couple and their respective families. The meal ends with a special Grace After Meals, followed by a repetition of the seven marriage benedictions over a cup of wine. For a week after the wedding relatives or friends invite the couple to a festive meal each evening. In order for the wedding benedictions to be recited it is necessary for a *minyan*, or quorum of ten males, to be present and for one of the guests to be a 'new face', i.e. someone who has not attended the wedding itself. These festive meals are known as *sheva berakhot*, 'seven benedictions', and with the growth among Jews of the practice of setting off on honeymoon immediately after the wedding they have been preserved only among traditionalists.

The Marital Sex Act

Despite seemingly puritanical attitudes towards the relations between the sexes, Judaism does not view the marital sex act as merely a necessary evil. The halakhic ideal for the married couple is what can only be described as holy sexual relations. The laws surrounding marital sex show an ambivalence between an affirmation of the sex act as a life-enhancing feature of God's world, and indeed according to kabbalistic teaching as symbolic of the inner structure of the divine, and an ascetic approach to one of the most powerful drives within man. In the *Talmud* contrary views are expressed about the way in which sexual intercourse between husband and wife should take place. Thus the wife of the first-second century sage, R. Eliezer ben Hyrcanus, reported that during the sex act her husband thought of himself as if driven by a demon, which one of the medieval commentators explains to mean that he hurried through the act as if a demon were driving him. Other remarks of his wife were interpreted to mean the R. Eliezer sought to diminish his own pleasure during sexual intercourse, adopting an ascetic attitude to the issue of sexual enjoyment.[23] This example was held up by the *halakhah* as a model of desirable behaviour in sexual relations between husband and wife. It does, however, conflict with other talmudic accounts about sages who clearly did not share R. Eliezer's viewpoint and treated sexual pleasure as a legitimate part of marriage, as well as with the talmudic maxim 'Everything which a man wishes to do with his wife, he may do'.[24]

The relative weight given in later halakhic literature to the two attitudes of modified asceticism and legitimate enjoyment varies between different authorities. On the whole, however, the more ascetic tendency predominates. Thus we find four respectable motivations for sexual behaviour quoted as substantial *halakhah* in the codes, and ranked in descending order of religious worth. (1) For the sake of having children. (2) For the benefit of the embryo being carried by his pregnant wife, for whom the rabbis consider sexual intercourse to be advantageous during certain stages of pregnancy. (3) To satisfy his wife's desire, there being a biblical *mitzvah* for the husband to have sex with his wife at specified times; this is the *mitzvah* of *onah*. (4) To satisfy his own desire in order to prevent himself sinning, although it were better if he could overcome his sexual desire in such a case.[25] The same halakhic sources add, following the *Talmud*, that men in different occupations have a duty to have sexual relations with their wives at intervals depending on their manner of work: either nightly, every second night, weekly, or monthly, as well as at the end of her period of menstrual separation. Men should not indulge in sex for their own pleasure, however, and they should certainly not excite their sexual desire at other times merely for the sake of enjoying sexual relations. Although the codes quote the views found in the *Talmud*, and among post-talmudic authorities, which take a less puritanical view of sexual pleasure, the main upshot of the discussion is that a man should sanctify himself even in those matters where he is allowed to indulge himself.[26]

Contemporary Jewish writers on the subject of traditional attitudes to sexual relations tend to over-emphasize the less ascetic ideal, while ignoring the main tenor of the codified *halakhah*, perhaps out of a desire to show that Judaism is consonant with modern ideas on the subject. Thus, for instance, Herman Wouk in a popular exposition of Orthodox Judaism writes that Judaism regards sex as 'the cord that secures the union of two lovers for life: for shared strength, pleasure and ease, and for the rearing of children.' He denies that the marriage of Jewish prophets, saints, and plain people has ever had any trace of concession to some supposed frailty or evil of the flesh.[27] This should be compared with the following statement of the *Shulchan Arukh*:

> One should not indulge in sexual intercourse too much . . . for this thing is very defective and senseless behaviour. But the less one engages in sexual intercourse the more praiseworthy. . . . And even when one does have sexual relations at the special times prescribed, one should not intend it for one's pleasure. Rather one should be like a man who pays off his debt, since one has a duty at these times, and also to fulfill the command of one's Creator in 'being fruitful and multiplying' [i.e. having children].[28]

The *halakhah* does emphasize that the husband should have consideration for his wife's pleasure during intercourse, and even recommends prolongation of the sex act to ensure her orgasm. This is only prescribed if the husband genuinely intends to give his wife pleasure through the prolongation, otherwise it is better to be as brief as possible in accordance with the practice of R. Eliezer mentioned earlier.[29] What is important for the *halakhah* are the intention, motivation and the thoughts of the husband prior to and during intercourse.

Naturally enough this programme of holy sex is a pietistical ideal, but even those halakhic works which allow a greater degree of human pleasure to be a legitimate part of the act agree on holiness as the main motivating factor to be striven for. Since intention is something which can be encouraged but ultimately must be left to the efforts of the individual Jew, the *halakhah* lays down a series of prescriptions about the correct manner of sexual intercourse. A husband should not force his wife into the sex act against her will. Nor should he have sexual relations with her if he despises her, or if either of them is in mourning, or drunk, or if he intends to divorce her, or if she immodestly invites intercourse. He should not look at her genitals or kiss her there. The position of the couple should not be with the woman on top, or with both partners side by side, but rather with the man above the woman. Intercourse should not take place in the presence of another person, if awake, nor in the same room as holy books or sanctified objects. The time of intercourse should be around the middle of the night, when people are sleeping, and it should not be performed with the light on.[30]

The Menstrual Cycle

An important part of the restrictions affecting sexual relations between husband and wife have to do with menstruation, or *niddah*. The Bible forbids a man 'to approach a woman in the *niddah* of her impurity, to uncover her nakedness' (Leviticus 18:19). The couple who have sexual relations while the woman is menstruating will be cut off from the midst of their people. The menstruating woman is considered ritually impure for seven days and any object she comes into contact with becomes defiled.[31] In Temple times and in the early post-Temple period, when purity and impurity occupied a large area of Jewish life, the restrictions on the *niddah* were severe to prevent her defiling objects of a ritual nature. The *Mishnah* even talks about a 'house of impurity', which presumably was occupied by women during their menstrual isolation.[32] A similar custom was still found until recently among the Judaizing Falashas of Ethiopia, though whether this practice was part of their Judaic heritage, or assimilated from neighbouring communities, is uncertain. With the destruction of the Temple, and the changes brought about in Judaism in its wake, many of the purity/impurity laws have ceased to have practical application. The only vestiges of the isolation of the *niddah* in contemporary Judaism relate to her attendance at synagogue, and her participation in public prayers. R. Moses Isserles, the joint author of the *Shulchan Arukh*, refers to the different customs on this subject:

> Some have written that a *niddah* woman, at the time she sees [blood], should not enter a synagogue, or pray, or mention the divine name, or touch a holy book. While some say she is allowed to do all of these, and that is the correct view. Nevertheless the custom in these lands is in accordance with the former view.[33]

Although the commentators on this passage mention other restrictions which some authorities impose on the *niddah*, e.g. that she must not look at the open scroll of the *Torah*, they dissent from a number of the prohibitions mentioned by Isserles.

The main significance of the *niddah* today is the prohibition on sexual relations during menstruation and for some days afterwards, and the necessity of undergoing a purifying bath in a *mikveh*, or ritual bath, at the end of this period. Halakhic literature on the subject of *niddah*, including a whole tractate of the *Babylonian Talmud* and seventeen chapters of the *Shulchan Arukh*, contains the many rabbinic additions to the biblical restrictions as well as such technical questions as the difference between menstrual blood and other discharges, the determination of a regular menstrual cycle, and the manner in which a woman should examine herself to discover the onset and termination of menstruation. The niceties of halakhic detail are important in unfortunate cases where a woman bleeds as a consequence of sexual intercourse or, where there is insufficient time interval between menses, in deciding whether or not she may have sexual relations at all. In general as time progressed the later halakhic authorities applied the *niddah* laws with greater stringency, claiming that they were not sufficiently expert to make the subtle differentiations between cases found in the earlier literature.

A woman is regarded as *niddah* during her menstrual bleeding and for seven days afterwards. She has to examine herself to ensure that bleeding has ceased before beginning the seven-day period, and also during that period in case bleeding recommences. The accepted practice is to begin counting the seven 'clear' days after five days have elapsed from the onset of bleeding, provided that the bleeding does not continue for longer. On the evening after the end of this period she attends the *mikveh*, and may resume sexual relations with her husband. The *mikveh* in which she has to bathe is a specially constructed bath containing a minimum amount of 'living' water, either rain water or that of some other natural water source. Once the bath is duly constituted then tap water may be added. The *mikveh* is also used by converts to Judaism, by male Jews just before the Day of Atonement or, in the case of Chasidic Jews, every Friday before Shabbat or even every day before prayers. It is also used to dip vessels bought from a gentile so that they may be used by Jews in the preparation of food.

In order to prevent husband and wife from infringing the *niddah* restrictions a series of precautionary measures are prescribed, which limit the relationship of the couple during this period. They should not act towards each other in a light-hearted manner, have physical contact, or sleep together in the same bed even if both are wearing clothes. The husband should not look at his wife when she is partially or wholly undressed, and they should curtail the tasks they usually fulfil for each other.[34] Although Orthodox Jews consider the *niddah* laws as a central part of Jewish life, only a small minority of Jews today actually abide by the letter of the law. Many Jewish communities do not have a *mikveh* in their vicinity, and Reform Judaism jettisoned the whole concept of *niddah* as belonging to archaic beliefs about ritual purity/impurity which no longer have significance for the modern Jew. Since the children born to a couple who do not keep 'family purity', as it is called, have no halakhic stigma attached to them and are fully Jewish, marriage between those who keep *niddah* laws and those whose parents did not is unaffected. In recent times there has been something of a revival in the use of the *mikveh* among Jewish women, partly perhaps due to efforts to modernize the design and decor of the *mikveh* itself. In Israel every bride must attend the *mikveh* prior to her wedding, and produce a certificate to that effect, before the officials of the state rabbinate will perform the ceremony. One of the reasons which the *Talmud* gives for the period of separation during and after menstruation is that it prevents the husband from taking his sexual relations with his wife for granted. When they renew their sex life, at the end of the *niddah* period, they are like bride and bridegroom again.[35]

Birth Control

Apart from the actual *mitzvah* of having a son and a daughter to fulfil the requirement of 'be fruitful and multiply', a large family is seen by Judaism as a divine blessing. In the modern period however, the advent of birth control techniques available to the average couple, and changed attitudes to family planning, have posed problems about the halakhic permissibility of limiting family size. In general there is some disagreement about the use of contraceptives, even after the minimum requirement of a son and a daughter has been fulfilled. There is an almost unanimous agreement that *coitus interruptus*, which involves 'wasting seed' and is viewed as tantamount to masturbation, is forbidden, although a minority view is found in the *Talmud* which allows such a practice where pregnancy would pose a problem for a nursing mother.[36] There is a similar consensus against the use of the condom among modern halakhists, with the exception of one leading American authority who regards it as something of a last resort.[37] The use of contraceptive techniques by the wife has won wider support where there is a health hazard in pregnancy. One pre-modern halakhist even goes so far as allowing a woman to use a diaphragm without any indication of pregnancy risk, as long as her husband has fulfilled the *mitzvah* of procreation.[38]

The extensive debate in the responsa literature about the permissibility of pre-coital and post-coital contraception by the woman is based on an ambiguous talmudic passage about the three categories of women who use a contraceptive device.[39] This passage is open to a broad interpretation, namely that some women must practice contraception in specific circumstances but that other women may if they wish, and to a narrow interpretation that only these three categories of women may use contraceptives but other women, not in the same circumstances, may not. The contraceptive pill has been accepted by some leading rabbis as one of the least objectionable techniques for family planning, once the requirement of 'being fruitful' has been satisfied, as long as there are no injurious side-effects or post-menstrual bleeding.[40] The intrauterine device, or IUD, is still something of an unknown entity as far as the *halakhah* is concerned, because its actual method of working is unclear and it may be an abortifacient.

Abortion

The subject of abortion raises different halakhic issues from that of contraception. It is generally agreed that the killing of an embryo does not constitute murder, although at least one rabbinic authority has sought to relate the two.[41] Whereas all halakhists view abortion as a prohibited act, in normal circumstances, there is no universal agreement as to the nature of this prohibition, nor whether it is a biblical or rabbinic one. Where there are medical grounds for performing abortion the different views about its permissibility depend largely on the various interpretations of the nature of the prohibition. It is an accepted ruling that if the mother's life is in danger through continued pregnancy then the embryo may be aborted to save the mother. Some authorities consider the state of mind of the mother, i.e. if the birth of the child could lead to suicidal despair on her part, as covered by this ruling. Others extend it to the threat to a child feeding on its mother's milk, the supply of which is affected by the pregnancy, whose life is thus endangered by the embryo, while a minority go further and allow abortion even if there is no actual threat to the mother's life, but pregnancy causes her great discomfort and pain. Other halakhists disagree with these lenient rulings, although they do not oppose abortion undertaken during the first forty days or three months of pregnancy in such circumstances, or if the child will be born deformed.[42] The common ground among these divergent opinions is consideration for the life of the mother, and an emphasis on the termination of pregnancy in its early stages where possible.

Divorce

The form which divorce takes in Judaism is modelled on the scriptural precedent:

> If a man takes a wife, and marries her, then if she does not find favour in his eyes, for he has found something unseemly in her, he shall write her a bill of divorce, and give it into her hand, and send her from his house.[43]

Here divorce is the prerogative of the husband, and takes the form of a document known as a *get* which must be delivered by him to the woman. The traditional *get* is written in Aramaic by a professional scribe specifically for the husband and wife concerned, and its core is the sentence, 'Behold you are permitted to every man.'[44] The full document also contains the names of husband and wife, their place of residence, the date, as well as a longer, unambiguous, formula of divorce. The document is signed by two witnesses. Extreme scrupulousness is necessary in preparing a *get* to ensure that no technical mistake might permit a woman not properly divorced to remarry. The correct spelling of personal names, places, rivers, towns, etc. occupies an inordinately large space in the responsa on this subject, since an accurate transliteration of Spanish, Polish, German, Turkish, English, etc., words into Hebrew characters is called for.[45] Because of the technical expertise necessary for the details of divorce procedure the *Talmud* warns:

> All who do not know the nature of divorce [procedures] . . . should not deal with them.[46]

Many serious divisions were caused within the Jewish community because the validity of a *get* prepared by one rabbi was called into question by other rabbis.

The divorce document has to be given by the husband of his own free will, but traditionally at least the wife did not have to consent, nor could she divorce her husband. In the tenth or eleventh centuries the leaders of the German Jewish communities forbade a husband to divorce his wife against her will, and this has been the accepted practice among Ashkenazi Jewry ever since. This interdiction is ascribed to R. Gershom ben Judah, the foremost German sage of his time, and is known as one of the elements in the *cherem* of Rabbenu Gershom since those who ignored it were threatened with being put in *cherem*, or excommunicated. Sefardi Jews have never accepted the restriction, although it is incorporated in the divorce laws of the State of Israel applicable to all Jews alike, as well as to non-Jews. If there is no mutual consent to the divorce by husband and wife, then one party may apply to the *Bet Din*, or Jewish law court, to compel the other party to participate in the proceedings. The grounds on which a wife may sue for divorce are that her husband is unfaithful, sterile, impotent, deprives her of economic sustenance, treats her cruelly, is irreligious etc.[47] If the *Bet Din* rules in favour of the wife, then they will put pressure on the husband to agree to a divorce. In ancient times they would beat the husband till he agreed, and this seeming paradox of forcing a man to give the *get* of his 'own free will' is explained by Maimonides as follows:

> He whom the law maintains that he should be forced to divorce his wife, and he does not want to divorce her, the *Bet Din* . . . beat him till he says, 'I want to' . . . Now why is this *get* not void for he is forced into it? . . . [The answer is] that this one who does not want to divorce, since he wants to be part of Israel, and wants to do all the *mitzvot*, and to keep far from sins, it is his evil inclination which attacks him. Once he is beaten till his evil inclination is weakened, and he says, 'I want to', he is already giving the divorce freely.[48]

With the exception of modern Israel, where a recalcitrant husband may be imprisoned till he agrees to a divorce, the Jewish authorities today have no power to force the husband to abide by the ruling of the *Bet Din*. At best they can use persuasion or social and economic sanctions. Sometimes the wife has to pay a large amount of money to her husband before he releases her by giving a *get*. It also happens that the wife refuses to accept a divorce from her husband, and if he is an Ashkenazi Jew he cannot remarry, since polygamy is also forbidden under the *cherem* ascribed to R. Gershom and his associates. Only if the husband can attain the agreement of one hundred rabbis can an Ashkenazi Jew remarry without first divorcing his wife. This latter procedure is used where the wife becomes mentally deranged, and therefore considered not to have a will of her own to accept the husband's *get*. Sefardi Jews, who halakhically may practise polygamy, do not need the agreement of a hundred rabbis to take a second wife, for they may either divorce their wives on their own initiative, or simply take an additional wife unless an anti-polygamy clause has been included in their original wedding contract. The most problematic situation arises where a husband disappears, and there is no shred of evidence to indicate that he is dead. His wife is known as an *agunah*, or 'chained' woman, who is considered a married woman until such evidence is forthcoming. Although the halakhic authorities expend great ingenuity in trying to release the *agunah* so that she can remarry, where there is no basis for the assumption that he has died there is nothing more that can be done for her. The husband whose wife disappears can have recourse to the *heter*, or 'permission' of a hundred rabbis since his prohibition on remarriage is only rabbinic, and applies to

Ashkenazi Jewry alone. The prohibition on the woman remarrying in such circumstances is considered to be biblical.

This disparity between the situation of the man and the woman in traditional divorce is one of the major bones of contention between Orthodox and Progressive Judaism. Even within Orthodoxy there are many critics of the system, particularly from within women's organizations, although ultimately they have to accept the limitations on halakhic flexibility. The Conservative Jewish leadership in the USA attempted to resolve the dilemma of the woman by a series of measures. One was the imposition of a monetary fine on the recalcitrant husband. This, of course, is only effective where the husband has not disappeared, and does not solve the *agunah* problem. An earlier attempt to solve the *agunah* problem, by having the husband authorize a Conservative *Bet Din* to issue a *get* on his behalf if he disappeared, had to be shelved when it came in for severe criticism from Orthodox halakhists. More recently a new proposal has been adopted by Conservative rabbis to activate the power which halakhists have, but do not use, to annul a marriage should there be a problem with the *get*. The couple have to agree, at the time of marriage, that should they obtain a civil divorce, but the husband refuse to give a *get*, the marriage will be annulled by the Conservative religious authorities. This would also be an option if the husband disappeared.

Old Age

Like most tradition-oriented cultures, Judaism sees the aged as an important element in the preservation and transmission of the heritage of the past. The biblical word for a sage is *zaken*, an elder, who was the natural leader of the community and to whom great respect was shown. This attitude carried over into talmudic Judaism where we even find the demand that great care must be taken with an elder who through senility has forgotten his learning.[49] The *Mishnah*, in outlining the various stages through which a person passes as he gets older, sees man come into his full strength at 30, achieve wisdom at 40, be fit to counsel at 50, enter old age at 60, and attain grey hair at 70.[50] The *halakhah* understands the commandment to 'rise before a grey-haired person, and honour the face of the old' to apply from the age of 70 onwards, whether or not the old person is a scholar. It applies even to a younger man if he is a sage.[51] Aside from the general demand to show respect for the elderly, there is also a separate *mitzvah* devolving on children to honour, and fear, their parents. According to some views this honour must also be extended to grandparents, although to a lesser extent.[52] The duty owed to parents is understood by the *halakhah* to consist of things like not contradicting their views, not calling them by their first name, not putting them to shame if they act badly to their children in public, and not losing one's temper with them. Children also have to feed and clothe their parents, to stand up when they enter, and to speak respectfully of them even after their death. If the parents' senility makes it impossible for a child to look after them, and show respect for them himself, he may leave them but must instruct others to care for them.[53] A child also has the responsibility for ensuring that his parents are properly buried, and for paying the funeral expenses.[54]

Death and Burial

In Judaism there are no sacramental last rites for a dying person. He is, however, asked by those around him to confess his sins, but they must make it clear that this does not mean that he will certainly die. He should be told that many who confessed their sins continued to live on, and that in any event confession will guarantee him a portion in the World to Come. If he is too weak to speak he should confess his sins in his heart. A short form of the confession on the death-bed, to which other suitable prayers may be added, runs:

> I acknowledge, O Lord my God, and God of my fathers, that my healing and my death are in Your hands. May it be Your will that You heal me with a perfect healing. But if I die may my death be an atonement for all the sins, transgressions, and iniquities which I have committed before You. Grant me my portion in the Garden of Eden, and let me attain the World to Come which is destined for the righteous.[55]

It is forbidden to interfere in any way with someone who is about to die lest one thereby hastens his death, an act tantamount to murder. This prohibition extends to activities such as anointing or washing the body, which are customary before burial, or to digging a grave for the dying person if he is aware of what is going on.[56]

It is a duty to remain with the dying so that they should not die alone. When they see that death is imminent those present rend their garments, and accept the righteousness of God's judgment with the benediction, 'Blessed be the truthful judge.' All water in the vicinity should be poured out of its containers, because it is believed to be contaminated by the angel of death and dangerous to drink.[57] Death is defined in the *halakhah* as the moment when all respiration ceases, and this is determined by placing a feather or a mirror near the face of the dying person. With developments in modern medicine a number of problems have arisen for the traditional definition of death, and rabbinic authorities are divided about how, if at all, it should be modified.[58] One of the main Modern Orthodox rabbinical groups in the USA has recently accepted brain death as a valid criterion of death, even though the patient may still be breathing with the help of a machine.

Once death has been established the arrangements for the funeral have to be undertaken immediately, since it is forbidden to delay burial. A shroud of white linen is prepared, and the corpse is washed thoroughly before being doused with a ritually prescribed amount of water. Among some Jews the body is then anointed with spices, and a raw egg mixed with wine is smeared on the head. There are many different customs about the preparation of the dead for burial, known as *taharah* or purification, and they are carried out by Jewish volunteer workers, the *chevra kadisha* or 'holy society', who also see to the burial proper. A dead Jew must be buried in consecrated ground, according to the *halakhah*, and cannot simply be interred in a non Jewish cemetery.[59] Orthodox Jews do not practise cremation, and most Orthodox rabbis would not officiate at a cremation even if the ashes are later buried in a coffin. Reform Judaism does not object to the practice of cremation, not sharing the Orthodox view which sees cremation as a denial of the belief in bodily resurrection in the messianic age.

The next of kin have to mourn for a dead relative, and the extent and severity of mourning depends on the closeness of the relationship, mourning for parents being the most stringent. From the time of death the mourner is known as an *onen* who must refrain from meat and wine, and does not have to perform any of the usual Jewish rituals. For the next seven days after the burial service, referred to as the *shivah* or 'seven', the mourner who is now known as an *avel* is in a complete state of mourning. He remains at home where prayer services are held, sitting on a low stool with his upper garment rent, and must not cut his hair, shave or wear leather shoes. Sexual relations are forbidden to an *avel* during this period, as are washing his body, working, studying *Torah* and listening to music, although he may eat meat and drink wine in moderation once the funeral is over. Only on the Sabbath day, when public mourning is forbidden, may he leave his house to attend synagogue. Relatives and friends come to the mourner's house to participate in the prayers and to comfort the mourner. During the services the *avel* recites the *Kaddish* prayer, which he will continue to recite for the next eleven months if the decreased is a parent, and each year on the anniversary of their death or *yahrzeit*. The *Kaddish* is an Aramaic prayer praising God and asking Him to grant peace and a good life. In no sense is it a prayer for the dead, although mourners often view it as such since they do not understand its meaning. The mourner says *Kaddish* in order to show that he is still willing to praise God despite the loss he has just suffered. This idea of accepting God's justice, however unfair the death of a loved one may seem, is a theme of a number of the prayers associated with death and mourning in Judaism. It is believed that after death the soul undergoes a cleansing period of purgatory, which lasts a full year for the wicked, hence the custom of only reciting the *Kaddish* for eleven months so as not to imply that the deceased was indeed wicked, which a full twelve months' recitation would indicate.

When the *shivah* is at an end the mourner enters a period of semi-mourning which lasts till the end of thirty days from the funeral. This is known as the *shloshim*, or 'thirty', and for its duration the *avel* should not cut his hair, wear new clothes, attend celebrations or sit in his usual place at the synagogue. Nevertheless he is allowed to work and to resume his place in society. Those who are in mourning for the death of a spouse, a child or a sibling end their mourning with the termination of the *shloshim*. For the death of a parent the mourning continues for a full year, although the hair may be cut when it becomes unsightly, usually after two or three months.[60] The process of mourning in Judaism can be seen as a gradual movement from isolation and separation to return to the rhythm of normal life. Not to mourn is considered by the *halakhah* as a manifestation of a hard and cruel disposition, but too much mourning is not advised. The mourner is presented with a highly ritualized structure into which he must fit from the first moment, and within which he must express his grief. The bewilderment and disorientation following on the death of a close relative are thus catered for by providing ritualized support, and by bringing in the community to visit and comfort the mourner. Many of the mourning laws, which obviously put considerable restraints on the economic and social life of the *avel*, are not maintained outside of traditional circles and Reform Judaism usually scales down both the period and the extent of mourning.

(1) The Ritual Year: from New Year to Tabernacles

The Day

The most important structure of the day for the traditional Jew is the sequence of prayers: evening *Arvit* or *Maariv* ('even-tide'), morning *Shacharit* ('dawn'), and afternoon *Minchah* ('offering'). These prayers, for which set times are stipulated in accordance with the times for the sacrifices once brought in the Temple, consist of one central prayer around which the service is built. This centrepiece, the *Shemoneh Esreh* ('eighteen'), is a prayer of nineteen benedictions, a special benediction having been added against heretics, specifically Jewish-Christians, in the late first-early second centuries. It is repeated virtually unchanged on each occasion, and has the following three-fold structure:

1   Praise of God, who is the God of the Patriarchs, provider of sustenance and healing, faithful to resurrect the dead, and holy (three benedictions).
2   Prayers for knowledge, repentance, forgiveness, redemption, healing, a blessed earth, ingathering of the exiles, righteous judges, destruction of heretics, reward for the righteous, rebuilding of Jerusalem, the coming of the Davidic Messiah, and a plea for the acceptance of prayer (thirteen benedictions).
3   Prayers for the return to Zion and the re-institution of the Temple Service, thanks for God's goodness and miracles, and a request for peace, mercy and life for Israel (three benedictions).

The *Shemoneh Esreh* has to be prayed while standing and facing Jerusalem, and it is often referred to as the *Amidah* ('standing').

Somewhat different versions exist among the various Jewish communities, but the essential structure is the same. When this prayer is said with a *minyan* quorum of ten adult males, it is first recited silently by each congregant, and then in the mornings and afternoons the prayer-leader repeats it aloud, originally for the benefit of those who did not know the prayer and who by answering *amen* after each benediction were deemed to have prayed themselves. At the repetition of the *Amidah* a special section known as the *kedushah*, 'holiness' is interpolated in the benediction praising God's holiness. This consists of verses from Isaiah (6:3), Ezekiel (3:12), and Psalms (146:10), recited by congregation and cantor. For the morning and evening services the *Amidah* is preceded by the recitation of the *Shema*[1] and its benedictions. The *Shema* occupies a central place in Judaism and serves as a credal affirmation in the absence of a formal creed. It is the first two portions of the *Shema* which appear in the *mezuzah*, the hand-written parchment scroll which must be affixed to one doorpost of every door in the Jewish home. It is these same two portions which, together with other scriptural passages,[2] make up the contents of the *tefillin* or phylacteries, the black leather boxes with black leather straps worn by the Jewish male on his head and left arm during the weekday morning services. The first verse of the *Shema*, 'Hear O Israel, the Lord is our God, the Lord is one', is also repeated by a dying person so that he may expire with the affirmation of the oneness of God on his lips. Outside of the *Amidah* and the *Shema* at morning and evening services, the three daily prayers are made up from scriptural verses and passages, particularly from Psalms, and from hymns and prayers composed in talmudic and post-talmudic times. The longest service is the morning one, which on Mondays and Thursdays also includes a reading from the *Torah* scroll.

Although the *Talmud* and the codes devote considerable detail to the exact times when each prayer may be said, the Chasidic mystics tended to pray at halakhically impermissible times. Though some justified their actions, which were severely criticized by halakhic purists, on kabbalistic grounds it is clear that behind their rebellion lay an irritation with 'prayer on demand'.[3] R. Mendel of Kotsk, a nineteenth-century Chasidic leader, is reported as saying that in Kotsk they had souls not clocks, i.e. that it was not possible simply to pray because the time for prayers had arrived since true prayer is an expression of the soul. Already in the *Mishnah* we find a view opposing fixed prayer because prayer has to be the supplication of the individual before God.[4]

The synagogue was traditionally a place of meeting, a focus of the life of the community, and though Jews are not supposed to talk during the service in most Orthodox synagogues this rule is not taken too literally. The atmosphere is therefore very informal, and the fact that Orthodox services are in Hebrew, and read from a *siddur* or prayer book, makes the personal involvement of the average Jew problematic. Some of the attractiveness of Reform services for the modern Jew lies in their use of the vernacular for many prayers, and in the wider variation between services, as well as in the greater decorum which is strictly maintained during divine worship. Informality and swaying violently while praying (*shokeling*) are preferred among Chasidic congregations, since they allow for maximum participation and a high degree of self-expression. At least one Chasidic group has tried to overcome the staidness of fixed prayers by encouraging its adherents to spend time each day talking aloud to God in their mother tongue. This practice of the Braslav Chasidim is known as *hitbodedut* or 'being alone' with God.

The Weekly Cycle and the Sabbath

Although the twenty-four-hour day, beginning according to Jewish calculation from sunset onwards, is an important feature of ritual time, it is the week which is the basic unit. The seven days of the week do not have individual names in Hebrew, they are simply referred to as 'First Day, (Sunday), 'Second Day' (Monday), etc. Friday is alternately referred to as 'the Sixth Day' or '*Erev Shabbat*' (i.e. Sabbath Eve). For ritual purposes each day is divided into two parts, night-time which begins at sunset, and daytime which is counted from the first morning light of dawn. The *halakhah* divides both day and night into twelve units, which will differ in duration between winter and summer, there being longer day units in the latter and longer night units in the former. There is some dispute as to whether the twelve day units should be calculated from dawn till star-time or from sunrise to sunset.[5] The practice of counting the twenty-four-hour day as beginning in the evening is based on the Creation story in Genesis (ch. 1), where it is said: 'And it was evening and it was morning.'

The Sabbath, known simply as *Shabbat*, begins on Friday evening before twilight which Judaism considered as a period of time indeterminate between day and night. In the separate references to *Shabbat* in the two versions of the Ten Commandments[6] we find an association between it and the Creation (Exodus), and between it and the Exodus from Egypt (Deuteronomy). The *Shabbat* thus emerges as an affirmation of God's creation of the universe and His control of the historical destiny of the Jewish people. Judaism regards *Shabbat* as a special gift from God to the Jews, and not as a ritual for the world at large. Indeed the gentile is forbidden to keep the Jewish *Shabbat* on pain of death,[7] and for this reason a gentile undergoing conversion to Judaism will not keep the *Shabbat* laws in their entirety until after conversion has taken place. The *Shabbat* is a sign between God and the Children of Israel that He made the world in six days and rested on the seventh, i.e. that the world is ultimately God's and not man's. The *midrash* depicts the seventh day as complaining to God that all the other days of the week have a partner, Sunday has Monday, etc., but she has no partner. God replies that the Congregation of Israel is her partner.[8] This image of Israel married to the *Shabbat* brings out the central place which this day has, both in ritual and in the Jewish imagination. Despite its importance the *Mishnah* admits that all the variegated laws of *Shabbat* are like mountains suspended on a hair, because of the paucity of scriptural references to the subject.[9] According to a talmudic view if the Jews would only keep the *Shabbat* properly for two consecutive weeks, they would bring about the messianic Redemption. This has been interpreted, by one modern rabbi, to mean that they must not only keep the two days of *Shabbat* but must also remain holy for the six weekdays in between.[10]

The *Shabbat* is inaugurated at home by the Jewish housewife lighting two candles, and by the man making *kiddush*, 'sanctification', over a cup of wine on his return from synagogue service. Another *kiddush* over wine or alcohol, with a somewhat different text of benedictions, is said on Saturday morning prior to lunch. The family dress in clean clothes in honour of the day, after a bath on Friday prior to the onset of *Shabbat*, and are expected to partake of three festive meals, one on Friday night and one on Saturday lunch-time, each consisting of two loaves of a specially baked bread known as *challah*, plus fish and meat, and a smaller meal on Saturday afternoon. During these meals *Shabbat* hymns (*zemirot*) are sung at the table which is decked with a white tablecloth. With the appearance of three stars on Saturday night *Shabbat* is over, and the evening service is followed by the *havdalah* ritual which is a ceremony of separation between the holiness of the *Shabbat* and the profane week ahead. It involves the use of wine or other beverages, spices which are meant to revive the Jew after the departure of an extra soul (*neshamah yeterah*) which is thought to alight on him for the duration of the *Shabbat*, and a special candle flame. During the course of the approximately twenty-five hours of *Shabbat* no profane work may be done. The *halakhah* goes to great lengths to enumerate the thirty-nine categories of forbidden work, and the many sub-categories. The Jew must rest from his control over the natural and social worlds, in order to realize that God alone is the creator and master of all that is. The rabbis, in the course of time, added categories of prohibited work of their own to further develop the message of *Shabbat* rest. Particularly important is the restriction on the kindling or use of fire, which the rabbis extended to cover electric power as well, some even maintaining that electricity would come under a biblical prohibition. Since no cooking may be done on *Shabbat*, food must be prepared on Friday and may be left on a covered flame to be used during *Shabbat*. This has given rise to a number of *Shabbat* dishes, which are cooked slowly overnight and served on Saturday lunch-time. The best known is the *cholent* stew of meat, beans and potatoes. A number of halakhic sources emphasize that hot food should be eaten on Saturday morning, both because it increases the joy (*oneg*) of *Shabbat* and because it contradicts the Karaite view that no fire is allowed to burn in a Jewish home on *Shabbat*.[11] In order to emphasize the *Shabbat* joy, and the affirmation of the goodness of the world which God has created, it is forbidden to fast on *Shabbat* or to show any public mourning, since both of these may be interpreted as a negative attitude to the created order of things. The only exception to fasting is a fast undertaken after a troublesome dream, for if such a fast is not allowed the conscience of the person who has had the dream will most probably disturb him throughout the *Shabbat*.

For the traditional Jew the *Shabbat* is a period of time beyond the natural order. He cannot prepare or plan anything on *Shabbat* which he needs for the coming week, and he is totally cut off from his normal weekday routine and problems. It thus became the symbol of sanctified, redeemed time implicit in the messianic era, and is thought of as a reflection in this world of the World to Come.[12] The Kabbalah expatiates on the theme of unity and harmony symbolized by the *Shabbat*, and the Zoharic tradition sees this day as the time when the conjugal union of male and female principles takes place within the sphere of the divine. A number of prayers and hymns, originating in kabbalistic circles but accepted by the wider Jewish community, stress the mystical symbolism of the *Shabbat* bride united with her divine bridegroom, out of the reach of the forces of evil which are impotent for the *Shabbat*'s duration.

The Month

The months of the Jewish year are lunar, beginning with the new moon and lasting either twenty-nine or thirty days. The ritual year is, however, solar with the festivals based on the agricultural seasons. Passover, for instance, is a spring festival, and the lunar year has to be intercalated with seven extra months every nineteen years to make up for a discrepancy of eleven days between lunar and solar years. In ancient times the new month was fixed by the sighting of the new moon, and witnesses to this sighting would testify before a special *Bet Din* in Jerusalem the head of which would proclaim the new month. A beacon would then be lit on the Mount of Olives, and a chain of signal beacons would carry the news to the Jewish communities in Babylonia. This practice was abandoned when Samaritans, who differed from the Pharisees over calendric details, lit their own fires and caused considerable confusion. Instead the *Bet Din* would send out messengers to distant communities with the tidings.[13]

In the fourth century CE the calendar was fixed, that is calculated in advance, and the sighting of the new moon ceased to be a factor in determining the month. In biblical times the New Moon festival ranked as an occasion for special sacrifices and celebrations. In later Judaism, however, it became a relatively minor festival marked out merely by additional prayers, such as the shorter *Hallel* (Psalms 113–118 with certain deletions) and an extra *Amidah* prayer (*Musaf*) commemorating the sacrifices once brought on this day. It is customary to announce the birth of the new moon (*molad*) in the synagogue, on the *Shabbat* preceding the new month, and among Jewish communities influenced by kabbalistic ideas the day before *Rosh Chodesh*, as the New Moon festival is known, is treated as a 'Little Day of Atonement' with fasting and penitential prayers.

Between the third and the fifteenth day of the new lunar month a small ceremony of blessing or sanctifying the moon takes place, usually held on a Saturday night. The moon must be visible in the night sky, if only for a fleeting moment. In the prayers for the sanctification of the moon Israel is compared to the moon which continually renews itself, and which does the will of its Creator in joy. The moon is now a lesser light than the sun, but in future times it will regain its former splendour and be as bright as the sun, similarly Israel will abandon its lesser status among the nations and regain its former splendour in the messianic age.

The New Year Festival

There are two points at which the Jewish year may be said to begin. The first is at the beginning of the spring month, *Nisan*, on the fifteenth day of which the Passover festival falls. This month is referred to in the Pentateuch as the 'beginning of months, the first month of the year'.[14] It is more natural, however, for the Jew to think of the new year as beginning on the first of *Tishri*, the seventh month from *Nisan*, when the Jewish New Year festival, *Rosh Ha-Shanah*, originally a one-day festival, is now celebrated for two days both in the Diaspora and in Israel. Since it falls at the beginning of the month it was necessary in ancient times to keep the thirtieth day of the previous month, *Elul*, as *Rosh Ha-Shanah* in case witnesses to the new moon came sometime during that day. If they did not come then the thirty-first day of *Elul* was declared to be the first of *Tishri*, and hence *Rosh Ha-Shanah*, the festival being kept for two days. If the witnesses came on the thirtieth of *Elul* the festival was a one-day festival, at least for Jerusalem and its environs, but further afield and particularly in the Diaspora it was still kept for both days.

The month of *Elul*, immediately preceding *Rosh Ha-Shanah*, is a time for soul-searching and repentance. The *shofar*, or ram's horn, is blown briefly every morning after prayers, with the exception of *Shabbat* and the day before *Rosh Ha-Shanah* itself. Beginning from the last week of *Elul*, the week during which the New Year festival falls, special prayers for forgiveness known as *selichot* are recited at dawn. All of this is a build-up to *Rosh Ha-Shanah* which is seen as a day of judgment on which the fortunes of the coming year depend.[15] This judgmental aspect makes the festival a solemn occasion, and it, together with the Day of Atonement which follows shortly after, are referred to as *Yamim Noraim*, 'Days of Awe'. Nevertheless *Rosh Ha-Shanah* is still a joyous festival, and this is explained by the *Talmud* as follows:

> The usual practice is for a man who is to be tried in a court to dress in black and to let his beard grow, since he does not know how his case will go. But Israel is not so. Instead they wear white, trim their beards, eat, drink and rejoice. For they know that the Holy One will perform miracles for them.[16]

Prior to and during the *Musaf*, the additional prayers for the festival, the *shofar* is blown according to the rabbinic interpretation of the biblical command that the day be one of horn-blowing (Numbers 29:1). In some communities a hundred notes are blown on the *shofar* in different combinations of its three basic sounds: *tekiah*, an unbroken note, *shevarim*, a note of three short sounds, and *teruah*, a note of nine or more short sounds.

Special foods are eaten during *Rosh Ha-Shanah* which are thought to be symbolic heralds of a good year ahead. In some communities the head of a fish, of a sheep, or other animal, is eaten to symbolize that in the coming year those who partake of it should be 'a head and not a tail'. For a similar reason the festive bread is dipped in honey, instead of the more usual salt, to symbolize a sweet year and an apple is also eaten dipped in honey. Another feature of the festival is the custom of wishing those one meets, 'May you be written and sealed for a good year', since it is believed that everyone's judgment is written in a heavenly book. It is also advised that one should not sleep on *Rosh Ha-Shanah* during the daytime so that one's luck should not, as it were, go to sleep in the year to come.[17] A late medieval custom which is popular among traditional Jews is to go to a river, sea or other place of flowing water on the afternoon of the first day of the festival, and symbolically cast away one's sins into the water. This ritual (*tashlikh*) is of unknown origin and it has been suggested that it was adapted from a non-Jewish rite. Its meaning for Judaism, as is brought out by the prayers and Psalms which accompany it, is simply a symbolic act of cleansing oneself for the new year, and some rabbis suggested that saying the prayers at home was just as effective.

In accord with the underlying theme of the festival, namely standing before God's judgment for one's sins, the prayers of *Rosh Ha-Shanah* emphasize that God, the divine judge, is indeed King of the universe. The Jews are His subjects passing before Him to receive judgment, and in the heavenly court Satan, the prosecuting attorney, prepares his brief which consists of the sins of Israel. The Jewish people turn in penitence to their King, seeking His forgiveness and mercy, and requesting a pardon not because of any merit of the accused, but for His name's sake. Special tunes are used in the synagogue to chant the prayers and readings which inculcate a sense of the awe of the occasion, and the story of the binding of Isaac (Genesis 22) is read. Like the other biblical festivals, Passover, Pentecost and Tabernacles, *Rosh Ha-Shanah* is a festival on which no profane work may be done. These festivals differ from *Shabbat* and the Day of Atonement in that food may be cooked on them, and food-associated work is allowed. Thus fire may be used, but not kindled, and articles may be carried in a public thoroughfare. Synagogue attendance, slack throughout the year except on the part of the devout few, picks up considerably for *Rosh Ha-Shanah*. Both Orthodox and Progressive synagogues find that their usual seating arrangements are inadequate, and they may have to hire premises for overflow services.

The Ten Days of Penitence

The first ten days of the month of *Tishri* are known as the Ten Days of Penitence. The day after *Rosh Ha-Shanah* is a fast day (*Tzom Gedaliah*) which has no intrinsic connection with the period but commemorates the assassination of Gedaliah, the governor of Judah who was appointed by the Babylonians after the fall of Jerusalem in 586 BCE. According to Jewish tradition his death led to the final elimination of Jewish life in the southern kingdom of Judah.[18] No exact date is given in the biblical sources which mention the incident (2 Kings 25:25; Jeremiah 41:1), but the third of *Tishri* is accepted as the day of his assassination. It obviously also suits the penitential mood, and compensates for any possible over-indulgence during the two preceding days. These ten days are marked by additions to the prayers: petitioning God to forgive the sins of the past year, to remember the Jews for life, emphasizing the kingship of God, and calling for repentance, which is known as *teshuvah* and means a turning back to God. Some communities also say the special penitential *selichot* at dawn, while it is the custom among pietistical Jews to read works of *musar* which lead man to a more inward and holy service of God. There is a general attempt to live in a stricter mode of ritual purity during this period.

The *Shabbat* before the Day of Atonement is known as the '*Shabbat* of Repentance', and is one of the two occasions in the year when the rabbi, in olden times, would preach a sermon, in this case dealing with the subject of *teshuvah*. For the additional reading from the Prophets (*haftarah*) chapter 14 of Hosea is chosen, beginning with the words: 'Return, O Israel, to the Lord Your God, for You have stumbled in your iniquity.' This period culminates in the day before the Day of Atonement when the atmosphere changes. It is a duty to eat well on that day, and many of the customary penitential prayers are not said. Among some Ashkenazi Jews, and among those Jews influenced by Kabbalah, the rite of *kapparot* is performed on the morning preceding the Day of Atonement. This rite entails taking a white cockerel or hen for a male or female, and passing it round the head three times saying: 'This is my substitute, this is my exchange, this is my atonement. This cockerel/hen shall go unto death, and I will go, and enter, into a good and long life, and into peace.' The animal is then ritually slaughtered, its intestines are thrown to the birds, and the meat is either given to the poor or an amount of money is given in its place and it is consumed. The custom is first mentioned in ninth-century Babylonia and R. Moses Isserles, the Ashkenazi joint author of the *Shulchan Arukh*, includes it as a normative practice. It aroused strong opposition, however, from some of the major halakhists of the Middle Ages who suspected it of pagan overtones. R. Solomon Adret writes in the thirteenth century:

> I found this custom [i.e. *kapparot*] widespread in our city together with other practices of a similar nature which were indulged in. They seemed in my eyes like Amorite ways, and I exerted great pressure on this issue. With divine mercy my words were listened to, and nothing of this and related matters has remained in our city.[19]

R. Joseph Caro, the Sefardi author of the *Shulchan Arukh*, says that one should deter people from adhering to this custom,[20] but despite these reservations the custom has become deeply rooted in Jewish life. Those who find it too pagan for their liking, and too likely to be misconstrued as an act of magical transference in which the cockerel receives the punishment due to man, use money for the ceremony instead of an animal. After the money is waved around the head with the appropriate formula it is given to charity. This then ties in with an old Jewish idea that charity is one of the things which helps to avert an evil decree.

The Day of Atonement, *Yom Kippur*, is the high-point of the process of repentance and the seeking of God's forgiveness. Since, however, it is believed that God can only forgive sins committed against one's fellow man after the latter has himself forgiven his malefactor, the sinner must seek his fellow's forgiveness prior to *Yom Kippur*. It is customary for Jews to approach those they have wronged and try to mollify them, but should they refuse to be reconciled after three attempts at winning forgiveness, the sinner is absolved from further efforts at propitiation. As a mark of ritual purification from sexual relations and seminal emission, or according to some views as a part of the process of repentance, it is prescribed that every Jew should bathe in a *mikveh* on the day before *Yom Kippur*, or at least pour a specified large amount of water over himself in one continuous flow. A practice which is relatively rare among contemporary Jews, although mentioned in the codes, is flagellation with a leather strap after the afternoon prayers, when there is a public confession of sins as formulated in the prayer book. This practice of flagellation was accounted conducive to repentance, and is still carried out by individual pietists though the flogging is usually more of a symbolic act than a real ordeal of suffering. The fast, which is one of the main features of *Yom Kippur*, begins just before sunset, and the last morsels of food have to be consumed with a little time to spare so as to add holiness to profane time.[21]

The Day of Atonement

In popular religious consciousness, as well as in halakhic literature, *Yom Kippur* is regarded as the high-point of the Jewish year, and indeed serves as a basic measure of a Jew's commitment to his traditions. Many Jews who do not participate in other rituals make a special effort to attend synagogue, or at least to fast, on *Yom Kippur*. In the modern State of Israel, where Jewish life is dominated by Orthodoxy, groups of secularist Jews make a point of going out for well-publicized picnics on *Yom Kippur*. This not only allows them to escape the heavy religious atmosphere of the towns, but is also the ultimate expression of defiance at the religious establishment. Aside from the fast, which like all fasts in Judaism involves complete abstention from food and drink, *Yom Kippur* is a day on which washing, anointing oneself, wearing leather shoes, and sexual relations, are all forbidden. As on *Shabbat*, it is forbidden to perform any type of profane work on *Yom Kippur*.

The service in the synagogue begins at evening with *Torah* scrolls being taken from the ark to the raised platform in the centre of the synagogue. The male congregants will be wearing their prayer shawls (*tallit*), which are normally only worn during daytime, and often also a plain white gown, or *kittel*, over their clothes. This manner of dress is given various interpretations, e.g. that white signifies purity and the forgiveness of sins, or that the *kittel* signifies the shroud worn after death and thus induces a sense of humility.[22] In the opening prayer the cantor asks permission from the heavenly host, and from the congregation, to pray with those sinners who may be excluded from the synagogue throughout the rest of the year, for one reason or another. This is followed by the *Kol Nidrei*, sung three times among Ashkenazi Jews in a haunting, solemn tune. The *Kol Nidrei* is essentially the annulment of vows, and was intended to free the Jew from those religious vows which he may have forgotten about. A number of halakhic authorities were unhappy about this rite of annulment, and even the leader of German Orthodoxy in the nineteenth century, R. Samson Raphael Hirsch, tried unsuccessfully to abolish the practice at one stage of his career.[23] The repeated accusations of gentiles that Jewish oaths could not be trusted because Jews could simply annul them at *Kol Nidrei*, though based on a misunderstanding of the kind of vows being annulled, led to great misery for the Jews down the ages and was a further incentive for those rabbis who wished to scrap the rite. The popularity of *Kol Nidrei* was such that it has survived the rabbinic caveats, and remained an integral part, for some Jews perhaps the most moving part, of *Yom Kippur*. The evening service which follows includes the public confession of sins, and the recitation of hymns emphasizing man's inadequacies but the overflowing measure of divine mercy.

During the next day there are long services in the synagogue with virtually no break until nightfall, when the *shofar* is sounded to herald the end of the fast. Different Jewish communities zealously preserve their traditional tunes for the chanting of the prayers, which are often sung with great relish by older members of the congregation for whom they bring back nostalgic recollections of accompanying their parents to synagogue in their youth. Among the central liturgical features of *Yom Kippur* are the memorial prayers for the dead (*Yizkor*) also recited at the end of Tabernacles, Passover, and Pentecost, a long-burning memorial candle having been lit prior to the fast in memory of deceased parents. There is also a lengthy recounting of the ceremonies undertaken by the high priest in Temple times, during which the congregation prostrate themselves at specified moments in imitation of Temple practice; the soulful lament over the ten sages who were cruelly martyred during the Hadrianic persecutions in the second century according to Jewish tradition; and the reading of the Book of Jonah during the afternoon service, to bring out the message that forgiveness is available to all those who repent and change their evil ways. The total effect of *Yom Kippur* can be one of considerable intensity and awe, with the fasting, the white clothes, the solemn melodies, the prostrations of cantor and congregation, and the prayers themselves, all contributing to an atmosphere both numinous and cathartic. Although the accepted halakhic view is that *Yom Kippur* only atones for sins which are genuinely repented of, it is clear that many Jews feel cleansed, and renewed, merely by undergoing the day-long ritual. Their life throughout the coming year may not differ substantially from their life during the preceding year, but nevertheless the belief that God has forgiven the past allows the future to be approached free from the burden of guilt.

Tabernacles

Five days after *Yom Kippur* the festival of Tabernacles (*Sukkot*) begins. The *sukkah* is a booth-like structure, with a roof of branches, built under the open sky which the traditional Jew lives in for the next seven days. In ancient times *Sukkot* was one of the three pilgrimage festivals, the other two being Passover and Pentecost, associated with the seasonal harvests. Like the other pilgrimage festivals *Sukkot* is connected in the Bible with the Exodus from Egypt:

> You shall dwell in booths seven days . . . so that your future genera-
> tions may know that I made the Children of Israel dwell in booths
> when I brought them out of the land of Egypt.[24]

With the destruction of the Second Temple, and the wide disper-
sion of the Jewish people outside Palestine, the harvest element of *Sukkot* became completely secondary. It is still present in various

festival rituals, particularly in the four species which must be waved together on *Sukkot*. This ritual is based on an exegesis of Leviticus 23:40, and the species consist of a palm branch (*lulav*), myrtle (*hadas*) and willow (*aravah*) sprigs, which are strapped together and held with an *etrog*, or special citrus fruit, to be waved during the recitation of the *Hallel* psalms (nos. 113–118) in the synagogue. The strange timing of the festival, falling as it does in autumn whereas the Exodus is commemorated in spring, is explained by the rabbis as containing a religious message:

> The commandment of *sukkah* is associated in Scripture with the Exodus from Egypt because the latter teaches the truth of the existence of a Creator, who has created all things according to His will. The booths, which Scripture relates He made us dwell in, are clouds of His glory with which He surrounded Israel, so that hot winds and the sun should not smite them. Although we went out of Egypt in the month of *Nisan* He did not command us to make a booth at that time, because those are the days of the onset of summer, and it is the practice of all men to make a booth for shade. Our making of them would not be recognizable as a commandment of the Creator. Therefore He commanded us to make them in the rainy season. We leave our house to dwell in a booth, and this will appear to all as a command of the King.[25]

It is clear that there are several layers of meaning built into the festival of *Sukkot*, the Exodus motif being only one of them, and the association with the autumnal harvest is one of the features which accounts for its timing. A particular feature of the agricultural nature of the festival is the water-drawing ceremony, which was performed by the Pharisees in Temple times after the first day of *Sukkot*. This was considered by the Sadducees as unscriptural, and the *Mishnah* recounts how an angry crowd of pilgrims pelted a Sadducean priest with their *etrog* fruits, when he poured the water libation on the ground instead of on the altar.[26] Talmudic literature describes the great joy accompanying the water-drawing festivities, the dancing, music and songs, and says, 'He who has not witnessed the rejoicing of the house of water-drawing, has never witnessed real joy.' The participants in the ceremony, who included the leading Pharisaic sages, were even said to be drawing up the Holy Spirit, so great was the religious fervour and enthusiasm during the proceedings.[27] Among Orthodox Jews today these water-drawing celebrations are still kept up, with the singing and dancing going on late into the night. An attempt is thus made to recapture the exuberance and joy of the ancient ceremony. Water, and the agricultural connection, appear more centrally in contemporary practice in the special prayers for rain initiated on the eighth day of *Sukkot*. This day, in fact two days in the Diaspora, is considered a separate festival known as *Shemini Atzeret*, but it is tacked on the end of *Sukkot*.

Generally speaking *Sukkot* is considered as the most joyous festival of the Jewish year, and is described in the liturgy as 'the time of our rejoicing'. *Shemini Atzeret* is the culmination of that rejoicing, which is expressed in the celebrations surrounding the completion of the yearly Pentateuchal cycle. These celebrations are known as *Simchat Torah*, the 'rejoicing of the *Torah*', and occur in Israel on the eighth day of *Sukkot* and in the Diaspora on the ninth. Two members of the congregation are elected to complete the reading of the Pentateuch and to begin it again with the first chapter of Genesis, respectively. The synagogue is filled with dancing worshippers who carry all the scrolls of the *Torah* in a joyous procession, accompanied by singing and flag-waving children. A party is usually thrown by the two congregants, at which large amounts of alcohol are drunk to enhance the atmosphere, and to the uninformed outsider an Orthodox synagogue on such an occasion presents a strange and indeed wild appearance. Samuel Pepys, who attended a *Simchat Torah* service in London on 14th October 1663, recorded in his diary:

> But, Lord, to see the disorder, laughing, sporting, and no attention, but confusion in all their services, more like brutes than people knowing the true God, would make a man forswear ever seeing them more; and indeed I never could have imagined there had been any religion in the whole world, so absurdly performed as this.

One other day of the festival of *Sukkot* stands out in the uniqueness of the rituals associated with it. This is the seventh day of the festival, *Hoshana Rabba*, which is not technically a festive day or *yom tov* but is marked by a number of significant rituals. On it the *hoshana* prayers (the English 'hosanna') are recited as the congregation carry their four species round the synagogue. These prayers call for God's salvation, and are followed by each Jew taking a bunch of willow sprigs and beating them till all or most of the leaves drop off. These customs go back to Temple ceremonies.[28] *Hoshana rabba* is also seen as the end of the period of divine judgment begun with the new year. A Jewish folk belief has it that if one does not cast a shadow on the evening of *Hoshana Rabba* one will not live out the year. A medieval custom, strongly reinforced by later kabbalistic ideas, is to stay awake the whole night of *Hoshana Rabba* reciting special texts. This was understood as a last effort of repentance, undertaken to awaken man's heart to *teshuvah*.[29]

The maintenance of all the *Sukkot* rituals, in every detail laid down by the *halakhah*, caused considerable problems to Jews living far from the setting in which these practices originated. The special citrus fruit was hard to come by, and exorbitantly priced, for Jews living in Europe and often a whole community could only obtain one set of the four species which everyone had to share. With the mass return of Jews to Israel this difficulty has been overcome and a whole *etrog* industry exists to supply the fruit from Israeli orchards to the Diaspora. Urban Jews, particularly those in high-rise apartment buildings, have always found it difficult to build a booth which was both open to the sky and close enough to be used for eating and sleeping in. In Israel, and in some Diaspora communities, this difficulty has been overcome by designing balconies in such a way that each tenant has at least one which is not under the balconies above, and on which an halakhicaly acceptable *sukkah* can be constructed. Among Reform Jews it is not usual for individuals to have a *sukkah* of their own, instead a *sukkah* is erected in a Reform synagogue which congregants use when they come to services on the festival.

(2) The Ritual Year: from Chanukah to the month of Av

Chanukah

Some two months after the end of the festival of *Sukkot*, on the 25th day of the Hebrew month of *Kislev*, the eight-day celebration of *Chanukah* begins. *Chanukah* is a Jewish festival of light, of extra-biblical origin, commemorating a miracle story associated with the Maccabean victory over the Seleucid rulers of Palestine circa 165 BCE. According to the *Talmud* when the Hasmoneans (as the Maccabees were known) re-dedicated the Temple they could only find one small jar of oil still containing the High Priest's seal and which was thus undefiled. This small amount of oil should only have lasted for one day at the most, but actually burned for eight days, which was sufficient time to prepare new purified oil. In the following year these days were declared as festive days.[1] A somewhat different version of the story is given in 1st and 2nd *Book of Maccabees*, where the festival either simply commemorates the re-dedication of the Temple, or was modelled on the eight-day Solomonic celebration of the Temple completion. The account in *Maccabees* also associates the eight days of the festival with the eight days of *Sukkot* which the Maccabean soldiers were unable to celebrate. A midrashic source relates the date of *Chanukah* to the erection of the Tabernacle by Moses in the wilderness, which should have been on the 25th of *Kislev* but was delayed. Divine Providence therefore arranged that the Hasmoneans should re-dedicate the Temple on this date.[2] The talmudic view of the origin and significance of *Chanukah* is the one accepted by traditional Judaism, and is the rationale behind the custom of kindling lights for eight days. It does not, however, appear as a theme in the special prayer for *Chanukah*, known as *Al Ha-Nissim*, which is added to the liturgy and which only mentions the victory, the re-dedication, and the necessity of giving thanks to God, as the motifs of *Chanukah*.

In terms of Jewish ritual it is not the military victory of the Maccabees, nor even the re-dedication of the Temple, which is celebrated. Rather it is the miracle wrought by God which enabled a small jar of oil to burn for such a long period which is emphasized as having religious worth. The outstanding ritual feature of *Chanukah* is the kindling of lights, one on the first night, two on the second, etc., and eight on the last night, followed by the singing of a hymn, *Maoz Tzur*. This has given rise to a whole ritual art form, the eight-branched candelabrum known as a *menorah* or in modern Israel as a *chanukiyah*. Although specially coloured candles are normally used for these lights, pious Jews endeavour to use olive oil with wicks, since the miracle involved a jar of olive oil. The *Chanukah* lights have to be kindled in a doorway or a window, so that they may be seen by passers-by, in order to 'publicize the miracle'. *Chanukah* is not a festival in the true sense, for there is no prohibition on profane work, and no *kiddush*, or sanctification, to introduce it. There are, in fact, no festive meals prescribed although various food customs, such as eating cheese pancakes and doughnuts, have developed in the course of time. Children are given presents of money and encouraged to play with a small spinning-top (Yiddish *dreidl*, Hebrew *sevivon*) on the sides of which are Hebrew letters, while adults, somewhat to the dismay of the halakhic authorities, have adopted the habit of playing cards during the festival. In modern Israel the heroic rebellion of the Maccabees, who regained their independence from foreign rule, is emphasized more than the traditional theme of a divine miracle since Israeli secularists can easily identify with it. For this reason the kindling of the *Chanukah* lights is popular among the non-religious sections of Israeli society.

Chanukah falls close to the winter solstice and one Jewish theologian, R. Judah Loeb of Prague in the sixteenth century, attempts to tie up this festival of light with the themes of darkness and light experienced in nature:

> You should know that it is fitting that it should be on the 25th of *Kislev* that light should go out to the world. For in the three preceding months the light of the sun is continually diminished. From then on the light grows.[3]

Between Chanukah and Purim

Approximately a week after *Chanukah* there is a day-long fast known as *Asarah be-Tevet*, 'the tenth of the month of *Tevet*', which remembers the day on which the siege of Jerusalem by Nebuchadnezzar began. Since *Tevet* is the tenth month from *Nisan*, the month of the Exodus, the *Talmud* understands this to be 'the fast of the tenth month' mentioned by the prophet Zechariah (8:19). Like all the minor fasts this one only lasts from dawn till nightfall, but it is unique in one respect. If it falls on Friday then the date of the fast is not changed, even though it is usually forbidden to fast just prior to *Shabbat*, because Ezekiel says of the day when the King of Babylon besieged Jerusalem 'write you the name of the day, even of this self same day', i.e. the day should not be brought forward or postponed, but commemorated on the correct date.[4]

In the following month the New Year for Trees is celebrated. This takes place on the fifteenth of *Shevat*, when penitential prayers are omitted from the liturgy and fasting is forbidden. It is customary to eat fruit, particularly the special fruits associated with the land of Israel in the Bible: grapes, figs, pomegranates, olives and dates. In modern Israel *Tu bi-Shevat*, as the festival is known, has become a time for tree-planting ceremonies in which school children participate throughout the country. *Tu bi-Shevat* is also important for religious Jews in Israel, because fruit which blossoms after that date is considered to belong to the new year as far as tithes and other agricultural laws are concerned.

Purim and the Month of Adar

The month of *Adar* (February/March), on the 14th of which the festival of *Purim* falls, is the most joyous month of the Jewish year. As the *Talmud* says,[5] 'When *Adar* comes in one should rejoice greatly.' On the 7th of *Adar* Moses was born and also died, according to Jewish tradition.[6] It is customary for the members of the Jewish burial society, the *chevra kaddisha*, to fast during the day and to break their fast at night with a celebratory meal. Since, according to the Jewish interpretation of the biblical account of the death of Moses, it was God Himself who buried him and 'no man knows his burial place' (Deuteronomy 34:6) it has also become the custom to remember on this day those Jewish soldiers whose graves are unknown. The festival of *Purim* falls, in most places, on the 14th of

Adar, but in cities with an ancestry going back to the time of Joshua, and a tradition of being walled cities at that period, it is celebrated on the 15th. The reason for this is that, according to the Book of Esther (9:18), the Jews of Shushan the Persian capital celebrated on the 15th, and in order not to denigrate the ancient cities of Israel their inhabitants do so as well. The back-dating of the walled cities to Joshua is explained by the fact that at the time of the Babylonian captivity, when the story of *Purim* is set, the cities of Israel were in ruins.[7]

The day preceding *Purim* is a fast known as *Taanit Ester*, the Fast of Esther, which is kept in all locations on the 13th of *Adar* in commemoration of the fast undertaken by Esther and the Jews for three days prior to her visit to the king (Esther 4:15). This particular fast only dates back to geonic times, and is not mentioned in the *Talmud*. *Purim*, like *Chanukah*, is not a genuine festival or *yom tov*, and work is allowed although generally discouraged.[8] The main features of the day are the reading of the *Megillah*, as the hand-written scroll of the Book of Esther is called, once in the evening and once during the day; the inclusion of a special *Purim* prayer (*Al Ha-Nissim*) in the liturgy; the giving of charity to the needy and the sending of gifts of food to at least one friend; and a festive meal which should be eaten in the afternoon. Jews are encouraged to drink alcohol to the point where they cannot distinguish between 'blessed be Mordecai' (the hero of the *Purim* story) and 'cursed be Haman' (the villain of the piece). Some authorities do not interpret this demand literally, and indicate that it is sufficient to drink a little more than usual and then to sleep, thereby not being able to distinguish between hero and villain.[9] That Judaism, which normally strikes a very sober tone in its rituals, should include a demand to drink to the point that one's discriminatory powers are dulled has been commented on at length in halakhic and kabbalistic literature. Some see the use of alcohol as reflecting the salvation of the Jews in the *Purim* story, which came about through the various drinking feasts attended by the Persian king. Others emphasize the more mystical dimension of transcending the everyday world of distinction between good and evil, Mordecai and Haman, to a level of harmony where opposites coalesce.

Around these halakhic requirements have grown up a series of customs which give *Purim* a distinctly carnival atmosphere. Jews dress up in masks and costumes, men often wearing female attire and vice versa, although this is normally a forbidden practice.

Children go from house to house in their costumes, acting out a drama usually based on the Esther story, known as a *Purim spiel*, and collecting money for charity. Students lampoon their teachers, and make up absurd interpretations of Jewish teaching. Whenever the name of Haman is mentioned in the reading of the *Megillah* the congregants bang, stamp, boo and make as much noise as they can to blot out his name. Three-cornered buns, filled with poppy seed, are customarily eaten, and known colloquially as 'Haman's ears' (Yiddish *hamantaschen*). Of all the Jewish festivals *Purim* is the most secular in nature, God not being directly referred to in the Book of Esther. It is also very much a folk festival, and is celebrated in modern Israel as a time of national carnival with large floats moving in procession through the streets of Tel Aviv. In a Jewish leap year an extra month is intercalated so that there are two *Adar*s, known as *Adar Rishon* ('first *Adar*') and *Adar Sheni* ('second *Adar*'). In such a case the second *Adar* is regarded as *Adar* proper, and *Purim* is celebrated during it.

Passover

The story of the Exodus, the consequent theophany on Mt. Sinai, and the wanderings of the Children of Israel in the wilderness prior to their entry into the Promised Land, are primary themes of Jewish religious consciousness. All exile is seen, typologically, as an extension of the Egyptian experience, and all liberation and redemption as an extension of the Exodus. The Passover festival, known as *Pesach*, is the festival of the Exodus par excellence, although it is also an agricultural festival associated with the barley harvest. *Pesach* lasts for seven days in Israel, and for eight in the Diaspora, with the first day and last day as *yom tov* in the former, and the first two and last two days as *yom tov* in the latter. The other days, like the intermediate days of *Sukkot*, are festive weekdays, *chol ha-moed*, during which profane work is allowed but restricted in scope. The day before *Pesach*, which begins on the 15th of *Nisan*, is a fast day for first-born males, or if they are too young their fathers must fast for them till they reach maturity. There is even an halakhic view that first-born females should fast, though this is not the accepted practice.[10] The reason for the fast most commonly given in Jewish literature is because first-born Jews were saved when the first-born Egyptians were slain in the tenth plague. In practice, however, the fast is not undertaken, instead a special meal is arranged to celebrate the conclusion (*siyyum*) of a talmudic tractate, and such a ritual meal overrides the fast.

The most outstanding feature of *Pesach* is the prohibition on eating, or even possessing, any form of leavened bread. The latter is referred to as *chametz*, and includes not merely bread which has been allowed to rise, but anything made of flour and water unless prepared under very stringent conditions. The staple food during the festival is unleavened bread, *matzah*, made from flour kept specially dry which is mixed with water and baked within eighteen minutes from the time it first becomes wet. *Matzah* is made either by machine or by hand, some strictly observant Jews using only the latter, and comes as square or oval-shaped flat wafers. Special kitchen utensils, crockery and cutlery must be used throughout the festival, since those used during the rest of the year have absorbed *chametz*. Orthodox Jews thus often possess a completely separate set of kitchen and table ware for *Pesach*, although certain items may be made usable for *Pesach* by either soaking, boiling or heating to red heat, such a process being known as *kashering*, from the Hebrew word *kasher*. Since all leaven must be removed before *Pesach*, an extensive 'spring cleaning' takes place in the weeks prior to the festival. On the *Shabbat* before Passover, known as *Shabbat Ha-Gadol*, the rabbi preaches a sermon reminding his congregants of aspects of the *Pesach* ritual. Individual Jewish communities have their own special restrictions for *Pesach*, which are strictly adhered to. Beans, peas and rice, for instance, are not used by Ashkenazi Jews. In order that unused *chametz* should not simply be thrown away it may be locked up and sold to a gentile to be bought back after the festival. This has to be done with a proper bill of sale, and the community rabbi usually acts as an agent in the sale. Whatever *chametz* is left unsold is ritually searched for on the evening before *Pesach*, and then is burnt and annulled on the following morning.

The first night of *Pesach*, or the first two nights in the Diaspora, is the highlight of the festival, and is known as *seder* ('order') night. A special ritual meal is eaten, often in the company of grandparents, aunts, uncles and cousins, as well as with invited guests. The meal is modelled on the family gatherings which came together in Temple times to eat the sacrificial Paschal lamb. Jews of very different levels of religious commitment still keep up the practice of having a *seder*, although for some the accompanying rituals are kept to a minimum and the evening is more of a family 'get together'. At a traditional *seder* the story of the Exodus is told from a specially prepared text or *Haggadah*. Many of these texts were produced with elaborate illustrations, translations into the vernacular, and in modern times even with a revised version of the story to suit the theology of Reform Judaism, or the secularist ideology of Israeli kibbutz socialists. Since the theme of the *Haggadah* is freedom from slavery it lends itself to adaptation, and has actually been re-written by politically radical American Jews as a manifesto of civil rights, and of freedom movements in the Third World. The traditional *Haggadah* is based on the prototype mentioned in the *Mishnah*,[11] but has grown to include poems and songs which are sung to rousing tunes to involve the children of the household.

The main rituals accompanying the recital of the *Haggadah* are: the drinking of four cups of wine in commemoration of the four expressions of redemption mentioned in the Book of Exodus (6:67), the first cup being used for the festival *kiddush*; the males sitting round the table all lean slightly to their left side, this being an ancient sign of the free man; the eating of vegetables dipped in salt water – a reminder of the tears of the Hebrew slaves; the four questions (*Mah Nishtanah*) which the children ask about the evening's rituals, and the head of the household's reply; the chanting of the *Hallel* psalms; the eating of at least a minimum amount of *matzah*; the eating of bitter herbs (*maror*), usually horseradish or lettuce, as reminders of the bitterness of slavery; and the general order of the table on which a *seder* plate with the various ritual foods is set, including a burnt shank bone symbolizing the Paschal sacrifice, and an egg symbolizing the festival offering, neither of which are actually eaten on the evening. At the end of the meal, before the concluding part of the *Haggadah* is recited, a last piece of *matzah* is eaten, this being known as the *afikoman*. This is a Greek word meaning a post-meal dessert accompanied by entertainment. Since the piece of *matzah* is the last thing eaten, and no dessert follows, the name became attached to the *matzah* itself. The *afikoman* is set aside at the beginning of the meal, and as it must be eaten before midnight there is a custom in some communities for the children of the household to try to 'steal' it. They then hold up the person conducting the *seder* to ransom, demanding a present in return for the *afikoman*. Around these rituals many other customs have grown up, such as pouring out a glass of wine for the prophet Elijah, opening the front door and inviting him in; tipping wine from the glasses as each of the ten plagues is mentioned, which is explained as a symbolic participation in the albeit necessary suffering of the Egyptians; and the wearing of the white *kittel* by the male participants or dressing up as the Israelites about to leave Egypt, each community having their distinctive style of *seder*, a style which is even being modified in the present day with such customs as leaving a vacant chair at the table to remember those Jews unable to celebrate *Pesach* freely.

The Omer

From the second night of Passover the *Omer* period begins, each day of which is counted by traditional Jews in accordance with an interpretation of Leviticus 23:15:

> And you shall count for yourself from the day after the *Shabbat* . . . seven weeks.

The counting goes on for forty-nine days, the fiftieth day being the festival of Pentecost, from the day on which the *Omer* ('measure' or 'sheaf') of barley was brought as an offering from the newly harvested crop to the Temple in Jerusalem. Although the Pharisees interpreted the phrase 'the day after the *Shabbat'* to refer to the second day of *Pesach*, the first day being a *yom tov* also being called *Shabbat* because no work is done on it, the Sadducees and later on the Karaites took it literally as referring to Sunday. They therefore always celebrated Pentecost on a Sunday seven weeks later. For contemporary Jews this whole agricultural/sacrificial dimension plays little part in their lives, its only significance being that new cereals cannot be eaten till after the second day of *Pesach*. There is some dispute among halakhists as to whether this prohibition applies outside the land of Israel.[12] The counting of the *Omer* still continues today, but the period has come to be one of semi-mourning and Orthodox Jews do not cut their hair or shave, and do not celebrate weddings, for most of these seven weeks. The origins of this mourning are unclear. The most common reason given for it is that in the second century the pupils of R. Akiva died during the *Omer* period. In practice there is no agreement about when the mourning begins and ends, and a variety of different customs are mentioned in halakhic literature.[13] There is, however, general agreement that the mourning is interrupted on the 33rd day of the *Omer*, known as *Lag Ba-Omer*, and this is a very popular date for weddings.

The nature of *Lag Ba-Omer* itself is obscure, and a number of explanations are given for its origin. The popular imagination has adopted a kabbalistic teaching that *Lag Ba-Omer* is the day on which the sage, and reputed author of the *Zohar*, R. Simeon bar Yochai finally revealed his secret teaching to his disciples and died. The day is one of great celebration among kabbalists, who describe R. Simeon's death as the wedding between his soul and God, and pilgrimages are made to the sage's tomb in Meron in the Galilee where large bonfires are lit and there is much singing and dancing. This pilgrimage is particularly important to Oriental Jews who camp at Meron and give the place the atmosphere of a fair. They also slaughter sheep there, to the annoyance of the Israeli health authorities. It is quite usual for a Jew from an Oriental community to undertake a vow to visit R. Simeon's grave in gratitude for some recovery from sickness or stroke of good fortune. Candles are lit on the tomb on *Lag Ba-Omer* and the *Zohar* is studied, while young boys who have entered their fourth year have their first haircut (*upsherinish*) at Meron, the hair being cast into the bonfires. Elsewhere in Israel the day is celebrated with bonfires, and with games involving bows and arrows.

Other days during the *Omer* period have attained the status of minor festivals in recent times among some sections of Jewry, and even interrupt the mourning restrictions. There is Israel Independence Day which is celebrated on the 20th day of the *Omer*, the 5th of the Hebrew month *Iyyar*, and is a national holiday in Israel, the day preceding it being a memorial day for those killed in Israel's wars. No set form of religious ritual has as yet been accepted for celebrating Independence Day, and whereas religious Zionists see it as commemorating an act of divine redemption with messianic overtones, anti-Zionist Orthodox Jews manifest public mourning at what they take to be the desecration of Jewish values by Zionists. Another national/religious festival is Jerusalem Day, commemorating the re-unification of the city after the 1967 war, which falls on the 43rd day of the *Omer*, the 28th of *Iyyar*. A day of a rather different nature, about which there is less controversy, is Holocaust Remembrance Day on the 12th day of the *Omer*, 27th of *Nisan*. Gatherings are held in Jewish communities throughout the world to remember the genocide of the Jewish people under the Nazi regime, and to celebrate Jewish resistance in the uprising of the Warsaw Ghetto. Since many Holocaust survivors are still alive the day has remained a fairly strong element of Jewish life. Whether it will survive the passing of the generation of the Holocaust remains to be seen.

Pentecost

Pentecost (*Shavuot*) is a one day festival (two days in the Diaspora) for which no fixed date is given in the Bible. It falls on the 50th day after the *Omer* offering is brought, and with the advent of a calendar based on calculation rather than the sighting of the moon it was assigned to the 6th of the Hebrew month *Sivan*. In the Bible it is described as a harvest festival (Exodus 23:16), but its main significance for later Jewish consciousness is its association with the revelation of the *Torah* at Mt. Sinai. The harvest element of the festival is subservient to the theme of the Sinai Covenant, and agricultural rituals and customs associated with *Shavuot* are re-interpreted in line with this theme. Thus it is a custom to decorate the synagogue with greenery for the festival, a custom opposed by some halakhists since it is too similar to Christian practices of decorating the church at harvest time,[14] which is explained as symbolizing the greenery surrounding Mt. Sinai. The custom of eating cheese and milk dishes on *Shavuot*, a custom connected with harvest festivals in other cultures, is given a variety of explanations linking it with Sinai, for instance that the Jews could only eat milk then because they were subject to the dietary laws after the revelation and needed time to ritually slaughter their cattle. Even the custom of baking special loaves of bread for *Shavuot*, which is a festival of the wheat harvest, is seen by some as an oblique reference to the *Torah*, the spiritual 'bread' of the Jews.

The first night of the festival is spent by some Orthodox Jews in a long vigil of *Torah* study, which ends with prayers at dawn. In Jerusalem whole congregations, after a night of study, make their way just before dawn to the Western Wall (or Wailing Wall) of the Temple mount to pray in the shadow of the Temple. The custom of a night-long vigil, known as *Tikkun Leil Shavuot*, is explained from a midrashic account of how the Israelites overslept at Sinai, and had to be awakened by Moses. Their descendants, therefore, stay awake all night to be ready to receive the *Torah* anew. The custom became institutionalized under kabbalistic influence, and a special book of readings was prepared to be recited during the vigil. On the day of the festival the Ten Commandments are read from the *Torah* scroll in the synagogue, as is the opening section of the Book of Ezekiel which is about the prophet's vision of the divine throne. It is also customary to read the Book of Ruth during the festival, since the story of Ruth is set in harvest time and Ruth's descendant King David is reputed to have died on the 7th of *Sivan*. A number of special hymns are sung in the synagogue in honour of the *Torah* and the Sinaitic theophany. In modern times two further dimensions have been added to the festival. Among Reform Jews it has become the period for the confirmation of young Jews, because they thus re-affirm the ancient covenant and because of the story of Ruth who voluntarily accepted the Jewish religion. In Israel the agricultural aspects of *Shavuot* have been resurrected on secularist kibbutzim, with ceremonies connected with the grain harvest and the ripening of the first fruits. This is in line with a general tendency among Israeli secularists to find a renewed land-based, rather than historical/ritual-based, religion of national identity to give meaning to the traditional festivals.

The Three Weeks of Mourning

The last part of the Jewish ritual year, leading up to the month of *Elul* and the New Year festival which follows it, is a period of intense mourning remembering the destruction of the First and Second Temples. It also encapsulates the whole Jewish experience of suffering in exile. The period begins with the fast of the 17th of *Tammuz* (which usually falls in July), 'the fast of the fourth month' mentioned by the prophet Zechariah (8:19) according to rabbinic exegesis. Jewish tradition relates five tragic events to this date, the most significant of which was the breach in the walls of Jerusalem prior to the destruction of the Second Temple. Originally the fast was held on the 9th of *Tammuz*, the date that Jeremiah (52:6) records the breach in the walls of Jerusalem during the First Temple period. Since the dates were so close together, and the destruction of the Second Temple was felt to be a greater tragedy for Jewry, the 17th of *Tammuz* came to represent the events of both Temples. The *Jerusalem Talmud* even claims that the original date of the 9th of *Tammuz* was simply a mistake, caused by the confusion of the times, and that the breach took place on the 17th of *Tammuz* on both occasions.[15] The period of mourning which follows the fast is characterized by a prohibition on weddings, on partaking of meat and wine during weekdays, on cutting the hair, on acquiring new garments, and on wearing freshly laundered clothes. In most communities these restrictions, with the exception of that on weddings, are only adhered to during the last nine days of the three weeks of mourning which end with the fast of *Tishah Be-Av*, the 9th of the month of *Av*. The *Mishnah* sees this month as a time of generalized sorrow for the Jews: 'When *Av* begins rejoicing should be minimized.'[16] With the exception of *Yom Kippur* the 9th of *Av* is the only fast which begins at sunset and lasts till nightfall of the next day. As a sign of mourning it is forbidden to wear leather shoes, which provide a modicum of comfort; no *Torah* study is allowed since it 'rejoices the heart', with the exception of passages whose theme is suffering; and for the first half of the day the Jew must not sit on a normal chair or seat. The synagogue is darkened, with only sufficient light for the congregants to read their prayers, and the mantle is removed from the ark containing the *Torah* scrolls. The *tallit*, or prayer shawl, and the *tefillin*, or phylacteries, are not worn till the afternoon service, and some of the more joyous parts of the liturgy are not said. The biblical Book of Lamentations is read to a mournful melody, and special prayers of lamentation, *kinot*, are recited.

All in all *Tishah Be-Av* is the most sorrowful day of the Jewish year. Tradition has it that both the First and Second Temples were destroyed on this day, although the actual burning of the First Temple is ascribed to the 10th of *Av* by Jeremiah (52:12). It is also associated with other tragic events in Jewish history, and has come to symbolize the bitterness of Jewish suffering down the ages. Zion and Jerusalem are remembered in tears, but the day is capped by the hope that next year the fast will be turned into a day of gladness as prophesied by Zechariah (8:19). In modern Israel voices have been raised advocating a re-assessment of the fast in the light of the return of the Jews to their homeland, but no rabbis have indicated a willingness to take such a drastic step as abolishing the fast altogether. Even the new liturgical formula introduced by R. Shlomoh Goren, changing the prayer bemoaning the destitute condition of Jerusalem into the past tense, has not been generally accepted, and R. Goren was one of Israel's Chief Rabbis.

12

The Synagogue, Home and Jewish Community

The Synagogue

Every Jewish community today is built round a synagogue centre, which may vary from an elaborate building with stained-glass windows to an ordinary house converted into a place of worship. Sometimes the synagogue is part of a community centre which caters for the wider needs of its members in the areas of social life and sports. The synagogue is referred to by Yiddish-speaking Jews as a *shool*, after the German word for school, because in Eastern Europe the synagogue was also a place of study. In effect there are two kinds of synagogue, the *bet ha-keneset* or 'house of gathering' which is the synagogue proper used for prayers and other liturgical rites, and the *bet ha-midrash* or 'house of exegesis' which is used for study as well as regular services. The halakhic status of these two types of buildings differs; thus while the former should be the tallest building in the locality and one should neither eat nor sleep in it, these rules do not apply to the latter.[1] They also differ in internal structure, furniture and atmosphere. A *bet hamidrash* is usually well stocked with books, and is furnished in a manner conducive to men sitting together in groups studying, while a *bet ha-keneset* has pews, a fixed platform or *bimah* in the centre, an ark with an embroidered curtain at the end of the building facing Jerusalem in which the *Torah* scrolls are kept, and in the case of Orthodox synagogues a separate gallery for women.

Each community of Jews has developed its own unique form of synagogue, reflecting the host society in which it lived and the particular customs and religious views of the congregants. Oriental Jews, a small minority of whom remove their shoes before entering the synagogue, arrange their seating around the walls of the building and the *bimah*, whereas most Occidental Jews sit in lines of pews facing towards Jerusalem. The atmosphere in Progressive temples, and in German Orthodox synagogues, is formal and decorous, while in a Chasidic prayer house or *shtibl* (literally 'room') there is a very informal aura and decorum is not thought of as compatible with heartfelt prayer. Other synagogues range between these extremes of Chasidic casualness and Teutonic formality with most Ashkenazi congregations tending towards the former. The requirements necessary for a synagogue to be suitable for prayers have long been a bone of contention between Orthodox and Progressive Judaism. The separate seating of women has been insisted on by Orthodox rabbis, and they have forbidden Orthodox Jews to pray in, and even to enter, Progressive synagogues where there is no *mechitzah* or partition between the sexes. When mixed seating was first introduced by Reform communities in the nineteenth century it was greeted by strong opposition from Orthodox rabbis in Europe. R. Moses Sofer, the leading halakhist of Hungarian Jewry, emphasized that the separation of the sexes was necessary to prevent thoughts of a sexual nature interfering with the worshipper's concentration, and thus making his prayers unacceptable to God.[2] His pupil, R. Moses Schick, wrote a responsum to one congregation where some Jews wished to introduce mixed seating:

> Heaven forbid for you . . . to remain silent against the licentiousness of these arrogant people. For according to the law we must make a separation between the sections for men and for women. . . . It is necessary . . . that the men should not see the women, for this leads to levity and other sins. We must protest against the situation and reprove the sinners.[3]

Other features of the synagogue service have also widened the rift between Orthodoxy and Reform. The public role of women in the service, such as counting them for a *minyan* or quorum, calling them to the *Torah* reading, allowing them to lead the service and even ordaining them as rabbis, have all been regarded as undermining traditional halakhic rules by Orthodox rabbis. The use of the vernacular for prayer, changes in the liturgy, choirs in synagogue, and the use of musical instruments to accompany the liturgical singing, though some of these features are found in Modern Orthodox synagogues, have generally been condemned by Orthodoxy as imitations of Christianity. The resistance to change on the part of the traditionalists expresses the value which communal prayers have in the eyes of the *halakhah*. For though it is possible to pray in private at home, there is a frequent insistence in rabbinic literature on the importance of public, congregational, worship. The synagogue itself began as an institution during the Babylonian captivity, after the destruction of the First Temple, and became the central element of Jewish public life after the destruction of the Second Temple. Today it is an integral part of Jewish communal religion, and has even replaced the home for some modern Jews as the focus of ritual life.

The Jewish Home

The Jewish home is the major centre of Jewish life and ritual, and there are a number of differentiating features which mark out a Jewish house. Traditionally each doorway of a Jewish dwelling should have a *mezuzah*, or hand-written parchment scroll with the *Shema* on it, affixed to the doorpost in accordance with a literal interpretation of Deuteronomy 6:9 and 11:20. The scroll is rolled up and usually inserted in a case which is then nailed to the doorpost. The pious Jew will touch his fingers to the *mezuzah* and then lightly kiss them as he passes through a doorway, or more frequently when he leaves the house. Many Jews, even if not Orthodox, will at least have a *mezuzah* on the front doorpost of their home, and it is commonly regarded as a kind of talisman guarding the house from evil. The advocacy of the talismanic qualities of the *mezuzah* is found among halakhists influenced by the Kabbalah, and is based on talmudic precedents.[4] The talismanic idea is also the source of the addition of various formulae to the *mezuzah* parchment, which led Maimonides, the leading halakhic rationalist, to complain:

> But those who write the names of angels, or holy names, or a verse, or seals, inside [the *mezuzah*] are included among those who have no portion in the World to Come. For it is not sufficient for these fools to have nullified the *mitzvah*, but they have treated a great *mitzvah*, which involves the unification of the name of the Holy One, blessed be He, and His love and service, as if it were an amulet for personal benefit, since their foolish hearts think that this is something which brings benefit in worldly vanities.[5]

It is also customary, though by no means mandatory, for a traditional Jewish home to have a plaque or painted sign on a wall facing Jerusalem. Among Western Jews this is known as a *mizrach* (literally 'east'), and often consists of the Hebrew letters of the word *mizrach* surrounded by a decorative motif. Among Oriental Jews one finds more elaborate plaques with drawings and kabbalistic formulae, often in the shape of a hand, which are hung on the wall and regarded as amulets. The *halakhah* stipulates that a small area of wall space in a Jewish house should be left unpainted or unpapered, as a memorial to the destruction of the Temple.[6] This sign of perpetual mourning has, however, fallen somewhat into desuetude among modern Jews.

The Family

Since the home is regarded as the focus of religious activity in Judaism, the family plays a role not only as the basic unit of social life but also as the primary milieu of ritual expression. All the festivals are permeated by home-based rituals, and the *Shabbat* is structured round the family meals. In a traditional family the male householder is the dominant person, both in matters of religion and as the master of the house. The *midrash* depicts the ideal wife as one who does the will of her husband, and Maimonides writes in his code:

> The sages have commanded [the Jewish] wife that she should be modest inside her house, and that she should not overindulge in levity before her husband. . . . The sages have also commanded the husband to honour the wife more than his very self, and to love her as himself . . . and not to make her fear him overmuch. His speech with her should be gentle, and he should not be touchy or angry. They have also commanded the wife that she should greatly honour her husband, and stand in awe of him.[7]

This traditional picture has been modified in modern times with the change in the roles and expectations of the woman. Among those Orthodox Jewish groups which live in self-imposed ghettos without walls, rejecting modern attitudes, and among some Oriental Jewish communities, one finds the closest approximation to the male-dominated home. The Jewish rituals themselves preserve something of the primacy of the male, though the popular stereotype of the Jewish wife and mother depicts her as a domineering and over-protective creature. It may be that the formal dominance of the husband was often simply a veneer for the informal role of the wife, who exercised the real power over her children and over her occasionally hen-pecked husband. Certainly the home and children were very much her preserve, since the husband would be away working, attending prayer services, or studying in the synagogue.

Dietary Laws

Central to the life of the Orthodox Jew, and to a lesser extent of the Progressive Jew, are the plethora of dietary requirements which shape Jewish food habits, and give the Jewish home a distinctive ritual atmosphere. Adherence to these requirements ranges from strict observance on the part of many Orthodox Jews, to only partial observance or complete rejection on the part of some Reform Jews and most Jewish secularists. Even those who neglect the ritual dimension of diet often tend to eat kosher-style food, which has emerged as a consequence of the traditional cuisine. For the Orthodox Jew eating is a ritual activity charged with religious meaning, to be preceded and followed by the appropriate benedictions and for some foods requiring the ritual washing of the hands. The dietary laws are seen as part of the attempt to sanctify the ordinary life of man, and to transmute him into a holy creature of God. The general term for permissible food is *kasher*, which has passed into English, via the Ashkenazi pronunciation, as 'kosher'. In the *halakhah* there are a series of technical terms applying to different areas of *kashrut*, but the term *kasher* is colloquially accepted as delineating all those foods which the traditional Jew may eat.

MEAT AND FISH

Certain species of animals are permitted, and others prohibited, in the Bible.[8] Animals which both chew the cud and have a cloven hoof, such as cattle, sheep, goats and deer, are permitted, while those which do not have these characteristics, or only have one *kasher* feature, such as camels (which chew the cud) or pigs (which have a cloven hoof), are forbidden. Fish which have fins and scales are likewise permitted, while all other sea creatures are prohibited. The situation with birds is slightly more complicated, since the Bible simply lists twenty-four species of forbidden birds, not all of which were known or could be determined by the *halakhah*. Birds are therefore considered *kasher* if there is a reliable tradition that they were eaten by Jews in the past, and different communities maintain their own customs with regard to such traditions. Certain kinds of locust are also mentioned as *kasher*, and Jews from countries where locusts are found, such as Morocco or the Yemen, eat those locusts about which they have a tradition of *kashrut*.

The *kasher* varieties of animals and birds need to be ritually slaughtered before they can be prepared as food. This ritual slaughter, *shechitah*, has to be done by a *shochet*, in practice a qualified adult Jewish male, although in theory a woman or minor could also perform the act.[9] *Shechitah* entails passing a completely smooth knife horizontally across the windpipe and gullet of the animal. This must be done in one swift act. It is forbidden to eat the flesh of an animal which has died naturally, or been killed through other methods, as it is to eat a limb torn off a living animal. With a non-domesticated animal, or a bird, the blood must be symbolically covered with soil or ashes in accordance with the rabbinic interpretation of Leviticus 17:13. A blessing should be made both over the *shechitah*, and, where applicable, over the covering of the blood. Neither fish nor locusts need to be ritually slaughtered, and may be eaten once dead however they have been killed. A slaughtered animal has to be carefully examined to ensure that it is not diseased, for if it is it will be considered *terefah* and unfit for consumption. The lungs need to be scrutinized with particular care, and other internal organs are investigated for punctures caused by the animal swallowing sharp objects.

Certain parts of the fat of domesticated animals are forbidden and must be removed, as must the sciatic nerve, known as 'the sinew of the thigh vein',[10] and in both domesticated and nondomesticated animals the major arteries are excised. Considerable expertise is needed for porging some of these forbidden parts, and it is usual for the whole hindquarters of the animal not to be consumed at all in most Diaspora communities rather than have it porged. Once all the forbidden parts are removed the meat of all types of animals has to be salted to remove blood. First the meat is soaked in water for about half an hour to loosen up the pores, then it is allowed to drain for a short time before being sprinkled all over with a coarse salt, and left for an hour. The meat is finally rinsed to remove the salt and any blood it has absorbed. This whole process used to be done by the housewife, but is more often performed by the butcher today prior to being sold. Liver cannot be drained of its blood by salting, and has to be grilled over a flame after having been cut across the surface and lightly sprinkled with salt. Meat may also have its blood removed by grilling rather than by salting, but the latter is the more usual procedure.

MEAT AND MILK

It is forbidden to cook and eat meat and milk together, according to the rabbinic interpretation of the thrice repeated biblical prohibition on boiling a kid in its mother's milk.[11] The *halakhah* extended this prohibition to all animals and birds, although the original biblical proscription was understood as referring only to domesticated animals. Fish and locusts are not included in the rabbinic extension of this prohibition,[12] but fish and meat are not cooked or eaten together on health grounds.

In order to maintain the complete separation between meat and milk the Orthodox Jew has two sets of kitchen ware, crockery, cutlery and washing-up facilities. These are kept apart, and sometimes the milk ware is specially marked to avoid any possibility of mixing it up with that used for meat. Utensils and dishes which are used for neither meat nor milk are called *parev*, and dishes may be prepared in them for use with either meat or milk. The separation between meat and milk extends as far as maintaining a time interval, ranging from six hours to one hour in different communities, after eating meat before milk dishes may be eaten. This is variously explained because of the particles of meat which remain between the teeth, or because of the fatty aftertaste in the mouth, which need time to dissipate. After milk foods all that is necessary is a cleansing of the mouth and hands before eating meat.[13] Just as the dietary laws restrict the use of meat to animals which are *kasher*, so animal by-products such as milk or eggs are only permissible if they come from *kasher* animals. The only exception is bees' honey, the bee itself not being *kasher*, which is allowed on the grounds that honey is never really part of the bee but is extraneous material carried by the insect.[14]

VEGETABLES AND FRUIT

Since insects and worms are forbidden by the *halakhah*, vegetables and fruits which may contain them must be examined and cleaned before use. Thus, for instance, lettuce must be thoroughly washed and then inspected to ensure that all small insects have been removed. Aside from this restriction there is a general prohibition on growing mixed seed plants together, on sowing a vineyard with other crops, and on grafting different kinds of trees onto each other. The details of these laws are complex, and the rabbis have their own system of taxonomy for deciding what are different botanical species. Some of these laws only apply to the produce of the land of Israel, while others affect the Diaspora as well. These restrictions are known as *kilayim,* and are based on passages in the Bible.[15] It is also forbidden to wear clothes woven from a mixture of wool and flax, and Orthodox Jews have new garments examined by an expert to ensure that no such mixture, *shaatnez,* exists in the material. The fruit of a new tree is forbidden for the first three years, and no benefit may be had from it. This restriction, based on Leviticus 19:23, is known as *orlah.* The fruit of the fourth year had to be taken to Jerusalem to be consumed there, or redeemed for money which was used to buy food to be eaten in Jerusalem. Nowadays the fruit of the fourth year is symbolically redeemed for a small coin. The same laws apply to vineyards.

There are a whole series of laws, originating in biblical times, concerning the produce of the land of Israel. Most of these laws only affect the farmer, but two important categories are part of the dietary laws of the Jewish consumer. The first is the need to tithe the produce of the Holy Land, the tithes being given to the priest, *kohen,* the levite, and either to the poor or alternatively during certain years to be taken to Jerusalem to be eaten there. Today it is customary simply to set aside a little over a hundredth part of the produce, to designate the tithes in this and in the rest of the produce, and to redeem those tithes which are redeemable for a small coin. Except for the small amount set aside, which may not be eaten, the rest of the food is now formally tithed and may be consumed. A further tithe applies to dough prepared for the baking of bread or cakes,[16] which originally applied only in Israel but was extended to the Diaspora. When the dough is kneaded a small amount of the tithe, known as *challah,* is set aside. This used to be given to a *kohen,* but since no priest is in a state of ritual purity today it is burnt instead. Traditionally the separation of *challah* was one of the *mitzvot* seen as the preserve of the Jewish housewife, although Jewish bakers also take *challah* from their products.

The second category of agricultural laws which affects the consumer directly is that concerning the produce of the land of Israel during the last year of the seven-year cycle, the *shemittah* or sabbatical year. The Bible prescribes a complete cessation of all agricultural labour during this year, and the *halakhah* extends this to forbid the produce of the Holy Land after it becomes unavailable in the fields, and also forbids trade in *shemittah* produce and limits the uses to which it may be put. In order to overcome what would be a severe economic hardship for Israeli agriculture, exports, and the home market, the Israel rabbinate has developed an halakhic solution to the *shemittah* problem. This involves selling all Jewish held land to a gentile for the duration of the year, since the sabbatical laws apply only to Jewish-owned land. Although this solution is based on the ruling of some of the leading sages of the last hundred years, it has been consistently opposed by other halakhists as invalid or ineffectual. The arguments of the two camps are essentially of a technical nature, but those who support the land sale solution are generally Zionist in outlook, and those who oppose it non-Zionist. While the majority of Orthodox Jews rely on the land sale, a minority of Orthodox Jews in Israel go to great lengths to buy produce of Arab-owned lands, or that imported from abroad, rather than eat *shemittah* produce.

WINE, MILK, CHEESE AND COOKED FOOD OF GENTILES

While the dietary laws have the incidental consequence that Jews who wish to keep them need to live in Jewish communities where the supporting institutions of *kashrut* are to be found, there is a further series of laws which has, as one of its aims, the limitation of social intercourse between Jews and gentiles. It is true that even with regard to some of the more basic *kashrut* laws many Jews only preserve them with any degree of strictness in their homes, and are willing to eat non-*kasher* food in restaurants and in the homes of others. With regard to those dietary restrictions, introduced by the rabbis to discourage socializing with gentiles and any subsequent intermarriage, there is perhaps greater laxity among Jews in modern society. Prominent among these latter restrictions are the prohibitions on gentile wine, and on food, even made out of *kasher* ingredients, cooked by a gentile. The prohibition on wine was originally introduced because of the idolatrous libations poured from wine, which made it anathema to Jews. Once such libations ceased the rabbis maintained the prohibition 'because of their daughters', i.e. to prevent the kind of conviviality brought about by drinking wine which might lead to intermarriage.[17] Not only is gentile wine forbidden, but the prohibition extends to Jewish wine handled by a gentile while in an unsealed container. Other alcohol, not wine-based, is permitted as long as it is drunk by the Jew at home, or casually among gentiles, but not where it would lead to the possibility of conviviality and intermarriage.[18]

The food cooked by a gentile (*bishul akkum*) is forbidden if its main ingredients cannot be eaten raw, and it is the kind of food served at 'a king's table', i.e. food of some importance. These qualifications enable traditional Jews to eat many of the foods prepared by gentiles, and some rabbis do not apply the whole prohibition of gentile-cooked food to mass-produced items such as tins or packaged goods, because no social intercourse with gentiles is involved. Where a non-Jewish cook is employed in a Jewish household a symbolic act of participating in the cooking, e.g. lighting the gas or stirring a pot, is undertaken by one of the Jewish members of the household to ensure the food is not wholly gentile-cooked.[19]

The prohibition on gentile milk is not to prevent social intercourse, but to ensure that the milk comes from a *kasher* animal. Theoretically a Jew should be present at the milking, and in some Orthodox communities gentile milk is produced under Jewish supervision. In the main, however, Jews rely on government regulations restricting the milk sold by dairies to cows' milk, and such reliance has been given halakhic sanction by R. Moshe Feinstein, a leading American rabbi, although his ruling has come in for some criticism.[20] Gentile cheese is also forbidden, although there is no general agreement among halakhists as to why this should be so if all the cheesemaking ingredients are *kasher*. While some medieval authorities believed that the prohibition did not apply any more, the majority of halakhists maintain that cheese remains forbidden even if made from vegetarian rennet, and can only be considered *kasher* if supervised by a Jew.[21]

Jewish Community

A traditional Jewish community needs a number of professionals who carry on its ritual and liturgical functions. Larger communities are usually served by more than one professional of each type, while smaller ones either manage with occasional professional help or else employ a man of many parts, a so-called *kol-bo-nik*, to act in a number of different roles. Modern communities, where the synagogue is part of a community centre, will also employ a number of professionals to act as programme directors, welfare workers, youth leaders, etc. The main traditional professionals, known somewhat derogatively as *kelei kodesh* or 'holy vessels', are as follows.

THE RABBI

The title 'Rabbi' means 'My Master' and was applied to a Palestinian sage in talmudic times whose major role was as a teacher. He was someone expert in the *Torah* and was ordained to decide cases of Jewish law, although he would usually earn his living by other means. This situation persisted well into the Middle Ages when some of the most famous rabbis were doctors or merchants who regarded it as prohibited to take money for any *Torah* teaching.

The justification for paying the professional rabbi is that he is not being paid for his religious work, but being compensated for other work he might have undertaken when he is engaged in rabbinical duties. Today the rabbi is usually paid by a congregation whom he serves as teacher, preacher, expert on religious law, officiant at marriages and funerals, and pastoral counsellor.

The Orthodox rabbi proper has received ordination, *semikhah*, from an already-ordained rabbi. In order to qualify for this ordination the candidate has to master certain sections of the *Shulchan Arukh* dealing with complicated questions of *kashrut*, and to be someone who knows and follows the halakhic prescriptions for everyday life. Of course such a training for ordination does not necessarily equip the rabbi of a modern synagogue for his task, and rabbinical seminaries run by Modern Orthodox and Progressive movements have a much wider curriculum for their rabbinical programme.

In larger Jewish communities there would be a full-time or part-time rabbinical court, or *Bet Din*, dealing both with specialized matters of divorce and conversion as well as with halakhic issues once well within the competence of the individual rabbi. The supervision of the ritual slaughter of meat, and the responsibility for a whole range of *kashrut* facilities, may well come under the aegis of the *Bet Din* whose members will have received a more thorough traditional training than most modern rabbis.

Although the generic term for the senior synagogue official is 'rabbi', not all who actually serve in this capacity have been ordained. The rabbi of a congregation is not a priest, and most of his functions can be performed by a learned Jew whether or not he has received *semikhah*. In Britain the spiritual leader of a community who has not been ordained will style himself 'Reverend', while in North America he would be referred to as 'Rabbi' out of respect for his position. Sefardi Jews generally prefer the title '*Chakham*' ('sage') to 'Rabbi', although in most Western countries they tend to follow Ashkenazi nomenclature. It is not unusual to find that a leading halakhic authority, with an international reputation, does not in fact hold any official position as a rabbi within the community. His piety and scholarship, rather than any formal title or status, have won him renown as a sage and his rulings on legal matters are accepted as authoritative.

THE CANTOR

According to the *halakhah* any adult male Jew may lead the prayers, read from the *Torah* and perform other synagogue rituals. The synagogue is a totally lay institution, and only the priestly blessing[22] needs to be delivered by a *kohen*. This blessing is delivered on the major festivals among Orthodox communities in the Diaspora, and more frequently in Israel. In Progressive synagogues it is the rabbi, rather than a *kohen*, who would deliver the blessing. Despite the possibility of lay participation many large synagogues employ a specially trained, full-time, cantor to conduct the services. He is known as a *chazan*, the title of a community official in talmudic times whose role as cantor dates back to the geonic period. The modern cantor, and the style of music he now uses, began to emerge in the nineteenth century with the emancipation of the European Jew. The Central European influence on cantorial music has, by now, been overlaid by Chasidic musical traditions as well as by Oriental Jewish melodies and modern Israeli compositions.

The ideal cantor should be free of sin, not have a bad reputation, be humble, and acceptable to the congregation. He should also possess a pleasant voice, but the *halakhah* stipulates that the piety and scholarship of the *chazan* are more important than the quality of his voice.[23] Nevertheless congregants have expectations of cantorial performance which demand an operatic style and virtuosity from the cantor, with considerations of piety playing very much a background role.

THE RITUAL SLAUGHTERER

The need for *kasher* meat necessitates the employment of a highly trained *shochet*, or ritual slaughterer, by the Jewish community. In smaller communities he might well combine this work with other religious duties, such as teaching, circumcision, and cantorial duties. Because of the responsibilities of his work the *shochet* has to be a completely trustworthy individual, who will usually possess a certificate of proficiency in ritual slaughter. In the past numerous communal disputes arose over *shochetim* whose slaughtering methods were suspect, and the rabbi should examine the *shochet* and his knife to ensure that he is up to the mark. If any serious deficiency is found the rabbi should declare him unfit, and the product of his slaughter as unsuitable for *kasher* consumption.[24] It is the *shochet*'s duty to examine the carcass of the slaughtered animal in order to detect any disease which might make it *terefah*, and therefore inedible by Jews.

Although Judaism accepts the eating of *kasher* meat as perfectly legitimate, there is considerable ambiguity felt towards the *shochet*'s work, and to the taking of life for the purposes of food. This is brought out in a talmudic tale about R. Judah the Prince who was afflicted with suffering because when a calf, on its way to slaughter, took refuge under his cloak he said to it: 'Go, for you were created for this.' The sufferings were brought upon him because he had no pity on the animal, and they only left him when, on a later occasion, he took pity on some house-mice that his servant girl was about to kill.[25]

MINOR FUNCTIONARIES

Aside from the three main categories of communal professionals, the rabbi, the *chazan* and the *shochet*, there are a number of minor roles which are often combined with each other or with employment of a different nature. There is the sextant or beadle, *shamash*, who looks after the synagogue and in olden times would call people to the daily prayers. There is the assistant cantor, *chazan sheni*, who often reads the weekly section of the *Torah* in synagogue, and leads the prayers during weekdays. There is also the *mohel*, who performs ritual circumcisions, the *melamed*, who teaches in the religion school or *cheder*, and the *sofer*, or scribe, who writes and repairs *Torah* scrolls, *mezuzah* parchments, *tefillin*, and bills of divorce (*get*) for the *Bet Din*.

LAY LEADERSHIP

The synagogue itself is run by elected officials, who serve in an honorary capacity and are in charge of all administrative matters. In an Orthodox synagogue the Board of Management, the synagogue president (*rosh ha-kahal*), and the warden (*gabbai*) will all be elected from among the male congregants. The ladies will form their own Ladies Guild or Sisterhood, whose usual role is fund-raising, catering preparations, and other secondary synagogue support activities. In a Progressive congregation the women play a more active role in synagogue management, and in some cases even act as full-time rabbis or cantors. The exclusion of women from positions of synagogue control in Orthodox congregations is based on an halakhic ruling, which lays it down that a reigning Jewish monarch has always to be a king and not a queen.[26] Orthodox opposition to females acting as rabbis or cantors is much more far-reaching, and involves basic assumptions about the different religious roles of men and women.

Communal Diversity

Jews are united with each other by a series of interlocking matrices of religious belief and practice, shared historical memories, and a deeply rooted sense of group identity and solidarity. For all that Jewish communities are pluralistic conglomerates, with differences not only between one Jewish community and another but also between sub-groups within the same community. A well known Jewish joke has it that if you put two Jews together you will obtain three opinions, and another one tells of the Jew who was shipwrecked on a desert island. When rescued he was found to have built two synagogues on the island, although he was quite alone as a castaway. He explained his strange action with the remark, 'One synagogue is for me to go to for prayer, and the other is the synagogue that I would never set foot in.'

One of the most long-standing divisions among Jews is that between Ashkenazim and Sefardim. The term 'Ashkenazi' in its narrow sense means someone of German origin, and 'Sefardi' means someone of Spanish origin, based on the medieval understanding of the use of the two terms in Genesis 10:3 and Obadiah 1:20.27 According to a popular, but over-simplistic notion, Jews from Central and Eastern Europe are Ashkenazim, having migrated there from Germany, and Jews from North Africa, the Levant, and the East are Sefardim, having come from the Iberian peninsula. In fact, however, while most Ashkenazi Jews share a common culture, a culture once based on Yiddish which was the Ashkenazi *lingua franca*, it is not possible to lump all other Jewish communities together as Sefardim. The Jews of Italy, the Yemen and Soviet Georgia have all preserved a distinctive Jewish culture of their own which cannot simply be classified as Sefardi. There is also a major distinction between many of the Oriental Jewish communities who absorbed some of the highly sophisticated culture of the Iberian Jews who migrated to their countries and integrated it with their own Jewish customs, and the Spanish and Portuguese Jews in Holland and the eastern Mediterranean. The latter preserved Ladino, a Spanish dialect, as their Jewish *lingua franca* after their expulsion from the Iberian peninsula in the 1490's, as well as many distinctively Spanish-Jewish cultural elements.

The Ashkenazim and Sefardim developed in relative isolation from each other in the late Middle Ages, with Ashkenazim living in Christian countries and Sefardim in Islamic ones. There was some intellectual cross-fertilization, with scholarly works finding their way from one sub-culture to the other, but these channels of communication varied considerably with time and place. The main differences between Ashkenazim and Sefardim are in their respective liturgical usages, halakhic norms, customs, methods of study, pronunciation of Hebrew, musical traditions, attitudes to their surrounding gentile cultures, the influence of the Kabbalah, and the superstitions assimilated on a popular level from their respective environments. There are no major theological differences between them that would act as a barrier to intermarriage between Ashkenazim and Sefardim, or prevent them attending each other's synagogues or participating in their rituals. Most of Ashkenazi Jewry today has adopted Western education and culture, and this has created a large social and economic gap between them and their Sefardi-Oriental co-religionists in Israel. The Ashkenazim there represent a socially advantaged group, while the Sefardim, whose culture is based on pre-modern Islamic models, represent the socially disadvantaged sections of society. Not so long ago, however, the Sefardim who had settled in Britain and the USA were socially more developed then the Eastern European Ashkenazi migrants who followed them to these countries. Even today there is a certain social stigma for a member of an old-established Sefardi family to marry an Ashkenazi. In Israel the stigma works the other way, and many Israelis of Ashkenazi origin are thought of as marrying 'down' if they take a spouse from a Sefardi-Oriental family. Whereas Yiddish preserves a number of derogatory terms for Sefardi Jews, and prejudicial folk-sayings about them, Oriental Jews in Israel refer to their Ashkenazi co-religionists as 'vuzz-vuzzim', a term mimicking the Ashkenazi manner of speech.

The differences between Ashkenazim and Sefardim are all found, to a greater or lesser degree, among the various sub-communities within these two sections of Jewry. Ashkenazi Jews pronounce their Hebrew in a number of different ways, and the different dialects of prayer found among German, Hungarian, Lithuanian, Russian and Polish Jews are as divergent as those between Ashkenazim and Sefardim themselves. The same is true of the differences between the pronunciation of Italian or Yemenite Jews and true Sefardim. Different liturgies and customs exist in these many Jewish sub-groups, as do attitudes to gentile culture, Kabbalah and popular superstitions. Various Ashkenazi or Sefardi communities look down on other communal elements who like them are Ashkenazim or Sefardim. There are bitter rivalries and prejudices between German and Polish Jews, between Poles and Russians, Hungarians and Russo-Poles, and between Roumanian Jews and other Eastern European Jewries. Many 'ethnic' jokes are told reflecting the negative qualities preserved by these stereotypes: German Jews are unimaginative, cold, and do everything by the book, Jews from southern Poland and Hungary are pious fools, Lithuanian Jews are impious scholars, Roumanian Jews are out-and-out thieves. Many of these prejudices, like those between Ashkenazim and Sefardim, have remained deeply ingrained in the consciousness of the older generation of Jews. For their children, however, the attitudes of parents and grandparents seem largely irrelevant to the realities of Jewish life in the West and in Israel. The old communal boundaries have largely broken down under the impact of Nazi persecution, the vast migration of Jews during the last forty years, and the centrality of Jewish national consciousness.

13

Trends and Movements within Contemporary Judaism

Religious Diversity

The divisions between Ashkenazim and Sefardim are essentially a matter of historical and geographical accident, the product of centuries of isolation and separate development. Those between Orthodox and Progressive Judaism are of a totally different nature, and often represent real differences in outlook and attitudes. Until comparatively recent times the Orthodox/Progressive schism affected only Ashkenazi Jews and those small numbers of Sefardim living in Western Europe. It had no effect on the large, traditional communities of Sefardim living in Islamic countries. It is only with the mass exodus of Jews from Arab and Asian lands since the establishment of the State of Israel that the tensions between tradition and modernity, underlying the Orthodox/Progressive split, have begun to affect them. There is, however, no significant movement among them to reform Jewish norms to bring them into line with modern beliefs. This is largely ascribable to the different milieu into which they are emerging from their cultural ghetto. The emancipation of European Jewry brought Jews into contact with a Christian world in which Christian values, albeit enlightened ones, were still operative. In modern Israel, where this new emancipation is taking place, the dominant non-Judaic culture is that of a secularized, post-industrialized, Western world.

Reform Judaism

Reform Judaism began in the eighteenth century with demands for change in Jewish practice and doctrine on the part of German Jewish intellectuals. The precursors of this demand for modernization still saw themselves as belonging to traditional Judaism, and advocated their innovations to make Jews and Judaism an acceptable part of gentile society. Thus Moses Mendelssohn tried to refine the language of his co-religionists by translating the Bible into German, a work begun in 1780. He wished to revise educational programmes to give Jews a better grasp of the Hebrew tongue, the Bible, and the moral values of Judaism. He also wanted to see vocational training introduced for Jewish youth, and a grounding in subjects like mathematics and literature, alongside traditional Jewish studies. The process which Mendelssohn and his disciples set in motion had its own inner momentum. Christianity seemed less alien to the emancipated, and educated, Jew, and since it had much in common with the Judaic heritage the passage to the baptismal font was a natural progression for some. Others, who baulked at the rejection of their own religious tradition, nevertheless wished to see the successful emancipation of the Jews and sought to bring about the changes in Jewish tradition which would ensure this. They also wished to be able to hold on to those who had already negotiated the process of acculturation, and found themselves alienated from the 'old world' synagogue.

The reforms introduced by Israel Jacobson into the service and liturgy, from 1810 onwards, were intended to enhance the rate of emancipation and to provide facilities for the already emancipated Jew. German hymns, the use of the organ, a mixed choir, a sermon in the vernacular, the shortening of the prayers, and the institution of a confirmation ceremony for boys, were all steps in this direction. Although Jacobson called his place of worship a temple, thus distinguishing it from the traditional synagogue, he saw himself as improving on pre-emancipation Judaism and not as creating a new religious movement. At the same time as these liturgical adjustments there was a general re-assessment of some elements of Jewish doctrine which seemed incongruous with the attitudes of the German Jew integrated into gentile society. Such ideas as the hope for a return to Zion, the rebuilding of the Temple in Jerusalem, and the reinstitution of animal sacrifices, were all out of phase with the outlook of emancipation.

This process of liturgical reform and doctrinal re-assessment, however, had no natural limits. A new prayer book was produced for the Hamburg Temple in 1819, and a controversial second edition came out in 1841 already reflecting the re-interpretation of ideas on the Messiah and on Zion. In the early stages the supporters of reform backed up their case with an appeal to halakhic precedent, even though such appeals were unacceptable to their more traditionalist opponents. With the development of a whole new intellectual climate associated with historical and literary studies on the Jewish past, the movement known as the Science of Judaism, an attempt was made to extend reforms into wider areas of Jewish life and ritual. The reformers now possessed an ideological perspective on the evolutionary patterns of Jewish religious growth. The division between traditionalists and reformers was now not simply a matter of resisting or promulgating cosmetic changes to halakhic practice, but a basic divergence of attitudes to the authority and character of Jewish teaching. There were radical thinkers both in Europe and America who wished to reshape Judaism anew, and jettison most of the rituals connected with diet, circumcision, the *Shabbat* and festivals. Their justification was that Judaism had grown through different cultures, absorbing external influences *en route*, and for it to exist in the modern world it must discard outworn forms and adopt new ones.

This diversity of approach between moderate reformers, such as Abraham Geiger, and radical reformers, such as Samuel Holdheim, has continued within Reform Judaism right down to the present day. It was characteristic not only of continental Europe, but of other areas to which the reforming movement spread. In Britain the first Reform congregation was founded in 1840 by a group of well-to-do London merchants, who had broken away from established Orthodox synagogues. Their attitudes to reform were of the moderate variety, and this has been the dominant pattern of British Reform Judaism ever since. The congregation they founded, the West London Synagogue of British Jews, accepted the authority and divinity of the Bible but took a more flexible attitude to the rabbinic tradition. The prayer book they published was closely modelled on the Orthodox *siddur*, with minor liturgical variations, and their theological position on the restoration of the Temple cult, the Messiah, and the return to Zion, did not reflect the caveats of some of the German reformers. It was only in 1902 that the more radical position became institutionalized with the foundation of Liberal Judaism. The latter even went so far as to advocate the change of *Shabbat* services from Saturday to Sunday. A leading member of early Liberal Judaism, Claude Montefiore, accepted that the Pentateuch was non-Mosaic, rejected Zionism as a negation of Jewish universalism, and took a sympathetic view of the teachings of Jesus and of Christianity. Lilian Montague, one of Montefiore's collaborators in the establishment of the Liberal Jewish movement, then known as the Jewish Religious Union, herself conducted services – a phenomenon unknown to the more traditionalist West London Synagogue. Indeed in 1903, when the fledgling Liberal congregation requested the use of the West London Synagogue premises, one of the conditions stipulated by the latter was that the sexes should be separated during divine service.[1]

The same moderate/radical division was found in the early days of Reform Judaism in the USA in the second half of the nineteenth century. Isaac M. Wise, a leader of the moderates and one of the founders of the Reform seminary Hebrew Union College in Cincinnati, was an architect of the Cleveland Platform laying down the basis for American Reform Judaism. The Platform recognized the divine nature of the Bible and the validity of the rabbinic tradition, despite the fact that Wise's personal views on these subjects were far from Orthodox. Wise wanted to hold the middle ground, and believed that any changes introduced into Jewish ritual and liturgy should be such as to promote a viable form of American Judaism. He thus abolished the separation of the sexes in synagogues, the second days of the festivals, and in 1873 even the covering of the head by male congregants. The more radical reformers led by David Einhorn, and later by his son-in-law Kaufman Kohler, opposed the somewhat tentative and pragmatic approach of Wise, and advocated a more consistent, thoroughgoing, reform. The Pittsburgh Platform of 1885, in the formulation of which Kohler was a leading participant, saw the Bible as containing the out-dated ideas of the past although still highly valued as the source of Judaism. Only the moral teachings of Judaism could be binding, together with any rituals which sanctified the life of the modern Jew. Dietary restrictions, national aspirations concerning Palestine, and doctrines such as the Resurrection or reward and punishment after death were all rejected. Over all the more radical wing of Reform Judaism has dominated American Reform Jewry.

Since the early days of Reform the movement has grown in numbers particularly in North America. Its organization there, the Union of American Hebrew Congregations, has nearly 800 affiliated synagogues today. Although there are still disputes between moderates and radicals about the place of traditional norms in Reform Jewish life, there is in general a movement back to tradition in some quarters, and a strong identification with Zionism and with the

State of Israel. Discarded rituals have been re-introduced into some radical Reform congregations, and the moderate Reform groups are re-examining aspects of rabbinic practice which were rejected in the early days of Reform. A particular controversy affecting Reform rabbis in the USA today is the issue of their participation in the celebration of mixed marriages between Jews and gentiles. While the Reform association of rabbis, the Central Conference of American Rabbis, has come out against such participation in principle, it has allowed individual rabbis to determine their own policy. The New York Board of Rabbis, comprising Orthodox, Conservative and Reform rabbis, passed a resolution in 1973 forbidding membership to those officiating at these mixed marriages. This led to the resignation of a number of Reform rabbis from the Board.

Some of the ongoing problems associated with Reform, such as the acceptance by Reform rabbis in the USA of the children of Jewish fathers and gentile mothers as Jews, the principle of patrilineal descent, and the general non-acceptance by traditionalists of Reform conversions to Judaism, have caused major divisions within Jewry. Yet they can be solved in theory, albeit with difficulty, by conversion or reconversion of those concerned in a traditional ceremony. One of the more serious long-term problems between Reform and traditional Judaism is the divorce procedure used by the former. A married woman who does not undergo a traditional divorce is still considered by the *halakhah* as married. Any children born from a subsequent marriage are *mamzerim*, and cannot marry freely among their co-religionists. Since Reform divorce procedures are not halakhically acceptable, a growing number of children born into Reform communities are *mamzerim*, and this stigma will be passed on to their children in turn. In the course of time Orthodoxy and Reform might become two totally endogamous groups. A possible solution to this problem, based on the writings of R. Moshe Feinstein, a leading American Orthodox rabbi, is to regard Reform marriages themselves as invalid, since there are no halakhically suitable witnesses present. This would mean that any children born from a subsequent marriage are not *mamzerim*, although they would be regarded as born out of wedlock.

Conservative Judaism

The same tensions between tradition and modernity which led to the rise of Reform Judaism in the post-emancipation period were also responsible for the beginnings of the Conservative Movement. Its ideological mentors were those European scholars who developed the so-called Historical School within the Science of Judaism. Zacharias Frankel, a founder of the Historical School, opposed the thoroughgoing reforms of contemporaries like Holdheim and Geiger, and walked out of the 1845 Frankfurt Rabbinical Conference in protest at their stand. His own view was that moderate reforms were necessary but that they should reflect the spirit of the Jewish past, and not violate it in subservience to modernity. Frankel produced an influential body of scholarly research into the history of Jewish tradition, showing how it developed with time, and thus the direction in which new developments could take place. He helped found, and headed, the Jewish Theological Seminary in Breslau, which served as a model for Conservative institutions, combining the traditional curriculum with historical scholarship. To reformers the reluctance of the Historical School to jettison 'outworn' forms of Judaism made it unacceptable, while to many of the Orthodox the new historico-critical approach was sacrilegious.

In the second half of the nineteenth century a number of American rabbis who had come from the traditional environment of Europe wished to modify the liturgy and practice of Judaism to bring it into consonance with American life. They were ill at ease with their radical Reform co-religionists, though they worked with them for a time to try and unite the Jewish congregations in America. Foremost among these was Isaac Leeser, who in 1843 began to publish a journal, the *Occident*, to serve as a vehicle for a revised, yet traditional, approach to Judaism. Leeser, together with other immigrant rabbis such as Sabbato Morais, Marcus Jastrow and Alexander Kohut, worked to preserve the centrality of Hebrew in the liturgy, the maintenance of the *Shabbat*, and *kashrut* observance. They also adopted traditional attitudes to the messianic hope, the question of Jewish national identity, and Zionism, thereby differing from the Reform leadership. Morais founded the Jewish Theological Seminary in New York, which began to train rabbis in the tradition of Historical Judaism in 1887. The Seminary originally wished to include Orthodox congregations among its supporters, but the latter found its approach to religion too modernist. The Seminary was thus forced to develop on its own, independent of both Orthodoxy and Reform. In 1902 Solomon Schechter was brought over from England to head the Seminary, and to pilot its independent theological stance. Schechter, who had received a talmudic training in Eastern

Europe and was then teaching rabbinics at Cambridge, had already attained an international reputation for his recovery of the hoards of ancient manuscripts hidden in the Cairo *genizah* or storehouse. It was Schechter's theological sophistication and administrative abilities, more than his scholarship, which enabled him to turn the fledgling movement into a major force on the American Jewish scene.

In 1913 Schechter founded the United Synagogue of America, modelled somewhat loosely after the United Synagogue in London, to unite all Conservative congregations in North America. Today this is the largest formal synagogue organization in the USA ahead of both the Reform and Orthodox organizations, and still growing at a faster rate than its two rivals. While the United Synagogue of America is made up of congregations whose approach to Jewish ritual varies greatly, the Seminary has always represented the most traditionalist stance in the Conservative movement. The tone for the Seminary's traditionalism was set by Schechter himself, who designated the higher criticism of the Bible as the 'higher anti-Semitism',[2] and who saw changes in Jewish ritual as necessarily emerging from the consensus of 'Catholic Israel'. This concept of 'Catholic Israel', the living body of Jews implementing their Judaism in life and practice, though never carefully defined by Schechter, has served as the ideological lynch-pin of Conservative attitudes.[3] Schechter was also involved with Zionism, though he saw it primarily as a revival of Jewish cultural nationalism and a preventative against assimilation, rather than as a secular political movement. In general he saw the reforming zeal of some of his co-religionists as an alien import, applying Christian attitudes to specifically Jewish forms of religious expression.

Schechter's disciples followed his traditionalist position, and though some subscribed to a critical approach to the Bible they were wary at first of implementing changes to the *halakhah* where these threatened to antagonize the Orthodox leadership. Conservative synagogues in the course of time introduced mixed seating, allowed the use of transport on *Shabbat*, abolished the levirate marriage and the restrictions on the marriage of a *kohen*, discontinued the use of *mikveh* by women, and brought English into the liturgy. These, and many similar changes like them, have given Conservative Judaism an identity which clearly sets it off from Orthodoxy and make it very much a North American product. As a movement it is still grappling with the attempt to formulate a doctrine of revelation to act as a foundation for Conservative theology, and for its approach to Jewish tradition. While most Conservative thinkers today reject the idea of the Pentateuch as revealed by God to Moses, they do wish to preserve an authoritative, divine, element in biblical and post-biblical Judaism but the identification of this authoritative, divine component in the tradition has proved singularly problematical.

An offshoot of Conservative Judaism is the Reconstructionist movement, founded by Mordecai Kaplan, a one-time member of the Jewish Theological Seminary staff. Kaplan's 'theology', found unacceptable by many of his Conservative colleagues, viewed Judaism as an evolving religious civilization in which rituals are folkways externalizing its collective existence, and God a projection of human ideals reflecting a cosmic process making for salvation. Reconstructionism represents a fourth stream in Jewish, especially American Jewish, life with a small but creative membership drawn largely from intellectual circles. The movement runs its own educational institutions and publications, and has an influence on the American Jewish scene out of all proportion to its size.

Orthodox Judaism

The different sub-groups which make up Orthodox Jewry today are a heterogeneous and diverse conglomerate. The term, which is merely a useful umbrella label for traditionalist Jews belonging to synagogues not affiliated to Conservative or Reform movements, was first coined by reformers to refer, somewhat derogatorily, to those who resisted change and modification in traditional Jewish life. In fact it is a misnomer, for whereas many traditionalist groups can be described as ortho-prax in so far as they subscribe to halakhic norms, there is no one doctrinal framework which unites them.

In the nineteenth century those European Jews who did not respond to emancipation by advocating radical changes in Jewish ritual or belief either simply continued with their nineteenth-century version of Jewish traditionalism, or tried to absorb modernity into a Jewish framework. The first option led to extremely conservative positions like that of R. Moses Sofer of Pressburg who attacked even moderate reforms under the slogan: 'What is new is forbidden by the *Torah*.' The Hebrew word for new, *chadash*, is used in rabbinical literature to refer to the new cereal crop which is indeed forbidden to be eaten until the *Omer* offering is brought on the second day of Passover. The slogan is thus a well-known halakhic rule which, by a play on words, was used by Hungarian Orthodoxy to sum up its attitude to the reformers. Sofer and his pupils in the Austro-Hungarian Empire led a counter-attack on reforms of any kind and insisted that the standards of nineteenth-century traditionalism should remain unchanged.

Another expression of this ortho-prax conservatism is found in the attitude adopted by the Chasidic leader R. Schneur Zalman of Liadi. The latter actively supported the Russian Tsar against Napoleon, despite the reactionary and anti-Jewish policies of the Tsarist regime and the more enlightened policies of Napoleon. R. Schneur Zalman saw the Napoleonic policy of pulling down the ghetto walls and modernizing the Jews as a threat to the traditional character of Jewish life. Both R. Moses Sofer and R. Schneur Zalman rejected *in toto* the secular culture of Europe and the consequential challenges it proffered to Jewish attitudes and behaviour.

A quite different response to emancipation was the Neo-Orthodoxy of R. Samson Raphael Hirsch in Frankfurt. While affirming the immutability of halakhic norms, except where the internal dynamic of the halakhic process itself led to the introduction of modifications, Hirsch fully accepted the value of European culture. For him a secular education and active participation in the life of the general community were not merely concessions to the times. There was an in-built necessity for Judaism to absorb the culture of the society in which it found itself, and to express Jewish ideas and values in its terms.

The slogan of Hirschian Neo-Orthodoxy was *Torah im derekh eretz*, *Torah* together with the way of the land, a phrase borrowed from rabbinic literature where it originally meant that *Torah* should be accompanied by a worldly occupation. Hirsch widened the meaning of the phrase and interpreted it as saying that *Torah*, i.e. Judaism, must go together with the culture, science and society of the place and period in which Jews live.

These two reactions to modernity on the part of traditionalists have, in fact, determined the dual nature of Orthodoxy up to the present. A minority of Orthodox Jews, including many of the leading rabbinic scholars, reject the advances of modern culture (even including modern dress), secular education, and participation in the intellectual and social life of gentile society. Although they have accepted purely technological developments, e.g. electricity, the motor car, the aeroplane, the telephone and modern medicine they prefer to live within a self-imposed cultural ghetto. Contact with the world outside this ghetto is kept to a minimum, usually determined by economic factors, and many of these so-called Ultra-Orthodox Jews would not watch television or read a daily paper. Naturally the extent to which individuals reject gentile culture varies considerably, but in the tight-knit communities of this type there are certain norms conformity to which is a condition of membership.

The larger grouping within Orthodox Judaism, which may conveniently be characterized as Modern Orthodoxy, is a direct descendant of the Hirschian approach even though most of its members would not actually accept Hirsch's ideological position. Modern Orthodox Jews wear Western clothes, attend universities, and accept the secondary cultural values of their host society. Like many of Hirsch's own followers the men will be clean-shaven and wear modern hairstyles. The majority of the women in such communities will not wear a wig, or *sheitel*, even though it would have been insisted on in Hirschian circles, and will wear hats for synagogue attendance.

Modern Orthodoxy has created its own educational institutions, both at high school and college level, the best known of the latter being Jews' College in London, Yeshivah University in New York, and Bar Ilan University in Israel. Although none of these institutions adopt a critico-historical approach to the teaching of Judaism their curricula manifest a modernity which makes them suspect in the eyes of the Ultra-Orthodox. For whereas Modern Orthodoxy is committed to the *halakhah*, it is flexible in its interpretation and implementation of halakhic standards. Tradition is viewed through a lens coloured by the values and assumptions of modern man, though it will not allow it to become subservient to these values.

The Modern Orthodox synagogue usually employs a rabbi who has undergone university training, and who preaches his sermons in the vernacular. While the sexes are segregated during worship the women's gallery is not curtained off, as in Ultra-Orthodox synagogues, and women play an active, if secondary, role in the life of the community. Many of the actual members of Modern Orthodox synagogues have taken their personal compromise between tradition and modernity far beyond the official limits of Modern Orthodox norms. Their practice of *kashrut*, Sabbath observance, or the *niddah* restrictions on marital relations, may not differ substantially from those of Conservatives or traditionally minded Reform

Jews. They define themselves as Orthodox Jews in terms of the synagogue and community to which they belong, rather than in terms of theological belief or ritual practice.

While Ultra-Orthodox leaders do not co-operate with Progressive Judaism, even on neutral ground, because they do not recognize a form of Judaism which they see as negating the essentials of Jewish faith, Modern Orthodoxy is divided on the extent of permissible co-operation. Hirsch himself insisted that Neo-Orthodox communities should function completely independently of Reform Judaism. This led to a split in the ranks of German Orthodoxy in the nineteenth century, and Hirsch's isolationism was attacked by a prominent Orthodox contemporary R. Seligman Bamberger.

Limited co-operation between Modern Orthodoxy, Conservative and Reform Judaism is more frequent today when all Jews share a common memory of anti-Semitism and the Holocaust, and a common need to support Zionism and Israel. Thus it is not unusual to find Modern Orthodox leaders working closely with their Progressive counterparts on communal and public relations issues. When it comes to matters of a religious nature, however, Modern Orthodox rabbis are far less happy about joint ventures because they feel that this will be interpreted as *de jure* recognition of Reform. Even the recent re-assessment of its attitude to traditional practices and its re-incorporation of some rituals by sections of the Reform movement has done little to bridge the gap between it and Modern Orthodoxy. The history of controversy and mutual antagonism is too strongly rooted, and the divergence in theology and practice too great, for the gap to be closed.

14

Jews and Gentiles

The history of the relationship between Jewish communities, living as a minority mostly among Christians or Moslems, and their hosts is one of intermittent degradation and persecution. Only in very few countries over the past two millennia did the Jews survive in relative tranquillity.

Generally speaking Jews fared considerably worse in Christian countries than they did in Moslem ones. In the latter they were a protected people who had to pay a special tax, were not allowed to wear the same clothes as Moslems, and were subject to a number of special restrictions. Actual forced conversion of Jews to Islam was rare, although it did take place, e.g. under the fanatical Almohades in twelfth-century Spain and North Africa, and in Iran at different periods under various Shiite rulers.

The situation of the Jews under Christendom was much more insecure, since they were exposed to a deep-seated animosity continually fired by claims about Jewish collective responsibility for the death of Jesus. At various times Jews were expelled from European states, forbidden to accept Christian converts to Judaism, had their economic behaviour limited to one or two main areas – particularly usury. They were subject to pogroms in which countless Jews were killed, raped and beaten-up, and Jewish property was pillaged or destroyed. They had to debate the merits of their religion against the claims of Christianity in contrived disputations which they could never really win. The *Talmud* was burnt and if allowed to be published was censored by Christian divines who considered it a work offensive to Christianity. Jews lived with the consciousness that for Christians they were an outcast people, spurned by God, to be mocked at by man, and if they were not forced more often to the baptismal font that was to serve as an example to Christendom of the fate of rejectors of Christ.

The memories of what happened which were passed on in Jewish books, liturgical poems, and commemorative rituals, reflect the purely negative aspects of the Jewish-Christian encounter. This had a profound effect on the way Jews in general, and Ashkenazi Jews in particular, saw the gentile – the *goi*.

The perpetrators of the persecution and humiliation were seen as the official representatives of Christendom: bishops, crusaders, local priests inciting an Easter mob, the Inquisition, simply pious, churchgoing lords and barons, or even at times the Pope himself. The Christian religion, its churches, its central symbol the crucifix, its icons, the very name of Jesus, thus came to be identified in the Jewish consciousness with cruelty and inhumanity. The feeling that Judaism was an infinitely superior religion to the Christian 'gospel of love' which seemed lacking in basic human values, was reinforced by Jewish suffering at the hands of Christians. The Jew willingly turned in upon himself, upheld by the belief that he was the Suffering Servant, suffering for the sins of the world. He lived in the dark night of exile but he looked forward to the dawn of a messianic day when the nightmare would have passed and he would come into his own.

The Christian Religion

Christianity, with its belief in the Trinity, its doctrine of the Incarnation, its use of statues of the crucified Jesus and of the Madonna, and its worship of saints, was seen by many Jewish thinkers as idolatrous, an accusation which could not be levelled against Islam. Thus Maimonides, who lived in Moslem countries and was not subject to pressure from the Church authorities, states categorically:

> Know that the Christian nation who go astray after Jesus, although they have different religious groupings, are all idolaters. . . . It is fitting to deal with them as one deals with idolaters.[1]

By contrast, medieval Jewish halakhists who lived in Christian countries were inclined to find halakhic grounds for treating Christianity as something less than idolatrous. Since there were pressing economic reasons for Jews to be able to engage in business with Christians, a more practical interpretation of the situation was called for where the *halakhah* would exclude such dealings with idolaters .

Although these reinterpretations of the *halakhah* allowed Jews to conduct basic commercial relations with Christians, few of the rabbis went so far as to advocate excluding Christians altogether from the category of heathens, about whom the *Talmud* has some very negative things to say.

The heathen *nochri*, or *goi*, was not considered to be on the same moral or socio-cultural level as the Jew, and he was thought to live an animal-like existence.[2] Whereas dealings between Jews are circumscribed by high demands of ethical or religious conduct, these demands do not apply in the contact between a Jew and a heathen. At best Jewish behaviour towards the heathen must be such as not to cause enmity or strife.

One of the few halakhists who excepted Christians from the class of heathens was Menachem Meiri (1239–1316) of Provence. He argued that Christians were civilized and God-fearing and could not be compared to the immoral heathen of talmudic times.[3] Other rabbis merely contented themselves with a passing remark in the introduction to their works, or when the subject of Jewish relations with the heathen first came up, disclaiming the application of what they wrote to contemporary gentiles. Perhaps sometimes this was a genuinely held belief, but it would more often appear to the Jewish reader as simply a way of getting round the censor or avoiding Christian antagonism.

Jewish and Gentile Souls

Among Jewish theologians in the Middle Ages there was more concern with trying to show the truth of Jewish teaching over Christianity and Islam than with the relative status of Jew and gentile. The most notable exception, however, is Judah Halevi who argues in his *Kuzari* that Israel differs totally in its spiritual make-up from other peoples. Each individual Jew is heir to a prophetic capacity which alone enables man to know the mind and will of God. Even the proselyte does not acquire this capacity when he becomes a Jew, since as we might put it today he lacks the 'spiritual genes' of the born Jew.

The talmudic antipathy to the *goi* is found, and in a stronger form, in the medieval and post-medieval mystical literature, particularly in the *Zohar* and in Lurianic Kabbalah. There, unlike in the *Talmud*, it is not so much a question of gentile practice which is at issue, but the very difference in essence between Jew and gentile. Whereas the *Talmud* seems to be denigrating the ethical and spiritual life of the *goi*, his lack of morality, his unwillingness to transcend the earthly, and his ignorance of the divine, the Kabbalah sees the difference as one of kind.

The *goi* belongs to the kabbalistic sub-world of the demonic. He possesses a lower-order soul than the Jew, who at least has the potential of reaching the dimension of the divine. Basing itself on a talmudic precedent which taught that Eve had been impregnated by the evil serpent, and her seed was thus tainted till the Sinaitic theophany removed the taint from Israel,[4] the mystics taught their own version of a doctrine of Original Sin. The *goi* was the tainted child of woman's carnal relationship with the serpent, the symbol of demonic powers. Since the gentile had not undergone the cleansing experience of the revelation of God's *Torah*, he remained half-human and half-demon.

This idea, even when allowance is made for the picturesque symbolism of the Kabbalah, seems to set up an unbridgeable gap between Jew and gentile and makes the whole notion of converts to Judaism problematic. The *halakhah* recognizes proselytes as full Jews, but how could their conversion bring about a change in the essential structure of the gentile soul? The *Zohar* itself solves the problem by viewing the convert as presented with a new soul from heaven, albeit one inferior to that possessed by Jews.[5] Other kabbalists saw the gentile convert as already having a Jewish soul which had been lost among the gentiles, for instance through the forced baptism of a Jewish ancestor. Conversion was in fact a Jew returning to the fold, and it was the hidden Jewish spark within which brought the convert back to Judaism.

Perhaps the clearest statement of the distinction between Jews and gentiles is found in the writings of the eighteenth-nineteenth century Chasidic master, R. Schneur Zalman of Liadi. According to the latter every Jew has two souls, an animal soul and a divine soul. The animal soul stems from the highest reaches of the demonic, it is the source of evil but also of natural goodness, such as mercy or benevolence, since its root is the 'shell of light' – the closest point of the demonic structure to the side of holiness. The divine soul is rooted in God, or is in some sense a part of God. The gentile not only lacks a divine soul, his animal soul stems from lower levels of the demonic than that of the Jew.[6]

Jewish Attitudes to Gentiles Today

Jewish self-consciousness and the Jew's interpretation of his position in the world were affected by continual persecution from the outside. They were also influenced by internal ideas about the gentile, and the special Jewish role of witnessing God's *Torah* and acting as a vehicle for the messianic redemption. Traditional Judaism saw human history, and the activities of the gentiles, as ultimately serving interests reducible to Jewish terms. Since the purpose of life was the worship and service of God, and since this purpose was fulfilled primarily, if not entirely, by the Jew through *Torah* and *mitzvot*, the whole of creation was seen as supportive of the ideals of Jewish life.

This idea is already contained in a talmudic teaching to the effect that at the creation God made a condition with the heavens and the earth: if Israel would accept the *Torah* at Sinai well and good, but if they refused it then the whole of nature would return to primeval chaos.[7] It was given modern expression in a parable ascribed to a leading twentieth-century sage R. Israel Meir Kagan (the *Chafetz Chaim*):

> A traveller who has never been on a train before sets out on a rail journey. Interested to find out how the train moves he wanders into the first-class compartment where well-to-do people are travelling in luxury. He asks them if they are driving the train. When they reply in the negative he goes into the second-class compartment making similar enquiries, and so on until he eventually finds the engine driver who is all grimy from shovelling coal into the engine's boiler. Only here is his question answered in the affirmative.

The parable quite obviously refers to the running of the world. It is not the rich and cultured members of gentile society who control the world, for all that they seem to have the reins of secular power in their hands. It is the outcast and rejected People of Israel whose service of God is what really keeps the world going.

The deep-rooted ideology of contrast between Jews and gentiles, and their different respective values within the divine economy, finds expression in many of the terms which Jews use among themselves to refer to gentiles. Apart from neutral terms such as *goi*, the most common Yiddish expression for a gentile is *sheketz* (often pronounced *sheigetz*) for a male and *shiksah* for a female. In origin this is a term of abuse. Ultra-Orthodox Jews often refer to Jewish secularists or modernists as *shekatzim*, since they are regarded as having forsaken all that is holy in imitation of the gentiles.

With the emancipation of the Jew in the nineteenth century and the reforming developments within Judaism, a whole new series of attitudes has emerged towards the gentile. More traditional Orthodoxy, which has preserved social and cultural distance from the gentile world, still tends to see the Jewish/gentile dichotomy in pre-modern categories. The gentile world is an unknown entity, viewed through the matrix of negative attitudes to the heathen (and Christian) expressed in Jewish literature. It is feared as the harbinger of violent anti-Semitism and the purveyor of anti-Jewish beliefs and lax, if not non-existent, sexual morality.

Modernizing Jews, whether Orthodox or Progressive, who come into regular contact with gentile culture and often into social contact with gentiles tend to overlook the more extreme aspects of their own tradition on the gentile question. In so far as they have an ideological position on the issue it will be based on more universalistic elements within that tradition which view the differences between Jews and gentiles as matters of religion and culture, rather than essence or soul. Two factors, however, affect the consciousness of the modernist Jew deeply and preserve something of the classical model outlined above. The first is the memory of the Holocaust which has ingrained a strongly held suspicion about the *goi* and his ability to eradicate anti-Semitism from his own culture. The second is the State of Israel, and renewed Jewish nationalism.

Many of the older generation of contemporary Jews lived among gentiles in pre-Holocaust Europe, and felt totally at home in such a milieu. This feeling of harmony and shared humanity was rudely shattered by the experience of German and European anti-Semitism which brought the age-old differences between the gentile and Jew into sharp relief once again. Jews often express the belief that even the Allies were lukewarm about Hitler's treatment of the Jews, and but for his expansionist policy would never have taken up the cudgels on the Jews' behalf. The failure of the Allies to launch an air-raid against the Auschwitz death-camp is taken to be indicative of their lack of concern.

Support for the State of Israel and for Zionism, in one form or another, is characteristic of most Diaspora Jews still committed to maintaining Jewish identity. The seeming indifference of many Western gentiles to Israel's struggle for survival, and the antagonism to Zionist aspirations, seems to reflect a pattern with which the Jew is only too familiar – an unheeding world turning a blind eye to Jewish suffering. Other nations have an automatic right to exist, but the Jewish people has continually to justify its existence to a Christian civilization which has consistently denied it such a right. The fact that it took the Vatican more than forty-five years from the birth of the State of Israel to grant it *de jure* recognition is seen as symptomatic of this attitude. Anti-Zionism is, therefore, felt by the Jew to be simply the latest form of anti-Semitism.

All this may be, in its extreme form, an expression of a specifically Jewish paranoia, but Jewish sensitivities on these topics affect Jewish attitudes to the gentile. The suspicion of the *goi* reaches back over many incidents of persecution. Its modern variant only strengthens the Jew's theological self-consciousness of the People of Israel as 'a people which dwells alone'.

Glossary

Adam Kadmon	Kabbalistic concept of primordial man, archetype of humanity.
Adar	Hebrew month usually falling around February / March.
Afikoman	Last piece of unleavened bread eaten at the Passover meal.
Aggadah	Non-legal material in rabbinic literature.
Agunah (agunot)	Wife whose husband has disappeared, or refuses to divorce her.
Aleinu	Prayer recited at the end of every service.
Al Ha-Nissim	'For the miracles'. Prayer recited on *Chanukah* and *Purim*.
Aliyah	'Going up' for Torah reading and also to the Land of Israel.
Amidah	'Standing'. Benedictions at the centre-piece of every liturgy.
Amorite Ways	Term for magical practices forbidden by Judaism.
Arvit	The evening service, also known as *Maariv*.
Asarah Be-Tevet	Fast of the tenth day of *Tevet*.
Ashkenazi	Jew of Central or East European origin.
Aufruf	The call up of a bridegroom to the Torah prior to his wedding.
Av	Hebrew month usually falling July / August.
Avel	A mourner.
Baal Teshuvah	A penitent who has turned from his sinful ways.
Bar Mitzvah	The religious maturity of the male child at the age of 13.
Bat Mitzvah	The religious maturity of the female child at the age of 12.
Bedeken	Yiddish. The 'covering' of the bride's face by the groom.
Bekeshe	Long black silken coat worn by Chasidim.
Berit Milah	'Covenant of circumcision'.
Bet Din	Jewish court of law, comprising at least three ordained rabbis.
Bet Ha-Keneset	'House of gathering'. Usual name for the synagogue.

Bet Ha-Midrash	'House of study'. Smaller synagogue used also for study.
Bimah	Central platform in the synagogue on which the *Torah* is read.
Bishul Akkum	'Cooked by gentiles'. Certain categories of forbidden food.
Bund	Yiddish socialist movement. Founded in Russia in 1897.
Chadash	New produce prohibited till the second day of Passover.
Chakham	'Sage'. Used by Sefardi Jews as an alternative title to 'Rabbi'.
Challah	Tithe taken from dough. Also used of special Sabbath loaves.
Chametz	Leavened bread forbidden during the Passover festival.
Chanukah	Eight-day festival of light, falling in December.
Chanukiyah	Modern name for eight-branched *Chanukah* candelabrum.
Chasid	'Pietist'. Member of the Chasidic movement, plural *Chasidim*.
Chavurah	'Fellowship'.
Chazan	Cantor. Originally meaning a synagogue official.
Cheder	'Room'. Traditional school for religious instruction.
Cherem	Excommunication. Social ostracism.
Chevra Kaddisha	'Holy fellowship'. Burial society whose members wash the dead.
Cholent	Ashkenazi name for hot Sabbath dish.
Chol Ha-Moed	'Festive weekdays'. Intermediate days of festivals.
Choshen Mishpat	Section of *Shulchan Arukh* dealing with civil and criminal law.
Chupah	Wedding canopy.
Devekut	'Cleaving' to God. Religious devotion.
Din	'Judgement'. The kabbalistic *sefirah* which is the source of evil.
Dreidl	Spinning top played with on *Chanukah*.
Ein Sof	The unlimited Godhead of kabbalistic thought.
Elul	Hebrew month usually falling around August / Sept.
Erev Shabbat	'Eve of the Sabbath'. Friday.
Erusin	First part of the marriage ceremony. Also known as *kiddushin*.
Etrog	The special citrus fruit of the festival of Tabernacles.
Even Ha-Ezer	Section of *Shulchan Arukh* dealing with marriage and divorce.
Gabbai	Synagogue warden, elected to office.
Gaon (pl. *geonim*)	Babylonian academy head, and by extension any great sage.
Gartel	Black silken cord worn by Chasidim as a belt for prayers.

Gehinnom	Hell-cum-purgatory where the dead are purged.
Genizah	Storehouse where worn-out sacred texts are kept.
Ger	Male convert to Judaism.
Ger Toshav	'Resident alien.' Gentile who keeps the Noachide Laws.
Get	Bill of divorce, delivered by the husband to the wife.
Giyoret	Female convert to Judaism.
Giyyur	'Conversion' to Judaism.
Goi	General term for gentile.
Golem	Artificially man, created through kabbalistic means.
Gush Emunim	'Block of the Faithful'. Group of messianic Zionists.
Haftarah	Prophetic section ending Sabbath and festival *Torah* readings.
Haggadah	The text recited at the Passover *seder* meal.
Halakhah	The Jewish path. The legal side of Judaism.
Hallel	Psalms of praise (nos. 113–118) recited on festive occasions.
Havdalah	Ceremony marking the termination of Sabbaths and festivals.
Heikhalot	'Halls'. Levels through which the *Merkabah* mystic passes.
Heter	'Permission'. Permissive halakhic ruling.
Hitbodedut	'Being alone', specifically being alone with God.
Hoshana	'Hosanna'. Prayers for salvation chanted on Tabernacles.
Hoshana Rabba	'Great Hosanna'. Seventh day of the festival of Tabernacles.
Iyyar	Hebrew month usually falling around April / May.
Kaddish	Aramaic prayer recited by the cantor and by mourners.
Kapote	Long black silken coat worn by Chasidim.
Kapparot	Atonement ceremony performed prior to the Day of Atonement.
Kappel	Yiddish name of skull-cap worn by Jewish men.
Kasher	General term for food permitted by the Jewish dietary laws.
Kavod	The Divine Glory. Term used by medieval mystics.
Kedushah	'Holiness'. Liturgical piece affirming the holiness of God.
Kelal Yisrael	Term for the whole community of the Jewish People.
Kelei Kodesh	'Holy vessels.' The religious functionaries of the community.
Kelim	'Vessels' containing the divine light in kabbalistic cosmogony.
Kelipah	The evil shell surrounding the elements of holiness in

the world.

Ketubbah	The marriage document.
Ketuvim	The Hebrew name for the Hagiographa.
Kibbutz	Collective village in Israel, plural Kibbutzim.
Kiddush	Sanctification over wine said on Sabbaths and festivals.
Kiddushin	The initial part of the marriage ceremony. Also known as *erusin*.
Kilayim	The prohibition on planting or grafting mixed species.
Kinot	Special lamentations recited on the fast of the 9th of *Av*.
Kippah	Hebrew name of skull-cap worn by Jewish men.
Kislev	Hebrew month usually falling around November / December.
Kittel	White garment symbolizing the shroud.
Kohen	Priestly descendant of the Temple priests.
Kol-bo-nik	'Man of many parts'. Religious functionary with several roles.
Kolel	Talmudic academy for married students.
Kol Nidrei	The annulment of religious vows prior to the Day of Atonement.
Kvater/Kvaterin	Godparents who bring the baby into the circumcision.
Lag Ba-Omer	The 33rd day of the *Omer*. A minor festive day.
Leom	National status on an Israeli identity card.
Lubavitch	Chasidic sub-group. Also known as Chabad.
Lulav	Palm branch used on the festival of Tabernacles.
Maariv	The evening service, also known as *Arvit*.
Maaseh Bereshit	Early Jewish mysticism involving cosmogonic speculation.
Maaseh Merkabah	Early Jewish mysticism leading to a vision of the divine throne.
Mah Nishtanah	Four questions asked by children at the Passover *seder* meal.
Mamzer	Child of an adulterous or incestuous union. Plural *mamzerim*.
Maoz Tzur	Song sung after kindling the *Chanukah* lights.
Maror	Bitter herbs eaten at the Passover seder meal.
Matzah	Unleavened bread eaten during the Passover festival.
Mazal Tov	'Good luck'. Common greeting on joyous occasions.
Mechitzah	Partition between the sexes in Orthodox synagogues.
Megillah	'Scroll'. Usually applied to the Book of Esther; plural *megillot*.
Melamed	Teacher of young children.
Menorah	Eight-branched candelabrum used on *Chanukah*.

Merkabah	The divine chariot seen in the visions of early Jewish mystics.
Metzitzah	'Sucking' the blood from the wound after ritual circumcision.
Mezuzah	The small parchment scroll affixed to door posts.
Midrash	Homiletical Bible exegesis and literary genre. Plural *midrashim*.
Mikveh	Ritual bath, originally constituted out of natural water source.
Minchah	Afternoon prayers.
Minhag	'Custom'. An important element of normative behaviour.
Minyan	Quorum of ten adult male Jews necessary for certain prayers.
Mitnaged	'Opponent' of the Chasidic Movement; plural *Mitnagdim*.
Mitzvah	'Commandment', and generally any religious act. Plural *mitzvot*.
Mizrach	'East'. Sign for the direction of Jerusalem in the Western world.
Mohel	Ritual circumciser.
Musaf	Additional service for New Moon, Sabbaths and festivals.
Musar	Ethical instruction.
Musarnik	Follower of the *Musar* Movement.
Nachas/Nachat	'Pleasure' felt by parents at the achievements of their children.
Neturei Karta	Anti-Zionist ultra-Orthodox group.
Neviim	'Prophets'. Hebrew name for the biblical prophetical books.
Niddah	Menstruant woman.
Nisan	Hebrew month, usually falling in Spring (around March / April).
Nochri	'Stranger'. Common term for a gentile.
Omer	Barley 'measure'. Also period between Passover and Pentecost.
Onah	The time when marital relations are prescribed.
Oneg	The joy of Sabbaths and festivals.
Onen	The status of a mourner prior to the burial of the deceased.
Orach Chaim	*Shulchan Arukh* section dealing with prayer and holy days.
Orlah	The forbidden fruit of a tree during its first three years.
Parev	Food which is not classified as meat or milk.

Peot	Side curls.
Pesach	The Passover festival.
Pidyon Ha-Ben	Redemption of the first born male child.
Pilpul	Dialectical casuistry.
Purim	Festival commemorating the story of the Book of Esther.
Purim Spiel	Mini-drama acted out on *Purim* by children in fancy dress.
Rosh Chodesh	Festival of the New Moon, beginning each lunar month.
Rosh Ha-Kahal	Elected head of the community.
Rosh Ha-Shanah	'Head of the year'. Jewish New Year festival, falling in autumn.
Sandek	The godfather who holds the child during the circumcision.
Sanhedrin	The supreme religious council of sages in ancient times.
Savoraim	Babylonian sages who edited the *Talmud*.
Seder	'Order'. The rituals of the Passover festive meal.
Sefardi	Jew originally of Iberian origin.
Sefirah	One of the ten kabbalistic structures. Plural *sefirot*.
Segulah	Act or rite thought to be magically efficacious.
Selichot	Penitential prayers.
Semikhah	Ordination of rabbis.
Shaatnez	Prohibited clothing woven from a mixture of wool and flax.
Shabbat	'Rest'. Saturday, the Jewish Sabbath, when labour is proscribed.
Shabbat Ha-Gadol	'The Great Sabbath'. The Sabbath before Passover.
Shacharit	The morning service.
Shadkhan	Matchmaker.
Shalom Zakhar	Celebratory meal held on Friday night prior to circumcision.
Shamash	Synagogue beadle. Yiddish *Shamas*.
Shavuot	The festival of Pentecost.
Shechitah	Ritual slaughter.
She'elot U-Teshuvot	'Questions and answers'. Responsa to halakhic queries.
Sheketz/Sheigetz	Pejorative term for gentile, fem. *shiksah*, pl. *shekatzim*.
Sheitel	Wig worn by married women to cover their natural hair.
Shekhinah	'Divine Presence'. The feminine aspect of the divine.
Shema	Biblical passages said twice daily proclaiming the divine unity.
Shemini Atzeret	A festival at the conclusion of Tabernacles.
Shemittah	The Sabbatical year during which the land of Israel lies

	fallow.
Shemittot	The kabbalistic doctrine of world cycles.
Shemoneh Esreh	Nineteen benedictions said thrice daily. Also called *Amidah*.
She'ol	Biblical term for the world inhabited by the spirits of the dead.
Sheva Berakhot	The seven marriage benedictions.
Shevat	Hebrew month falling around January / February.
Shiddukh	Arranged marriage.
Shivah	'Seven' days of intense mourning for the loss of a near relative.
Shloshim	The first thirty days of mourning.
Shochet	Ritual slaughterer.
Shofar	Ram's horn blown at the New Year and on various occasions.
Shokeling	'Swaying' violently while praying.
Shool	'School' Yiddish term for synagogue.
Shtibl	'Little room'. Yiddish term for an informal synagogue.
Shtreimel	Fur hat worn by Chasidim on Sabbaths and festivals.
Shulchan Arukh	'Laid Table'. Main Jewish law code.
Siddur	Ashkenazi name for the weekday and Sabbath prayer book.
Simchat Torah	'Rejoicing over the *Torah*' at completing the *Torah* readings.
Sitra Achra	'Other Side'. Kabbalistic name for the forces of evil.
Sivan	Hebrew month usually falling around May / June.
Sofer	Scribe.
Sukkah	'Booth' in which Jews live during the festival of Tabernacles.
Sukkot	'Booths'. The festival of Tabernacles.
Taanit Ester	The Fast of Esther held on the day preceding *Purim*.
Taharah	'Purification'. The preparation of the dead for burial.
Tallit	Prayer shawl. A small *tallit katan* is worn under the clothing.
Tammuz	Hebrew month usually falling around June / July.
Tanakh	The Hebrew Bible.
Tannaim	Sages of the mishnaic period.
Targum	Aramaic translation of the Bible. Plural *targumim*.
Tashlikh	Ceremony of casting away sins on the New Year festival.
Tefillin	Black boxes with biblical passages, worn on weekday mornings.
Tenaim	Engagement ceremony.

Terefah	Ritually slaughtered animals with defective internal organs.
Teshuvah	Repentance, literally a 'turning back' to God.
Tevet	Hebrew month usually falling around December / January.
Tiferet	The main masculine *sefirah*, according to kabbalistic teaching.
Tikkun	'Rectification' to restore harmony, according to Kabbalah.
Tikkun Leil Shavuot	All-night vigil of the first night of Pentecost.
Tishah Be-Av	The fast of the 9th of *Av* remembering the Temple destruction.
Tishri	Hebrew month usually falling around September / October.
Torah	'Teaching'. The Pentateuch and / or all of traditional lore.
Tu Bi-Shevat	The 15th of *Shevat*, celebrated as the New Year for Trees.
Tur/Turim	Thirteenth-century code. Prototype for the *Shulchan Arukh*.
Tzaddik	Great-souled 'righteous man'. Plural *tzaddikim*.
Tzimtzum	The contraction of the Godhead prior to the creation.
Tzom Gedaliah	Fast of Gedaliah on the third of *Tishri*, usually in September.
Upsherinish	Cutting off the hair of a boy at the age of 3, leaving his sidecurls.
Yahrzeit	Yiddish term for the anniversary of a death.
Yamim Noraim	'Days of Awe' The New Year and the Day of Atonement.
Yarmulke	Yiddish name of skull-cap worn by Jewish men.
Yeshivah	Educational institute for talmudic studies. Plural *yeshivot*.
Yetzer Ha-Ra	The evil inclination in man.
Yetzer Tov	The good inclination in man.
Yichud	Prohibition on being alone with a member of the opposite sex.
Yichus	Status derived from descent from a famous ancestor.
Yishuv	The Jewish community in the land of Israel.
Yizkor	Memorial prayers for the dead.
Yom Kippur	The Day of Atonement.
Yom Tov	A festival on which most profane work is prohibited.
Yoreh Deah	Section of the *Shulchan Arukh* code.
Zaken	An elder.
Zemirot	Sabbath table songs.
Zionism	Movement for the return of Jews to Palestine.

Notes

Chapter 1   Some Basic Categories and Complexities

1   Matthew 23:15.
2   *Contra Apion* 2:40.
3   *Wars of the Jews* 2:20:2.
4   TB *Pesachim* 87b.
5   *Yad:Melakhim* 11:4.
6   These laws are associated with God's command to Adam in Genesis 2:16. According to Maimonides, *Yad:Melakhim* 8:11 those gentiles who keep the Noachide Laws because they believe them to be commanded by God in the Bible will have a portion in the World to Come. This is not true if the laws are merely kept because reason dictates them. Maimonides' ruling puzzled many of his commentators since its source, the fourth century *Mishnat Rabbi Eliezer* was only rediscovered in the twentieth century. This may account for the more commonly held view which simply allocates a portion in the World to Come to all righteous gentiles.
7   TB *Chagigah* 13a.
8   TB *Sanhedrin* 58b.
9   *Tosefta Sanhedrin* 13:2.
10   *Sefer Mitzvot Gadol* Asayin 74.
11   Y. Leibowitz, 'An Interpretation of the Jewish Religion', in *Judaism Crisis Survival, Paris*, 1966.
12   'Trend' is used here instead of 'denomination', since the latter invites misleading comparisons with Christianity. The exact divisions between Orthodoxy, Conservatism and Reform differ from country to country. It is therefore simplest to define each group by the label it applies to itself.

Chapter 2   Main Religious Doctrines

1   *Yad:Teshuvah* 3:7.
2   *Guide for the Perplexed* 1:51–60.
3   Reconstructionist ideas are systematically expounded by the movement's founder, Mordecai Kaplan, in his *Judaism as a Civilization*, New

York, 1934.
4   *Pirkei de R. Eliezer*, ch. 13.
5   *Book of Beliefs and Opinions* 4:1.
6   TB *Berakhot* 18b.
7   *Zohar* 1:191a.
8   M *Sanhedrin* 10:1. An important passage for understanding the early rabbinic conception of the soul is the tannaitic teaching, quoted in TB *Niddah* 30b, to the effect that there are three partners who share in the making of man, his two parents and God. Whereas his parents supply the organic materials, God gives man spirit, soul, the shine of his face, sight, hearing, speech, locomotion, knowledge, understanding and intellect. It is thus apparent that spirit and soul are not simply identified with the personality of man or with his mental make-up.
9   TB *Sanhedrin* 91a.
10 TB *Shabbat* 152b.
11 TB *Berakhot* 18a.
12 Cf. 1 Samuel 28.
13 TB *Berakhot* 62a.
14 *Genesis Rabbah* 1:4.
15 M *Avot* 3:14, *Genesis Rabbah* 1:1.
16 Proverbs 3:19.
17 *Ibid*. 8:30. This is, admittedly, ⟨ ⟩ y one of several possible translations.
18 *Zohar* 3:152a.
19 Cf. especially *Nefesh Ha-Chaim* 4 ⟩.
20 Hebrew *ben Torah*, meaning lite₁ ly 'son of *Torah*'.
21 TB *Avodah Zarah* 3b.
22 TB *Sotah* 14a.
23 We have used this term to refer Conservative and Reform Judaism, since 'Non-Orthodox Judaism' ₁n awkward expression.
24 TB *Sotah* 3a.
25 TB *Yoma* 86b.
26 *Ecclesiastes Rabbah* 1:15.
27 M *Avot* 4:17.
28 *Ibid*. 2:15.
29 TB *Rosh Ha-Shanah* 17a.
30 TB *Berakhot* 17a.
31 TB *Makkot* 24a.
32 M *Sanhedrin* 10:1.
33 Maimonides, *Yad: Teshuvah* 3:₍ ₁as an alternative reading simply referring to those who deny th₍ ₎ctrine of the Resurrection.
34 *Sabbath Prayer Book*, New York, 45, pp. 562–3.

Chapter 3   The Bible and Revelation

1   R. Judah L. Fishman (Maimon) ₁ntroduction to vol. 6 of I. Halevi, *Dorot Ha-Rishonim*, Jerusalem, 1⟨ ⟩.

2   TB *Menachot* 29b.
3   TJ *Peah* 2:4.
4   TJ *Sanhedrin* 10:1.
5   M *Sanhedrin* 10:1 TB *Sanhedrin* 100b.
6   M *Yadaim* 3:5.
7   TB *Shabbat* 30b.
8   TB *Megillah* 7a.
9   TB *Shabbat* 13b.
10 *Ibid.* 30b.
11 TB *Baba Batra* 12b.
12 M *Avot* 5:24.
13 Nehemiah 8:7–8.
14 M *Megillah* 4:4–10.
15 TB *Megillah* 3a, but cf. the version of this story (about Aquilas), in TJ *Megillah* 1:9.
16 Quoted by Y. Komlosh, *The Bible in the Light of the Aramaic Translations* (Hebrew), Tel Aviv, 1973, p. 33, from *Shaarei Teshuvah*, Leipzig, 1859, no. 330.
17 TB *Berakhot* 8a.
18 *Tur: Orach Chaim* 285.
19 R. Aaron Greenbaum in M. M. Kasher, *Torah Shelemah* vol. 24, Jerusalem, 1974. p. 264.

Chapter 4   The Origins and Growth of Jewish Thought

1   Exodus 21 :24. The views of the talmudic sages are found in TB *Baba Kamma* 84a.
2   Cf. G. Vermes, 'The Etymology of "Essenes" ' in his *Post-Biblical Jewish Studies*, Leiden, 1975.
3   This is brought out in the study of *Shabbat* laws among the Qumran community by L. H. Schiffman, *The Halakhah at Qumran*, Leiden, 1975. The Qumran scrolls have greatly increased our understanding of exegetical and halakhic traditions among the Jews of Palestine prior to the destruction of the Second Temple.
4   *Tosefta Chullin* ch. 2. The story is also found with embellishments in TB *Avodah Zarah* 16b, *Ecclesiastes Rabbah* ch.1, and various later *midrashim.*
5   Records of these anti-Christian enactments are preserved in TB *Gittin* 45b, TB *Chullin* 13a, TB *Shabbat* 116a and TB *Berakhot* 28b.
6   TB *Shabbat* 116a.
7   TJ *Shabbat* 6:9.
8   TB *Chagigah* 3b.
9   *Antiquities of the Jews* 17:2:4.
10 TJ *Berakhot* 9:5, TB *Sotah* 22b.
11 Cf. Luke 18:9–11.
12 *Sedeh Chemed: Peat Ha-Sadeh* 1:70.
13 For a modern statement of this view by a leading Orthodox rabbi see

L. Jung, 'The Rabbis and the Freedom of Interpretation' in *Guardians of Our Heritage*, edited by L. Jung, New York, 1958.

14   Menachem Meiri, introduction to his *Bet Ha-Bechirah* on *Avot*.

15   '*Tosefot Maaseh Rav*' in B. Broida, *Bet Yaakov*, Jerusalem, 1884, quoted in Y. Even Shmuel (tr.), *Sefer Ha-Kozari*, Tel Aviv, 1972, p. 13.

16   *Yad:Teshuvah* 3:7.

17   Rabad *ad loc*. There are other versions of this criticism which tone down the harshness of 'greater and better men than he'. Cf. J.Albo, *Sefer Ha-Ikkarim* 2:1, and *Kesef Mishneh* to the *Yad ad loc*.

18   *Guide for the Perplexed* 3:51.

19   See the commentary of Ibn Falaquera to the *Guide ad loc*.

20   *Guide* 2 :25.

21   *Idem.*

22   Cf. *Ibid.* 3:26–7.

23   *Ibid.* 3:47.

24   *Ibid.* 3:32, 36.

25   *Leviticus Rabbah* 22:8.

26   *Mitpachat Sefarim*, Lemberg, 1870, p. 56.

27   *Yad:Mamrim* 3:3.

28   *Tractatus Theologico-Politicus* chs. 1 and 2.

29   *Ibid.* ch. 3.

30   *Ibid.* chs. 4 and 5.

31   *Ibid.* ch. 6.

32   *Ibid.* ch. 7.

33   *Ibid.* chs. 8–10.

34   *Chakham Tzvi* no. 18.

Chapter 5   The Growth of Modern Jewish Thought

1   *Igrot Ha-Rayah* vol. 1, no. 24.

2   cf. Scholem, 'Martin Buber's Hasidism' first published in the magazine *Commentary* 32 (1961) and subsequently reprinted in *The Jewish Expression*, ed. by J. Goldin, New York, 1970, and in G. Scholem, *The Messianic Idea in Judaism*, London, 1971.

3   This theme is reiterated in a number of Wiesel's works, but most forcefully in his novel *Night*.

Chapter 6   The Jewish Mystical Tradition

1   M *Chagigah* 2:1.

2   *Ibid.*

3   Genesis 5:24.

4   TB *Sanhedrin* 65b. The tradition that kabbalists could create a *golem* or artificial man, is a widespread one. Popular legend ascribed such activity to R. Judah Loeb, the great Jewish theologian of sixteenth-seventeenth century Prague. Elijah, the Gaon of Vilna, told one of his pupils that he had started to create a *golem* in the 1730s, before

his thirteenth birthday, but desisted when he received a sign from heaven. G. Scholem has shown how the *golem*-making process was actually a spiritual exercise among the kabbalists themselves. See his 'The Idea of the Golem' in *On the Kabbalah and its Symbolism*, New York, 1969.

5   *Heikhalot Rabbati* 1.
6   *Shir Ha-Yichud*, for Tuesday.
7   Bachya ben Asher, commentary to Genesis 32:10.
8   *Bet Yosef* to *Tur:Orach Chaim* 25.
9   *Tikkunei Zohar* 30.
10   *Etz Chaim* 1:2.
11   *Mitpachat Sefarim* p. 82.
12   The leader of the powers of evil.
13   Ahijah the Shilonite, the prophet who presided over the split between the Northern and Southern Kingdoms after the death of Solomon, was the Besht's heavenly mentor. It is significant that Ahijah, like the Besht, led a populist revolt against autocratic rule.
14   The *kelipah* or shell symbolizes the force of evil trapping the divine sparks.
15   The Besht's anguish has been interpreted as signifying the removal of messianic immediacy from Chasidic ideology. Cf. G. Scholem, 'The Neutralization of the Messianic Element in Early Hasidism', *Journal of Jewish Studies*, 1970, reprinted in his *The Messianic Idea in Judaism*, London, 1971. This view has been criticized by other scholars who point out the messianic tone of the whole letter.
16   *Noam Elimelekh*: *Devarim*.
17   *Nefesh Ha-Chaim* 3 :4.
18   Ch. Zaitchik, *Ha-Meorot Ha-Gedolim*, Jerusalem, 1969, p. 165.

Chapter 7   The *Halakhah*

1   TB *Berakhot* 5a.
2   See S. Lieberman's essay, 'The Publication of the Mishnah' in his *Hellenism in Jewish Palestine*, New York, 1962.
3   *Netivot Olam, Netiv Ha-Torah*, ch. 15.

Chapter 8   (1) The Ritual Lifetime: Childhood and Youth

1   *Tosefta Shabbat* 6:4.
2   Elijah of Vilna's *Biur Ha-Gra* on *Shulchan Arukh*: *Yoreh Deah* 196:6.
3   *Yad*: *Avodat Kokhavim* 11:10.
4   TB *Shabbat* 67a; *Shulchan Arukh*: *Orach Chaim* 301:27.
5   Genesis 3:16; M *Shabbat* 2:6.
6   TB *Niddah* 31b.
7   *Yad*: *Isurei Biah* 1 1:15.
8   TB *Baba Batra* 16b.
9   TB *Gittin* 57a.

10 Exodus 4:25; *Shulchan Arukh*: *Yoreh Deah* 264:1.
11 *Ibid.* 265:11.
12 *Idem.*
13 *Pirkei de R. Eliezer* 29.
14 M *Shabbat* 19:6.
15 *Shulchan Arukh*: *Yoreh Deah* 264:3.
16 Genesis 17:14 and Rashi *ad loc.*
17 *Shulchan Arukh*: *Yoreh Deah* 263:2.
18 TB *Shabbat* 137b.
19 Cf. *Yad*: *Isurei Biah* 13:6.
20 TB *Yevamot* 48b.
21 *Shulchan Arukh*: *Yoreh Deah* 263:5.
22 *Zohar* 2:86a.
23 *Chesed Le-Avraham* 2:52.
24 Exodus 13:2; Numbers 3:12.
25 *Yad*: *Nachalot* 1:1.
26 TB *Sukkah* 42b.
27 Leviticus 19:27.
28 Numbers 15:37.
29 *Shulchan Arukh*: *Even Ha-Ezer* 22 :2.
30 M *Sotah* 3:4.
31 *Shulchan Arukh*: *Yoreh Deah* 246:6.
32 *Zohar* 1:1 26b.
33 R. Israel Meir Kagan in his *Likkutei Halakhot* to tractate *Sotah.*
34 Cf. J. D. Eisenstein (ed.), *Otzar Yisrael*, New York, 1906 – 13, vol. 8, p. 266.
35 *Tiferet Yisrael*, ch. 56.
36 *Yad*: *Ishut* 2:1, 10.
37 I. Abrahams, *Jewish Life in the Middle Ages*, New York, 1975, p. 32.
38 *Shulchan Arukh*: *Orach Chaim* 225:2.
39 *Igrot Moshe*: *Orach Chaim* no. 104.

Chapter 9 (2) The Ritual Lifetime: Sexual Behaviour, Marriage and Old Age

1 *Yad*: *Ishut* 1:1– 4.
2 *Shulchan Arukh*: *Even Ha-Ezer* 21:1–6.
3 *Ibid.* 22: 1–19.
4 *Ibid.* 23, *Tosefot* to TB *Niddah* 13a and Nachmanides *ad loc.* For the whole subject of female seed see D. M. Feldman, *Marital Relations, Birth Control and Abortion in Jewish Law*, New York, 1974, ch. 7.
5 *Zohar* 1:188a.
6 *Shulchan Arukh*: *Even Ha-Ezer* 23.
7 Leviticus 18:22, 20:13, *Shulchan Arukh*: *Even Ha-Ezer* 24 and *Bayit Chadash* to *Tur ad loc.*
8 *Shulchan Arukh*: *Even Ha-Ezer* 20:2.
9 TB *Yevamot* 63b, *Shulchan Arukh*: *Even Ha-Ezer* 1:1.

10   *Ibid.* 1:3–4 and *Turei Zahav ad loc., ibid.* 1:5,8.

11   *Tosefot* to TB *Gittin* 41b, Rabbenu Nissim on *Alfasi* to TB *Kiddushin* 41a.

12   TB *Kiddushin* 12b.

13   *Leviticus Rabbah* 8:1.

14   Cf.J. Trachtenberg, *Jewish Magic and Superstition*, New York, 1970, p. 173.

15   J.D. Eisenstein, *Otzar Dinim u-Minhagim*, New York, 1917, p. 428.

16   *Shulchan Arukh: Even Ha-Ezer* 64:1, TB *Berakhot* 54b.

17   J. Werdiger, *Edut Le-Yisrael*, Bnei Braq, 1965, p. 6.

18   TJ *Bikkurim* 3:3, TB *Yevamot* 63b, Werdiger, *op. cit.*, p. 7 quoting Maharam Mintz.

19   TB *Eruvin* 18b, *Pirkei de R. Eliezer* 12.

20   Isserles in *Shulchan Arukh: Yoreh Deah* 319:3, *Bet Shmuel* to *Even Ha-Ezer* 30:5, *Chatam Sofer* responsa on *Even Ha-Ezer* no. 98, *Ketav Sofer* responsa on *idem.* no. 47.

21   *Mordekhai* on *Kiddushin* no. 488, *Tosefot* to TB *Kiddushin* 9a.

22   *Shulchan Arukh: Even Ha-Ezer* 55:2, *Bet Shmuel* to *idem.* 55:1.

23   TB *Nedarim* 20b and Rabbenu Nissim *ad loc., Tur: Even Ha-Ezer* 25, *Orach Chaim* 240.

24   *Shulchan Arukh ibid.*, TB *Berakhot* 62a, TB *Nedarim* 20b. *Tur ibid.*

25   *Tur ibid.* and *Shulchan Arukh ibid.* with variations.

26   *Idem.* quoting TB *Yevamot* 20a.

27   Herman Wouk, *This is My God*, New York, 1976, p. 141.

28   *Shulchan Arukh idem.* 25:2.

29   TB *Niddah* 31b, *Tur ibid.*

30   *Shulchan Arukh idem.* 25:5.

31   Leviticus 15:19–24, 18:19, 20:18.

32   M *Niddah* 7:4.

33   *Shulchan Arukh: Orach Chaim* 88.

34   *Shulchan Arukh: Yoreh Deah* 195, 196.

35   TB *Niddah* 31b.

36   *Shulchan Arukh: Even Ha-Ezer* 23:1, TB *Yevamot* 34b.

37   R. Moses Feinstein, *Igrot Moshe: Even Ha-Ezer* no. 63.

38   *Yam Shel Shlomoh* on M *Yevamot* 1:8.

39   TB *Yevamot* 12b.

40   *Igrot Moshe, idem.*, vol. 2, no. 17, R. Eliezer Waldenberg, *Tzitz Eliezer*, vol. 9, no. 51.

41   R. Elijah Mizrachi on Exodus 21:22.

42   For a full discussion of the different views see D. M. Feldman, *op. cit.*, chs 14 and 15, J. D. Bleich, *Contemporary Halakhic Problems*, New York, 1977, ch. 15.

43   Deuteronomy 24:1.

44   M *Gittin* 9:3.

45   See, for instance, I.J. Weiss, *Minchat Yitzchak*, vol. 1 , nos. 102–3, where the author, a leading halakhist, discusses the correct way to

transliterate the names 'Louis' and 'Rose' in Hebrew characters.

46 TB *Kiddushin* 13a.
47 *Shulchan Arukh*: *Even Ha-Ezer* 119:6, 154.
48 *Yad*: *Gerushin* 2:20.
49 TB *Berakhot* 8b.
50 M *Avot* 5:21.
51 Leviticus 19:32, *Shulchan Arukh*: *Yoreh Deah* 244:1.
52 Exodus 19:12, Leviticus 19:3, *Shulchan Arukh, idem.* 240:24 and *Turei Zahav ad loc.*
53 *Ibid.* 240.
54 Cf. Y. Grunewald, *Kol-Bo al Avelut*, New York, 1965, p. 174.
55 *Shulchan Arukh idem.* 338.
56 *Ibid.* and *Siftei Kohen ad loc.*
57 *Ibid.* 329:3 – 5.
58 J.D. Bleich, *op. cit.*, ch. 16.
59 *Shulchan Arukh idem.* 352, 362.
60 *Ibid.* 380 – 93.

Chapter 10   The Ritual Year: from New Year to Tabernacles

1 Deuteronomy 6:4–9, 11:13–21, Numbers 15:37– 41.
2 Exodus 13:1– 10, 11–16.
3 Cf. L. Jacobs, *Hasidic Prayer*, London, 1972, ch. 4.
4 M *Berakhot* 4:4.
5 *Shulchan Arukh*: *Orach Chaim* 89:1 and *Biur Halakhah ad loc.*
6 Exodus 20:8–11, Deuteronomy 5:12–15.
7 TB *Shabbat* 10b, TB *Sanhedrin* 58b, *Yad*: *Melakhim* 10:9.
8 *Genesis Rabbah* 11:8.
9 M *Chagigah* 1:8.
10 TB *Shabbat* 118b. The interpretation mentioned is that of R. Solomon Breuer quoted in his son's approbation to *Shemirat Shabbat Kehilchatah* by J.I. Neubert.
11 *Shulchan Arukh*: *Orach Chaim* 257:8.
12 TB *Berakhot* 57b.
13 M *Rosh Ha-Shanah* 2:2– 4,7.
14 Exodus 12:2.
15 TB *Rosh Ha-Shanah* 16a.
16 TJ *Rosh Ha-Shanah* 1:3.
17 TB *idem.* 16b, *Shulchan Arukh*: *Orach Chaim* 583:2.
18 *Yad:Taaniyot* 5:2.
19 *She'elot u-Teshuvot Ha-Rashba* 1 :395.
20 *Shulchan Arukh*: *Orach Chaim* 605.
21 *Ibid.* 606:4, 607:6, 608:1.
22 *Ibid.* 610:4, Isaiah 1:18.
23 Cf. N. Rosenbloom, *Tradition in an Age of Reform*, Philadelphia, 1976, pp. 68–70.
24 Leviticus 21:42–3.

25   *Tur*: *Orach Chaim* 625.
26   M *Sukkah* 4:9.
27   *Ibid*. 5:1, TJ *Sukkah* 5:1.
28   *Yad:Lulav* 7:22, M *Sukkah* 4:16.
29   Cf. R. Isaiah Horowitz, *Shnei Luchot Ha-Brit*: *Amud Ha-Shalom*.

Chapter 11   (2) The Ritual Year: from Chanukah to the month of Av

1   TB *Shabbat* 21b.
2   *Pesikta Rabbati* 6:5.
3   *Chiddushei Aggadot* on TB *Shabbat* 21b.
4   Ezekiel 24:2, *Shulchan Arukh*: *Orach Chaim* 550:3.
5   TB *Taanit* 29a.
6   *Tosefta Sotah* 7.
7   TJ *Megillah* 1:1.
8   TB *Megillah* 5b, *Shulchan Arukh*: *Orach Chaim* 696:1.
9   *Ibid*. 695:2.
10   *Ibid*. 470:1.
11   M *Pesach*im 10.
12   *Shulchan Arukh idem*. 489:10 and commentaries.
13   TB *Yevamot* 62b, *Shulchan Arukh idem*. 493:1.
14   Cf. *Mishnah Berurah* to *Orach Chaim* 494:3.
15   TJ *Taanit* 4:5.
16   M *Taanit* 4:6.

Chapter 12   The Synagogue, Home and Jewish Community

1   *Shulchan Arukh*: *Orach Chaim* 151:1,3.
2   *She'elot u-Teshuvot Chatam Sofer*: *Choshen Mishpat* 190.
3   *Idem*. *Maharam Schik*: *Orach Chaim* 77.
4   TJ *Peah* 1:1, TB *Avodah Zarah* 11a.
5   *Yad*: *Mezuzah* 5:4.
6   *Shulchan Arukh idem*. 570:1–3.
7   *Tanna de-vei Eliyahu* 9, *Yad:Ishut* 15:18–20.
8   Leviticus ch. 11, Deuteronomy ch. 14.
9   *Shulchan Arukh*: *Yoreh Deah* 1:1.
10   Leviticus 7:25, Genesis 32:33.
11   Exodus 23:19, 34:26, Deuteronomy 14:21.
12   *Tur*: *Yoreh Deah* 87 and *Shulchan Arukh idem*. 87:3 and commentaries.
13   *Shulchan Arukh idem*. 89:1–2.
14   TB *Bekhorot* 7b, *Shulchan Arukh idem*. 81:8.
15   Leviticus 19:19, Deuteronomy 12:9.
16   Numbers 15:20, Ezekiel 44:30.
17   TB *Shabbat* 17b, *Shulchan Arukh idem*. 123:1.
18   *Ibid*. 114:1 and commentaries.
19   *Ibid*. 113:1, 4.

20 *Igrot Moshe*: *Yoreh Deah* 47–9.
21 TB *Avodah Zarah* 35a, and *Tosefot ad loc.*, *Shulchan Arukh idem.* 115:2.
22 Numbers 6:24.
23 *Shulchan Arukh*: *Orach Chaim* 53:4–5.
24 *Idem. Yoreh Deah* 1:2 and commentaries.
25 TB *Baba Metzia* 85a.
26 *Yad*: *Melakhim* 1:5, *Sifre*: *Shoftim* 157.
27 Cf. *Targum Yonatan ad loc.*

Chapter 13 Trends and Movements within Contemporary Judaism

1 Cf. M. Leigh, 'Reform Judaism in Britain' in D. Marmur (ed.), *Reform Judaism*, London, 1973, p. 35.
2 N. Bentwich (ed.), *Solomon Schechter*: *Selected Writings*, Oxford, 1944, p. 146.
3 It appears most recently in a closely argued defence of Conservative Judaism as the true heir of rabbinic Judaism against its Orthodox critics in R. Gordis, *Understanding Conservative Judaism*, New York, 1978.

Chapter 14 Jews and Gentiles

1 Commentary to the *Mishnah* beginning of *Avodah Zarah*, also *Yad*: *Avodah Zarah* 9:4. Both passages were deleted from the usual printed editions by the Christian censor.
2 TB *Yevamot* 62a.
3 The attitudes of some of the main medieval rabbis are analysed in J. Katz, *Exclusiveness and Tolerance*, New York, 1969.
4 TB *Shabbat* 146a.
5 *Zohar* 2:95b.
6 *Tanya* chs 1 and 2, based on the Lurianic Kabbalah, cf. *Etz Chaim* 49:3.
7 TB *Shabbat* 88a.

Select Bibliography

General Reference works

Encyclopaedia Judaica, Keter, Jerusalem, 1972, 16 vols plus year-books. (This is the most up-to-date work of reference for Jews and Judaism.)

The Jewish Encyclopaedia, originally published by Funk & Wagnalls, New York, 1901–6, reprinted by Ktav, New York, 12 vols (Although out of date many of the articles are of a high quality, and still of some interest.)

G. Abramson (ed.), *The Blackwell Companion to Jewish Culture*, Basil Blackwell, Oxford 1989. (Concerned more with cultural, than religious, aspects of Jewish life.)

S. W. Baron, *A Social and Religious History of the Jews*, Jewish Publication Society of America (JPS), Philadelphia, 1952–83, 18 vols including Index to vols 1–8. (A massive effort by the author, although still incomplete at his death.)

L. Ginzberg, *The Legends of the Jews*, JPS, Philadelphia, 1968, 7 vols. (A collection of all midrashic legends on the Bible, with invaluable footnotes, and a comprehensive index.)

L. Jacobs, *The Jewish Religion: A Companion*, Oxford University Press, Oxford 1995. (A series of articles on all the major aspects of Judaism.)

Primary Sources

The *Mishnah*, tr. H. Danby, Clarendon Press, Oxford, 1933.

The Babylonian Talmud, tr. under the editorship of I. Epstein, Soncino, London, 1936, 35 vols.

A. Cohen, *Everyman's Talmud*, Dent & Sons, London, 1949.

Midrash Rabbah, ed. H. Friedman and M. Simon, Soncino, London, 1939.

C. G. Montefiore and H. Loewe, *A Rabbinic Anthology*, JPS, Philadelphia, 1960.

The Zohar, tr. H. Sperling and M. Simon, Soncino, London, 1931–4.

The Wisdom of the Zohar, by I. Tishby, tr. D. Goldstein, Littman Library, Oxford 1989. (Main teachings of the *Zohar* grouped according to subject matter.)

General Works on Jews and Judaism

L. Blue, *To Heaven, with Scribes and Pharisees*, Darton, Longman & Todd, London, 1975. (A good, if occasionally somewhat eccentric, introduction to Jewish life by an unconventional British Reform rabbi.)

M. I. Dimont, *Jews, God and History*, Signet Books, New York, 1962. (A popular survey of Jewish history by an American Reform rabbi. Easy to read if not always reliable.)

I. Epstein, *Judaism*, Penguin Books, Harmondsworth, 1959.

L. Finkelstein (ed.), *The Jews: Their Religion and Culture*, Schocken, New York, 1971.

M. L. Margolis and A. Marx, *A History of the Jewish People*, Harper & Row, New York, 1965. (The standard one-volume history of the Jews. Somewhat dry but a classic of its kind.)

L. Roth, *Judaism. A Portrait*, Schocken, New York, 1960. (A Jewish intellectual draws a picture of Judaism as he sees it.)

S. Sharot, *Judaism: A Sociology*, David & Charles, Newton Abbot, 1976.

A. Unterman, *Dictionary of Jewish Lore & Legend*, Thames & Hudson, London 1991. (Deals with the folklore and customs of Jews.)

Main Religious Doctrines

I. Epstein, *The Faith of Judaism*, Soncino, London, 1968. (An Orthodox scholar interprets Jewish belief in the light of modern thought.)

M. Friedlander, *The Jewish Religion*, Shapiro Vallentine, London, 1953.

L. Jacobs, *Principles of the Jewish Faith*, Valentine Mitchell, London, 1964. (A detailed analysis of Maimonides' Thirteen Principles and what they can mean to the modern Jew.)

J. Neusner (ed.), *Understanding Jewish Theology*, Ktav, New York, 1973.

S. Schechter, *Studies in Judaism*, Meridian Books, New York, 1958. (Ch. 3, 'The Dogmas of Judaism' is an essay which has attained the status of a minor classic.)

Jewish Thought: Rabbinic Period

A. Corre (ed.), *Understanding the Talmud*, Ktav, New York, 1975.

L. Finkelstein, *The Pharisees*, JPS, Philadelphia, 1962.

G. F. Moore, *Judaism in the First Centuries of the Christian Era*, Harvard University Press, Cambridge, Mass., 1966.

G. Vermes, *Jesus the Jew*, Fontana/Collins, London, 1976. (An attempt to see Jesus against the background of first-century Palestinian Judaism.)

Jewish Thought: Medieval Period

J. D. Bleich (ed.), *With Perfect Faith: The Foundations of Jewish Belief*, Ktav, New York, 1983. (Readings from the Medieval philosophers on Jewish doctrine.)

J. Guttmann, *Philosophies of Judaism*, Routledge & Kegan Paul, London, 1964. (The standard work on Jewish philosophy.)

I. Husik, *A History of Medieval Jewish Philosophy*, Meridian Books, New York, 1960.

S. Katz (ed.), *Jewish Philosophers*, Keter, Jerusalem, 1975. (A collection of articles by various scholars originally published in the *Encyclopaedia Judaica*, to which the editor has added a section on the modern period.)

H. Lewy, A. Altmann and I. Heineman (eds), *Three Jewish Philosophers*, Meridian, New York, 1961.

Jewish Thought: Modern Period

S. H. Bergman, *Faith and Reason*: Modern Jewish Thought, Schocken, New York, 1961.

E. Berkovits, *Major Themes in Modern Philosophies of Judaism*, Ktav, New York, 1974. (A series of critical essays on leading Jewish thinkers.)

E. Fleischner (ed.), *Auschwitz: Beginning of a New Era* (Holocaust), Ktav, New York, 1977.

N. N. Glatzer (ed.), *Modern Jewish Thought: A Source Reader*, Schocken, New York, 1977.

N. Rotenstreich, *Jewish Philosophy in Modern Times*, Holt, Rinehart & Winston, New York, 1968.

J. Sacks *Crisis and Covenant: Jewish Thought After the Holocaust*, M/c U.P., Manchester, 1992 (The British Chief Rabbi explores theological responses to the Holocaust, Israel and the challenges of modern knowledge to tradition.)

The Jewish Mystical Tradition

D. R. Blumenthal (ed.), *Understanding Jewish Mysticism: A Source Reader*, Ktav, New York, vol. I, 1978; vol.II 1982. (A selection of mystical texts with introductions and commentaries.)

M. Buber, *Tales of the Hasidim: Early Masters*, Schocken, New York, 1968.

——, *Tales of the Hasidim: Later Masters*, Schocken, New York, 1969. (Although the author allows himself considerable license in re-telling these stories, this is still one of the best introductions to the Chasidic ethos.)

J. Dan *The Teachings of Hasidism*, Behrman House, New Jersey 1983. (A series of readings, with footnotes, selected from the main Chasidic masters.)

R. Eisenberg *Boychiks in the Hood: Travels in the Hasidic Underground*, Harper, San Francisco, 1995. (A Yiddish-speaking secularist's account of his exploration of different Chasidic sub-groups.)

L. Jacobs *The Jewish Mystics*, Kyle Cathie, London, 1990. (Selected readings from Jewish mystical texts from earliest times to the present.)

L. I. Newman (ed.), *The Hasidic Anthology*, Bloch, New York, 1944.

H. Rabinowicz, *The World of Hasidism*, Valentine Mitchell, London, 1970.

G. Scholem, *Major Trends in Jewish Mysticism*, Schocken, New York, 1961. (The standard introduction to Jewish mysticism by the leading scholar of the subject.)

G. Scholem, *On the Kabbalah and its Symbolism*, Schocken, New York, 1965.

A. Unterman, *The Wisdom of the Jewish Mystics*, Sheldon Press, London, 1976.

H. Weiner, *91/2 Mystics: The Kabbala Today*, Collier Books, New York, 1969. (A very readable journal of the author's contact with contemporary Jewish mystics and scholars of mysticism.)

Halakhah and Jewish Law

J. D. Bleich, *Contemporary Halakhic Problems*, Ktav, New York, vols I-IV, 1977–95. (An Orthodox rabbi discusses modern applications of Jewish law.)

M. Elon (ed.), *The Principles of Jewish Law*, Keter, Jerusalem, 1975. (A collection of articles by various scholars originally published in the *Encyclopaedia Judaica*. Edited by the leading expert on Jewish law.)

S. B. Freehof, *The Responsa Literature*, JPS, Philadelphia, 1959.

——, *A Treasury of Responsa*, JPS, Philadelphia, 1963.

L. Ginzberg, *On Jewish Law and Lore*, Atheneum, New York, 1970. (A collection of articles by one of the leading scholars of the last generation.)

L. Jacobs, *Theology in the Responsa*, Routledge & Kegan Paul, London, 1975.

Jewish Ritual

A. P. Bloch, *The Biblical and Historical Background of Jewish Customs and Ceremonies*, Ktav, New York, 1980. (An analysis of the origins and development of Jewish rituals.)

D. M. Feldman, *Marital Relations, Birth Control and Abortion in Jewish Law*, Schocken, New York, 1974. (A major study of a highly complex area of Jewish life.)

J. Goldin (tr.), *Code of Jewish Law*, Hebrew Publishing Co., New York, 1927. (A translation of the *Kitzur Shulchan Arukh*.)

I. Grunfeld, *The Jewish Dietary Laws*, Soncino, London, 1972.

A. J. Heschel, *The Earth is the Lord's and the Sabbath*, Harper Torchbooks, New York, 1966. (Beautifully written account of Jewish life in Eastern Europe and the significance of the Sabbath.)

A. Z. Idelsohn, *Jewish Liturgy and its Development*, Schocken, New York, 1960.

I. Jakobovits, *Jewish Medical Ethics*, Bloch, New York, 1967. (Standard study of the subject by a leading Orthodox rabbi.)

M. Lamm, *The Jewish Way in Death and Mourning*, Jonathan David Publishers, New York 1969 (A major survey of Orthodox burial and mourning rites).

J. Magonet (ed.), *Jewish Explorations of Sexuality*, Berghahn Books, Oxford, 1995 (A collection of articles dealing with Jewish responses to different aspects of sexuality.)

Jewish Community

I. Abrahams, *Jewish Life in the Middle Ages*, Atheneum, New York, 1975. (A finely written survey of all aspects of Jewish life. A minor classic.)

J. L. Blau (ed.), *Reform Judaism: A Historical Perspective*, Ktav, New York, 1973.

W. B. Helmreich, *The World of the Yeshivah: An Intimate Portrait of Orthodox Jewry*, Yale U.P., London 1986. (A sociological study of the attitudes and lifestyles of American Orthodox Jews.)

S. Heschel (ed.), *On Being a Jewish Feminist: A Reader*, Schocken Books, New York, 1983. (A collection of articles by Jewish feminists reflecting their concerns with male chauvinism within Judaism.)

D. Landau, *Piety & Power:The World of Jewish Fundamentalism*, Secker & Warburg, London, 1993. (A study of right-wing religious groups by an Israeli jounalist.)

D. Rudavsky, *Modern Jewish Religious Movements*, Behrman House, New York, 1967. (Traces the history of the major movements, and the ideas behind them.)

J. Sacks, *One People? Tradition, Modernity, and Jewish Unity*, Littman Library, London, 1993. (A major attempt by a leading Orthodox thinker to deal with what unifies diverse Jewish groups.)

M. Sklare, *Conservative Judaism*, Free Press, Chicago, 1955. (An important study which remains valuable despite being out of date.)

M. Zborowski and E. Herzog, *Life is with People: The Culture of the Shtetl*, Schocken, New York, 1974.

H. J. Zimmels, *Ashkenazim and Sephardim*, Oxford University Press, London, 1958.

Index